# TWO YANKEE DIPLOMATS
IN 1830s SIAM

# ITINERARIA ASIATICA

THAILAND
*Volume X*

LA THAILANDE
*Tome X*

ORCHID PRESS
*Bangkok 2002*

# TWO YANKEE DIPLOMATS
# IN 1830s SIAM

by

Edmund Roberts
and
W.S.W. Ruschenberger, M.D.

Introduced and edited
by
Michael Smithies

*First published: 2002*

Edmund Roberts and
W.S.W. Ruschenberger, M.D.
TWO YANKEE DIPLOMATS IN 1830s SIAM
Introduced and editied by Michael Smithies
*First published: 2002*


Published by
ORCHID PRESS
P.O. Box 19
Yuttitham Post Office,
Bangkok 10907, Thailand

Printed in Thailand

ITINERARIA ASIATICA est une série de réimpressions d'ouvrages
contenant des descriptions et récits de voyageurs en Asie

ITINERARIA ASIATICA is a series of reprints of books
containing first-hand descriptions and narratives by travellers in Asia

© (Introduction and Notes)Orchid Press 2002

This book is printed on acid-free long life paper which meets the
specifications of ISO 9706/1994

ISBN 974-524-004-4

# TWO YANKEE DIPLOMATS IN 1830s SIAM: ROBERTS AND RUSCHENBERGER

edited by
Michael Smithies

## CONTENTS

| | |
|---|---|
| ILLUSTRATIONS | 8 |
| PREFACE AND ACKNOWLEDGEMENTS | 9 |
| GENERAL INTRODUCTION | 10 |

**PART I: THE TREATY MISSION OF 1833**

Roberts' introduction ................................................................... 20

1. (Ch XVI) ...Arrival at the mouth of the River Menam – Packnam – Procession to the Government House – Reception – Governor – Siamese temples – Interview with the Siamese Foreign Minister – Prima Donna – Feats of strength – Siamese females – Fire at Bang-kok – White elephants – Embalming – Shaving-head ceremony and feast – Fox-bats ............. 25

2. (Ch XVII) Presentation at the Palace of Bang-kok – Description – Royal elephant – White elephants – King of Siam – Great temple of Gautama – City of Bang-kok – Temple of Wat-Chan-Tong, and Figure of Budha – Banyan tree – Fire-feeders – Missionaries ..................................................... 52

3. (Ch XVIII) Chinese junks – Mechanic arts of Siam – Amusements – Dancing snakes – Annual oath of allegiance – Description of the capital – Embassy from Cochin-China – Education in Siam – Palace ............................................................. 72

4. (Ch XIX) Procession to the funeral pile of Wang-Na or Second King – Origin of Budhism in Siam – Sommona Kodom – Atheistical Principles of Budhism – Budhist

commandments – History of Siam – Government –
Titles of the king – Officers of the government..................................90

5. (Ch XX) Ancient laws of Siam – Legal oaths –
Punishment for debt – Divorces – Population of Siam –
Stature and complexion of the Siamese – Division of time –
Boundaries and possessions of Siam – Marine of Siam –
Imports – Inland trade – Currency – Treaty of Commerce –
Table of Exports.............................................................................106

6. (Ch XXI) Departure from Bang-kok for Singapore... ...................120

Appendix: Annual revenue obtained by the Government of
Siam from farms and duties; Annual expenditure...........................121

Taken from Edmund Roberts, *Embassy to the Eastern Courts of Cochin-China, Siam, and Muscat: in the U.S. Sloop-of-War Peacock, David Geisinger, Commander, during the years 1832-3-4.*

### PART II: THE RATIFICATION MISSION OF 1836

Ruschenberger's introduction..........................................................126

1. (Vol I, Ch XXIII)... Letter to the First Minister of Siam –
Sichang Islands and their inhabitants – Flying fox – Religious
temple – A talapoin – Siam roads ..................................................128

2. (Vol I, Ch XXIV) Prince Momfanoi – Departure for
Bankok – Paknam – Bazaar– Governor's house – Reception
by the governor – The captain of the port – Paddy-mill –
Female costume – Siamese twins – Uncomfortable lodgings.............133

3. (Vol I, Ch XXV) Siamese etiquette – Junk of ceremony –
Gaudy crew – Portuguese officers – Arrival in Bankok– Feast
of Paknam – Voyage up the Meinam – Mission-house at Bankok......142

4. (Vol II, Ch I) City of Bankok – Sampans – Amphibious
child – Population – Chinese residence – Commerce –
Revenue of Siam – Taxes – Gambling – Lottery – Cowries –
Division of time – Extent of the Siamese empire – King's
titles – Government, religion, and priests.........................................149

5. (Vol II, Ch II) Succession of the throne – Visit to
Momfanoi – The Royal Adelaide – Momfanoi's pets –
His private museum – The Khon Paa – A Siamese sword –
Musical instrument – A treat of ant's eggs – Phrenological

examination – Character of Momfanoi – A white ape –
Physical character of the Siamese – Siamese heads –
Sensuality of the Siamese – Their arrogance, etc.. ..........................166

6. (Vol II, Ch III) Public visits – Siamese badges of nobility –
Visit to the Phya-ratsa-pa-vade – Dwelling of the Second
Minister – A Siamese harem – Dr. Bradley – Siamese ladies –
Visit to the Phya-si-pi-pat – Dramatic exhibition.............................178

7. (Vol II, Ch IV) American missionaries – Their disinterestedness – Beneficial results of their ministry – Dispensary of the
missionaries – Missionaries in Bankok – Appearance of a
wat – Mechanics at work – The bazaar by day and by night –
Siamese theatricals..........................................................................186

8. (Vol II, Ch V) Delivery of the treaty – Sia-Yut'hia – Hall
of Justice – Procession of elephants – Spotted elephant –
Wat P'hra-Si-Ratanat – The Queen's wat – Sacred library –
Siamese prince and princess – Return to Paknam – The
governor – Departure from Paknam – Cholera on board ship............198

9. (Vol II, Ch VI) The King of Lagor – Entertainment of
board – Siamese curiosity and etiquette – Measurement of
the brig – Audience with the King of Siam – The procession –
Siamese soldiers– The audience hall – His Majesty and court –
Ceremonious entrance – Form of audience........................................206

10. (Vol II, Ch VII) Delivery of the Siamese treaty – Visit to
the Phya-Si-Pi-Pat – Departure of the embassy from Bankok –
Copy of the treaty............................................................................215

11. (Vol II, Ch VIII) Departure from Siam... ...................................226

Taken from W.S.W. Ruschenberger, *Narrative of a Voyage round the
World during the years 1835, 36, and 37; including a narrative of an
Embassy to the Sultan of Muscat and the King of Siam…*

CHRONOLOGY                                                                 228

INDEX                                                                      229

# ILLUSTRATIONS

1. Woodcut of a Siamese temple, from John Crawfurd, *Journal of an Embassy to the courts of Siam and Cochin-China*, London 1828........29
2. Paklat, from F.A. Neale, *Narrative of a Residence at the Capital of the Kingdom of Siam*, London 1852..................................... 31
3. The floating city, Bangkok, from F.A. Neale, *Narrative of a Residence at the Capital of the Kingdom of Siam*, London 1852.............. 33
4. The Portuguese consulate and missionary houses, from F.A. Neale, *Narrative of a Residence at the Capital of the Kingdom of Siam*, London 1852. ....................................................44
5. A War Elephant, from Anna Leonowens, *The English Governess at the Siamese Court*, London 1870...............................54
6. Woodcut of 'the front of the main building of the King of Siam's palace', from John Crawfurd, *Journal of an Embassy to the courts of Siam and Cochin-China*, London 1828....................55
7. View of a watt or temple, from F.A. Neale, *Narrative of a Residence at the Capital of the Kingdom of Siam*, London 1852........62
8. The Temple of the Sleeping Idol, from Anna Leonowens, *The English Governess at the Siamese Court*, London 1870..............63
9. Chinese cook on the Meinan, from F.A. Neale, *Narrative of a Residence at the Capital of the Kingdom of Siam*, London 1852........ 75
10. Mr Hunter's house, from F.A. Neale, *Narrative of a Residence at the Capital of the Kingdom of Siam*, London 1852........................ 91
11. Map by J. Walker showing Siam and Cochin-China, from John Crawfurd, *Journal of an Embassy to the courts of Siam and Cochin-China*, London   1828............................124
12. Siamese Buddhist priest, from John Thomson, *The Straits of Malacca, Siam and Indochina*, London 1875, reprinted Oxford University Press, Singapore, 1993....................130
13. Prince Chau Fa Noi, Chulamani, from frontispiece to F.A. Neale, *Narrative of a Residence at the Capital of the Kingdom of Siam*, London, 1852.....................................................134
14. The King of Siam's state barge, from John Thomson, *The Straits of Malacca, Siam and Indochina*, London 1875, reprinted Oxford University Press, Singapore, 1993.....................143
15. Priests at breakfast, from Anna Leonowens, *The English Governess at the Siamese Court*, London, 1870..............................164
16. Siamese lady, from John Thomson, *The Straits of Malacca, Siam and Indochina*, London 1875, reprinted Oxford University Press, Singapore, 1993. ...............................................183
17. Siamese musicians, from F.A. Neale, *Narrative of a Residence at the Capital of the Kingdom of Siam*, London, 1852.....................194
18. Siamese actor and actress, from Anna Leonowens, *The English Governess at the Siamese Court*, London, 1870...........195
19. Gateway of the Old Palace, from Anna Leonowens, *The English Governess at the Siamese Court*, London, 1870.......... 201

# PREFACE AND ACKNOWLEDGEMENTS

Of the various Western accounts of Siam in the first half or the nineteenth century, the best known is that of Crawfurd (1828), who came in 1822 and unsuccessfully tried to prise a trade treaty from the court in Bangkok; Finlayson (1826), Crawfurd's surgeon, also published an account of this mission. Burney's mission of 1826 was rather more successful, but the vast quantity of papers generated by his stay, published in five volumes, still needs to be presented in a more accessible form than is now available.

Neale (1852) has long been available in reprint, but Abeel (1835), Bruguière (1831/1844), Earl (1837), Gutzlaff (1834), Malcom (1839), Malloch (1852), Moor (1837), Pallegoix (1834/1839/1845), Richardson (1839), and Tomlin (1832) are, with two exceptions, difficult to lay hands on, and sometimes not very rewarding when one does, being rather boring accounts of missionary endeavour. Bradley's missionary efforts are well known, but much of his published work on his own press appeared later in the century. None attempted to present a complete survey of Siam, such as Bishop Pallegoix's until recently still untranslated *Description du royaume Thai ou Siam* (1854), and Sir John Bowring's *The Kingdom and People of Siam* (1857) indubitably were.

The contributions of the Americans Roberts and Ruschenberger to the literature on Siam in this period tend to be overlooked, even though both have appeared in reprints in the last thirty years, because they were combined with accounts of Muscat and Cochin-China, as well as long narratives about reaching and returning from these places via Brazil and Cape Horn. Here the accounts of Siam only are presented, the first, being Roberts' text of his mission in 1833, and the second Ruschenberger's record of the ratification mission of 1836. Of the two, that of Roberts, being the head of the first American diplomatic mission to Siam, is the more interesting; he died before his second journey was completed, and Ruschenberger, the ship's surgeon, gave his account of that journey. However, Ruschenberger's excessive interest in the now discredited science of phrenology can make for tiresome reading. But no other account is available of this second mission, and it therefore has rarity value.

I must record my thanks to Anthony Farrington of the British Library for his unfailing help in answering queries and assistance in obtaining material, and to the many persons whose brains I have picked for obscure points in the texts.

I hope that bringing together these two early American accounts of Siam in the Third Reign will make them available to a wider public than has hitherto been possible.

Michael Smithies
Bua Yai, Korat
7 May 1998

# GENERAL INTRODUCTION

The British and the Americans each made two attempts to establish diplomatic relations with Siam during the reign of Rama III, Phra Nangklao (r. 1824-51), at its beginning and at its end. None of these attempts was entirely successful; indeed, the last two, by Joseph Balestier representing the United States in March and April 1850, and Sir James Brooke representing Britain in August and September the same year, were total failures, for the conservative king was dying and no new initiatives could be contemplated until his successor, who was to be Prince Mongkut – Chao Fa Yai in these accounts – enthroned.

The first attempt by Western powers to establish formal relations with the Chakri dynasty in Siam took place in 1822 with the mission of Dr John Crawfurd, representing the Governor-General of India and not the British monarch. Crawfurd was as old South-East Asian hand, having served under Raffles in Java, and was to be appointed resident of Singapore from 1823-1826, but he was not an accomplished diplomat and his mission produced no results, not even a trade treaty, which was his chief object. Even if he had been a skilled envoy, he was unlikely to have obtained any results from his mission, for the Siamese court was firmly against giving up its lucrative trading privileges to the benefit of British merchants; nor was it inclined to leniency in its dealings with the Sultan of Kedah, its vassal. Crawfurd dealt with Prince Chetsadabodin, Rama II's eldest son by a royal concubine who superintended foreign affairs sand trade. However, Crawfurd's mission did, indirectly, secure recognition of the British occupation of Penang; the island had been ceded by the Sultan of Kedah, and the British were not entirely sure of their claims to the territory, obtained in 1785, and that of Province Wellesley on the mainland, ceded in 1800.

Captain Henry Burney, who followed Crawfurd to Bangkok in December 1825, was altogether more pliant and patient, and had the advantage, not only of being well-connected, but of speaking Siamese as well as Malay. The First Anglo-Burmese War started in 1824 and Britain wished to reduce Siamese pressure on Perak and Selangor, and above all end restrictive Siamese trade practices. Burney was lucky in that while in Bangkok the Burmese ratified the Treaty of Yandabo in February 1826, ceding to Britain Arakan, Assam, Manipur, and

Tenasserim, thus bringing the British up to the Siamese frontier. Prince Chetsadabodin now reigned as Phra Nangklao and the Siamese were willing to appear conciliatory before the representatives of the power which had overcome Siam's traditional enemy. They did not, however, deliver much in their treaty, concluded in June 1826; the terms of trade were marginally better than before, eliminating a host of taxes and imposts by fixing a single duty based on the measurement of a ship's size; arrangements were made for defining the British Burmese-Siamese boundaries and settling disputes, the Siamese position in the Malay states was recognized, but the British were not given the right to establish a consular resident in Bangkok, one which the Portuguese had obtained, though his position was closer to trade representative than consul.

The Americans were keen to have increased trade relations in the Far East, a cause espoused by Senator Levi Woodbury of New Hampshire and John Shellaber, American consul in Batavia, who hoped to be appointed to lead the mission to negotiate a number of commercial treaties. But Woodbury was appointed President Jackson's secretary of the navy, and he nominated on 26 January 1832 Edmund Roberts, the husband of a relative of his, as special agent of the United States to negotiate trade treaties with Muscat, Siam, and Cochin-China.

Roberts was born on 29 June 1784 at Portsmouth, New Hampshire; his father was similarly named, and died when his son was a child; his mother died when he was sixteen and he was left in the care of a bachelor uncle, Captain Joshua Roberts, a merchant then operating out of Buenos Aires. He understudied his uncle's business operations and on his death succeeded to a substantial fortune at the age of twenty-four. He returned to Portsmouth and married Catherine Langdon, who came from a locally important family, in 1808. The effects of the Napoleonic Wars on trade, and the activities of French and Spanish privateers ruined his business and he is said to have lived in financially straightened circumstances until his death.

He was appointed American consul in Demerara, British Guiana, in 1823 but apparently did not take up his post. He borrowed money in 1827 and chartered a brig, the *Mary Ann*, sailing to Zanzibar. Government trade monopolies and delays caused him to protest to the Sultan of Muscat, then the ruler of Zanzibar, who however favoured his enterprise; he visited Bombay and returned to the United States.

His appointment in 1832 as special agent to negotiate trade treaties would have gone some way to relieving his financial exiguity.

Roberts was also authorized to negotiate with Japan if he felt it possible, but his additional mission, according to the *Dictionary of American Biography*, of investigating the operations of the British East India Company was to be secret and he was given the official employment of clerk to the commander of the sloop *Peacock* with a salary of $1,500 a year. However, this is hardly likely to have fooled anyone, since Roberts was the chief negotiator in the trade discussions in Siam and elsewhere.

He went first to Cochin-China, but points of etiquette caused him to abandon attempts to negotiate (the government of the ultra-conservative Confucian emperor Minh Mang was not one to give way before jaunty Westerners). So he went on to Siam in February 1833, securing a treaty of amity and commerce, which in fact gave no more than Burney had obtained, and on the trade side, since the export of rice was prohibited, was without significant consequence. In fairness to both Roberts and Burney, though, it has to be said that subsequent to the signing of their treaties with Siam, the number of British and American ships calling at Bangkok increased significantly.

Roberts left Siam on 6 April 1833 and sailed on the sloop-of-war, the *Peacock*, accompanied by the schooner, the *Boxer*, to Muscat, where he signed on 21 September 1835 a treaty of amity and commerce with the Sultan. This was altogether more substantial, granting the American consul extraterritorial powers, and fixing duties at five per cent. He returned to Portsmouth, NH, in April 1834. In March 1835 he was instructed by the Secretary of State, Forsyth, to return to Muscat and Siam to exchange the ratifications of the treaties he had negotiated, and to try to negotiate treaties with Cochin-China and Japan. He sailed, as Ruschenberger tells us, in the same ship, the *Peacock*, this time commanded by Captain Stribling, accompanied by the schooner, the *Enterprise*, with Captain Campbell in command, and the two ships being under the command of Commodore Kennedy. He concluded his visits to Muscat and then Siam, where he was from 25 March 1836, leaving on 20 April, but fell ill and died in Macao on 12 June 1836. His account of his journey in 1833 was published posthumously (which may account for the many typographical errors in proper names). His introduction makes clear he had handed in his manuscript for publication before he left the United States in 1835 on his second and fatal journey, possibly to his wife's relative Levi Woodbury. The book is said to have 'suffered from official censorship', perhaps at Woodbury's hands.

Very little is known about William Ruschenberger, who was surgeon to the expedition of 1835-7 to ratify Roberts' treaties. He is not mentioned in Roberts' account of the first mission in Siam, when the ship's surgeon appears to have been Dr Ticknor, mentioned four times in various visits near Bangkok. Ruschenberger seems to have been far more preoccupied by the then fashionable interest in phrenology than in preventive medicine. After visiting Rio, Muscat, Zanzibar, Ceylon, Java, Siam, and Cochin-China, Edmund Roberts (as noted above) and a ship's lieutenant, Campbell, fell ill and died in Macao, possibly of cholera, which had affected the ship and caused some deaths even before it left Bangkok.

Undaunted by Roberts' death, Commodore Kennedy proceeded to Canton, Taiwan, Hawaii (preceded by a burial at sea), California, Mexico, Peru, rounded Cape Horn, called at Rio and Bahia, and eventually came home to Norfolk, Virginia, while Ruschenberger continued his phrenological observations.

An inaccurate account of Roberts' mission appears in the pages of F.A. Neale's *Narrative of a Residence at the Capital of the Kingdom of Siam* (London, National Illustrated Library, 1852). Neale was in Bangkok from 1840-41, a mercenary officer in Siamese service. Discussing 'Recent Embassies to Siam', he writes:

*The last embassy to Siam of any note or importance was that from the United States of America, under the charge of Mr. Eliot [sic], the Envoy. The "Peacock", American sloop of war, which had then been for several years cruising on a scientific and exploring expedition in the Eastern Seas, was, one fine morning, quite unexpectedly, reported to have anchored off the Bar of Siam, much to the delight of the European residents at Bangkok, especially the American missionaries, and not a little to the discomfort of the Siamese, who looked upon these visitations from men of war as neither more nor less than the precursor to a general invasion of their country, and considered the officers and men of the expedition as so many spies, who, under the plea of scientific acquirements, were laying plans and devising schemes for the easiest and most effectual method of subduing the empire. Not a leaf was plucked nor a stone picked up by the*

> *curious and learned that accompanied the expedition to add to their stock of mineralogical and botanical curiosities, but the act was attributed to some sinister purposes. Regularly paid and enlisted spies dogged their every movement, and reported proceedings regularly at head quarters. The reception of the mission was barely civil, and exacted only so much respect as was inculcated by a wholesome dread of consequences, and the fact of a vessel of war, well armed and equipped, being actually on the spot, ready at a moment's warning to vindicate the honour of the American flag. Many tempting propositions were made by the Envoy in his endeavours to persuade the Siamese Government to swerve a little from the cold and rigid formalities attendant on the then existing treaties between Siam and other European Powers, and Brother Jonathan [the missionaries] strove mightily and warily to ingratiate the officers of state, so that their influence might tend to facilitate pending negotiations; but all was in vain. Gifts and civilities were received and returned – assurances given and faith pledged that the amelioration of the interests of both parties should be always a weighty consideration; but further than this, nothing could be effected. No ratified treaty or written document could be obtained; and the "Peacock" sailed again, taking with her the Envoy and his party; the officers highly delighted with the many pleasant hours they had passed in the society of European friends, both in following up the wild sports of the East and in the more social enjoyment of dinner parties and picnics; but the diplomatic portion of the expedition sadly chagrined to think that all their efforts for the bettering of American traffic had been as futile and void of success as all the like embassies had heretofore proved. Oysterlike, the Siamese King vastly preferred being entirely dependent for all the comforts and luxuries of this life upon the resources that were enclosed within that shell – his own kingdom.* (Neale 1852, 227-8)

Apart from getting the name of the envoy wrong, and assuming a scientific disguise to the mission, Neale incorrectly states that no treaty was signed. One was, virtually identical to that obtained by Burney (whose mission Neale does not mention at all) seven years earlier, and apart from the regularization of imposts, was of little major significance.

Substantive change was only to occur in Siam's relations with Western powers after the death of Rama III in 1851 and the accession of Prince Mongkut as king. The Bowring Treaty of 1855, concluded after just a month spent by the Governor of Hong Kong in Siam (from 24 March to 25 April), coming after the Second Anglo-Burmese War of 1852, greatly changed the trading position. It limited import duties to three per cent, export duties to an average of five per cent, granting rights to British subjects to reside and own land in Siam, and enjoy extraterritoriality under the protection of a resident British representative. Government monopolies, the mainstay of trading for nearly two centuries, were abolished except in the case of opium.

Sir John Bowring, not one to let the grass grow under his feet, published in 1857 in London his comprehensive survey in two volumes, *The Kingdom and People of Siam*. Volume II includes a summary of various Western diplomatic missions to Siam, and, drawing on Moor's *Notices of the Indian Archipelago* (1837), includes the following comment on that of Roberts in 1833:

> *The treaties of commerce existing with the Siamese Government at the time of my Mission were two – that of Captain Burney (in 1826), and that signed by Mr. Edmund Roberts on behalf of the United States, dated 20th March, 1833, and ratified by the King of Siam on the 14th April, 1835, having been previously ratified by General Jackson on behalf of the American Government. The conditions of the American Treaty are:-*
>
> *1. Perpetual peace between the United States and Siam.*
>
> *2. Right of buying and selling in Siam; munitions of war and opium excepted among imports, and rice among exports; liberty of United States' subjects to obtain passports authorizing them to quit the country when no legal objection exists.*
>
> *3. Ships to pay, instead of import and export duties, a tonnage-duty of one thousand seven hundred ticals per Siamese fathom (£212-10s.); but a vessel arriving in ballast to pay one thousand five hundred ticals (£137-10s.) per fathom. Tonnage-duty not to be charged where a vessel only calls to refit, to victual, or to obtain information.*
>
> *4. Diminution of duties, if granted to vessels of other nations, to be equally granted to vessels of the United States.*
>
> *5. Hospitality and protection to be accorded to all shipwrecked vessels of the United States, – the expenses of salvage to be repaid to the King of Siam.*
>
> *6. An American debtor to be released on the cession of all his property*

to Siamese creditors.

7. Usual rental to be paid for warehouses, in which the goods landed shall not be subject to taxes.

8. American citizens brought by pirates to Siam shall have their persons protected and their property restored.

9. United States' citizens shall respect the laws and ordinances of Siam.

10. If any but the Portuguese obtain the right to nominate consuls to reside in Siam, that right shall be given to the United States' government.

The United States' Treaty with Siam was signed on Wednesday, the last day of the fourth month of the year of the Dragon (Siamese era 1194), corresponding, as just mentioned, to 20th March, 1833. It was signed in duplicate in Siamese and English, but Portuguese and Chinese translations are annexed. The contracting parties were the Chao Phaja Phra-klang (minister for foreign affairs) and Edmund Roberts, minister of the United States. The terms of the treaty are so little favourable to commerce, that it could confer no benefit on either America or Siam, and it has remained a dead letter from the first. During the negotiations at Bangkok, it was, however, exhibited to us handsomely bound.

Mr Roberts proposed to form a treaty of friendship and commerce, to which the Siamese made no objections. He endeavoured, however, to make a more advantageous one than the English did [with Burney's treaty of 1826]; but that, the Siamese said, could not be done: they would agree to allow the Americans to trade on the same footing as the English, but more could not be granted. After some trouble and delay, a treaty was drawn up after the Siamese fashion; but then came the fight for alterations, amendments, etc. Mr Roberts had an audience of the King, and only one. The treaty is written in the Siamese, Chinese, and Portuguese languages, and commences with the same style as the English one, with 'Somdet Phra Puttie Chau Yu Hua' etc, which is translated in the treaty 'the great and magnificent King,' instead of the literal and divine titles which are alike applied to their god and their King. [Bowring's note: The literal meaning of the Siamese is, "the Lord God Buddha is at the head."] Mr Roberts was very anxious to obtain the treaty sealed in duplicate, in order to forward one copy to the United States from Batavia or elsewhere; and, after having gone to the trouble of drawing up three copies, the foolish old Pra-klang could not be induced to sign the duplicate, being fearful, it is presumed, that Mr Roberts only wanted to sell the duplicate to some other state! – so that Mr R. went away with only *one copy sealed. The Pra-klang was reasoned with, and told that were he to sign a hundred copies no harm could befall the country, all being of the same tenor and date; but it was of no avail.*

*The presents given by Mr Roberts did not produce the desired effect, though valuable in themselves: indeed, to a Court like Siam they were rendered in some sense valueless, through their ignorance. The presents to the King consisted of a pair or two of beautiful watches set with pearls of some value, some silver baskets, and abundance of China silks. To the Pra-klang, also, Mr Roberts gave presents of a good amount, but he did not visit any of the inferior princes. The amount of the presents might be about two thousand or two thousand five hundred dollars; while the returns consisted of a little sugar, sticlac, pepper, tin, gambodge, benjamin, anguella-wood, sapan-wood, and inferior cardamums; the whole of which might be worth one thousand or one thousand five hundred dollars. The Siamese knew the presents were bought in China, which did not please them much; and it is said that at one time they were not disposed to accept them. The original presents intended for the Cochin-Chinese and Siamese Courts were sent out from America in a separate vessel, but she had not arrived in China before the Peacock left. But this the Siamese would not credit...*" [Bowring's note: Moor's Notices of the Indian Archipelago, p.203]

*Mr Roberts was desirous in inserting in the treaty a clause by which liberty should be granted to send a consul; but the Pra-klang would not consent, though the King is said to have told him to agree to it. The Pra-klang informed Mr Roberts that Captain Burney had asked permission for an English consul to reside at Bangkok, but was refused.*" [Bowring's note: Ib., p.204] (Bowring 1857, 203-9)

The Bowring Treaty was to be the model of a number of similar treaties concluded soon afterwards with the United States, France and other Western countries; that with the United States, was signed in Bangkok on 29 May 1856 by Townsend Harris. The earlier efforts of Burney and Roberts were to fructify something like a quarter of a century later in the Bowring Treaty and its counterparts with other powers. Neale was right in one thing; Phra Nangklao was not greatly interested in the outside world or in trade with the West. But the outside world could no longer be ignored when the British had reduced Burma to an inland statelet and the pace of change in the region quickened. King Mongkut had the prescience to realize this, as had his younger brother, Prince Chudamani, Chao Fa Noi, who figures so largely in the pages of Roberts and Ruschenberger, and who was made *upparat* or Second King on Mongkut's accession. But in the third reign they had to bide their time.

The following editions of Roberts and Ruschenberger are known:

Edmund Roberts, *Embassy to the Eastern Courts of Cochin-China, Siam, and Muscat: in the U.S Sloop-of-War Peacock, David Geisinger, Commander, during the years 1832-3-4*, Harper and Brothers, New York 1837, reprinted Scholarly Resources Inc, Wilmington, Delaware, 1972. Appearing here are the Introduction pp.5-8, and Chapters XVI-XXI, pp.227-319, 426-7.

W.S.W. Ruschenberger, *Narrative of a Voyage round the World during the years 1835, 36, and 37, including a narrative of an Embassy to the Sultan of Muscat and the King of Siam*, Carey, Lea and Blanchard, Philadelphia, 1838, and Richard Bentley, London, 1838, reprinted Dawsons of Pall Mall, Folkestone and London, 1970. Appearing here are Vol. I Introduction pp.v-viii, Chapters XXIII-XXV pp.416-450, and Vol. II, Chapters I-VIII, pp.1-144.

For this edition, the original spelling and punctuation in each text have been retained, even where this leads to inconsistencies between the two texts (e.g. Roberts' Packnam, Bang-kok, Budha, Menam; Ruschenberger's Paknam, Bankok, Boudha, Meinam) and within the texts (e.g. Roberts' tumeric and turmerick, Ruschenberger's wât and wat).The texts are full of nineteenth century prejudices which, at this distance in time, are occasionally funny, but in Ruschenberger's case in particular, can become tiresome. The footnoting has been, as far as possible, kept to a minimum.

# PART I: THE TREATY MISSION OF 1833

EMBASSY

TO THE

EASTERN COURTS

OF

COCHIN-CHINA, SIAM, AND MUSCAT;

IN THE

U.S. SLOOP-OF-WAR PEACOCK,

DAVID GEISINGER, COMMANDER,

DURING THE YEARS 1832-3-4

BY

EDMUND ROBERTS.

# [ROBERTS']
# INTRODUCTION

HAVING some years since become acquainted with the commerce of Asia and Eastern Africa, the information produced on my mind a conviction that considerable benefit would result from effecting treaties with some of the native powers bordering on the Indian Ocean.

With a view to effect an object apparently so important, I addressed a letter to the Hon. Levi Woodbury, then a Senator in Congress from the state of New Hampshire, detailing the neglected state of our commerce with certain eastern princes, and showing that the difference between the duties paid on English and American commerce, in their dominions, constituted of itself a very important item in profit, in favour of the former.

Subsequently to this period, Mr. Woodbury was appointed to the secretaryship of the Navy, and consequently became more deeply interested in the success of our floating commerce.

Scarcely had his appointment been confirmed before the melancholy news arrived, that the ship Friendship, of Salem, Mass., had been plundered, and a great portion of her crew murdered, by the natives of Qualah Battu.

As an important branch of our commerce to the pepper ports on the western coast of Sumatra was endangered by the successful and hostile act of these barbarians, it was deemed necessary that the piratical outrage should be promptly noticed by a national demand for the surrender and punishment of the aggressors.

About this period, the U.S. ship-of-war Potomac was nearly ready to proceed to her station on the western coast of South America, by way of Cape Horn, but her destination was immediately changed for the western coast of Sumatra, accompanied by instructions to carry into effect the measures of government against the inhabitants of Qualah Battu.

As our government was anxious to guard against any casualty which might befall the Potomac in fulfilling her directions, it resolved to despatch the United States' sloop-of-war Peacock and schooner Boxer, to carry into effect, if necessary, the orders of the first-named vessel, and also to convey to the courts of Cochin-China, Siam and Muscat, a mission charged to effect, if practicable, treaties with those respective powers which would place American commerce on a surer basis, and on an equality with that of the most favoured nations trading to those kingdoms.

A special or confidential agent being necessary to carry into effect the new measures of government, I had the honour to be selected for that duty, at the particular recommendation of the Secretary of the Navy.

The summary chastisement of the inhabitants of Qualah Battu, and the complete success of Com. Downes, in the performance of the duties assigned by government, rendered a visit from the Peacock to that place unnecessary, and thus left the objects of the mission more fully open to a complete and minute investigation. How far they have been faithfully accomplished, I leave to the candid and impartial judgment of those who peruse the details of the Embassy, in the following pages.

At the period of my visit to the courts of Siam and Muscat, American commerce was placed on a most precarious footing, subject to every species of imposition which avarice might think proper to inflict, as the price of an uncertain protection.

Nor was it to pecuniary extortions alone that the uncontrolled hand of power extended. The *person* of the American citizen, in common with that of other foreigners, was subject to the penalties of a law which gave the creditor an absolute power over the *life*, equally with the property, of the debtor, at the court of Siam. As an American, I could not fail to be deeply impressed with the barbarity of this legal enactment, and its abrogation, in relation to my own countrymen, detailed in the Embassy, I consider as not the least among the benefits resulting from the mission.

With the courts of Siam and Muscat, it will be seen, I was enabled to effect the most friendly relation, and to place our commerce on a basis in which the excessive export and import duties, previously demanded, were reduced fifteen per cent.

If in the attainment of these benefits some sacrifice of personal feeling was at times made for the advantage of American commerce, the dignity of my country was never lost sight of, nor her honour jeoparded by humiliating and degrading concessions to eastern etiquette.

The insulting formalities required as preliminaries to the treaty, by the ministers from the capital of Cochin-China, left me no alternative, save that of terminating a protracted correspondence, singularly marked from its commencement to its termination by duplicity and prevarication in the official servants of the emperor. The detail of the various conversations, admissions and denials, on the part of these eastern ministers, in the pages of the Embassy, exhibits their diplomatic character in true, but not favourable colours.

The unprotected state of our trade from the Cape of Good Hope to the eastern coast of Japan, including our valuable whale-fishery, was painfully impressed on my attention in the course of the Embassy. Not a single vessel-of-war is to be seen waving the national flag over our extensive commerce from the west of Africa to the east of Japan: our merchantmen, trading to Java, Sumatra and the Philippine islands, are totally unprotected. The extent of this commerce may be estimated from the fact that there arrived in two ports in Java during one year, one hundred and one ships, the united tonnage of which, amounted to *thirty-eight thousand, eight hundred and seventy-seven tons*. To this may be added the whale-fishery on the Japanese coast, which likewise calls loudly for succour, and protection from the government. The hardy whaler—the fearless adventurer on the deep—yielding an immense revenue to his country, amid sufferings and privations of no common order, certainly claims at the hand of that country, protection from the savage pirate of the Pacific. Among this class of citizens too, we may look for those bold and determined spirits who would form the bulwark of our national navy. The protection of this important and prolific branch of commerce is, in every point of view, a political and moral advantage. I indulge the hope that it will become the object of special legislation, and that the hardy sons of the ocean, while filling the coffers of their country, may enjoy the protection of her flag.

The various tables relative to exports, imports, currencies, weights and measures, in the various places visited by the Embassy, will, I trust, be found greatly beneficial to the commercial enterprise which, yearly, extends from the Cape of Good Hope to the China sea. They have been compiled in some instances from direct observation, and in others, from the best authority which could be obtained. While it has been my special object to render the pages of the Embassy a guide to the best interests of commerce, I have not been unmindful of the claims which the general reader may have on a work embracing a view of that interesting quarter of the world, the eastern and southern portion of the eastern hemisphere; its natural scenery, productions, language, manners, ceremonies, and internal political regulations, will be found in the Embassy. The picture may not be at all times of a pleasing character; it has rather been my object to give the original impression, than to decorate it with any factitious colouring. When visible demonstration could be obtained, I have always resorted to it, in drawing my conclusions; and in those cases in which this best auxiliary was denied me, I have given the testimony of travellers from other countries, who preceded me in visiting the courts touched at by the Embassy, and whose details have received the sanction of the world.

The abject condition of morals among the inhabitants of the Indian ocean, will naturally interest the philanthropist: while rejoicing in the high moral tone of society which distinguishes his own happy land, he will look with an eye of compassion on those regions where the worship of the Supreme Being gives place to the mysterious idolatry of Budha [sic], or the external ceremonies of Confucius.

The searcher after literary information will find in the account of the literary institutions of China much interesting and useful matter for observation and reflection. In relation to the strictness of her collegiate examinations, and the high grade of learning necessary to secure their honours, some useful hints may be derived to our own collegiate institutions.

In the appendix will be found a curious literary document in relation to the aborigines of the Malay peninsula, particularly of the negroes called Semang, accompanied by specimens of the Semang language in two dialects, for which due credit has been given in the Embassy.

The philologist will doubtless receive this accession to the common stock of inquiries into the origin of language, with considerable gratification. A philosophical investigation of the relationship existing between the varied families of the earth, and their common origin, may perhaps yet be based on the analogy existing between their language and dialects.

The phraseology of the epistolary document from the Sultan of Muscat to the President of the United States, with that contained in the letter from Tumbah Tuah to Captain Geisinger, at Bencoolen, furnishes specimens of that figurative and high-wrought diction, for which the Oriental nations are distinguished.

As I am about to undertake another voyage to exchange the ratifications of the treaties alluded to in the Embassy, to form others in places not yet visited, and to extend, if possible, our commerce on advantageous terms, still farther east than India or Cochin-China, I beg my readers will consider the present volume as a prelude to much further and varied information to be derived under more favourable auspices—more intimate knowledge of eastern forms—and that caution which should ever be the child of experience.

In concluding my introductory remarks, I would freely acknowledge my obligation to the works of those authors who have preceded me in visiting the nations to which the Embassy was directed. I deemed it important that no useful information, from whatever source derived, should be withheld from my countrymen. Wherever ocular or audible demonstration could be had, I have recorded the facts as they were presented, in the most simple and unadorned manner: I had not in view the flights of rhetorical composition, but the detail of useful intelligence.

My country claimed at my hands, the faithful fulfilment of arduous and responsible duties. If, in the information furnished in the Embassy, her requirements have been accomplished, my ambition is satisfied.

E. R.

# CHAPTER XVI

ARRIVAL AT THE MOUTH OF THE RIVER MENAM—PACKNAM—PROCESSION TO THE GOVERNMENT HOUSE—RECEPTION—GOVERNOR—SIAMESE TEMPLES—INTERVIEW WITH THE SIAMESE FOREIGN MINISTER—PRIMA DONNA—FEATS OF STRENGTH—SIAMESE FEMALES—FIRE AT BANG-KOK—WHITE ELEPHANTS—EMBALMING—SHAVING-HEAD CEREMONY AND FEAST—FOX-BATS.

...On the sixteenth February [1833], at noon, we were abreast of cape Liant[1] and the islands in its vicinity; the latter are high and bold of approach. Their latitude and longitude are laid down in the charts too far to the southward and eastward. On the eighteenth we came to anchor in four fathoms of water, about ten miles from the mouth of the river Menam.

The Ko Si-Chang[2] islands bore as follows: The most southern and westward of the group, S. S. E. ¾ E. ; centre, S. E. ½ S. The mountain of Bang-pa-soe,[3] on the main land, E. S. E. The entrance of the eastern or main branch of the Menam, and the easternmost land in sight, W. S. W. The land is very low, even with the water's edge, and covered with trees; that at the entrance on the starboard hand, is a little more elevated. On the nineteenth the tide had fallen to nineteen. We weighed again, and stood a mile or two to the southward, and anchored in five fathoms. The latitude and longitude of the anchorage is in latitude 13º 26´ N., and longitude 100º 33´ E., as was ascertained by frequent lunar observations and by four chronometers. During the height of the river, when it is swollen by the periodical rains, sixteen feet of water may be found on the bar. At high spring tides, in the dry season, twelve to thirteen feet, and eight to nine in common tides. The above-named islands, by some navigators called the Dutch islands, possess a safe and beautiful harbour, formed between the principal, or

---

[1] Cape Liant in the south-east tip of land, by modern Sattahip, giving entrance to the upper part of the Gulf of Thailand.

[2] Ko Sichang, by Siracha, also known, as Roberts says, as the Dutch Islands, is still today a harbour for ships too big to enter the Chao Phya River.

[3] Bang-pa-soe, more commonly Bang Plasoi, is the old name for Cholburi, at the back of which is a high mountain.

Si-Chang island, and the next in magnitude, called Koh-kam. They are inhabited only by a few fishermen, and produce *some* yams, bananas, capsicums, gourds, and cucumbers. A boat was despatched to them to obtain water, if possible, but it could not be found in sufficient quantities to furnish the ship. We had no other resource, but to send upward of forty miles for it, to Bang-kok, or else to take the brackish water of Packnam. Water, we were informed, could only be had at the Si-Changs during the rainy season.

A boat was sent to the governor of Packnam on the eighteenth, to inform him of the arrival of the ship, &c., and a letter was sent to the minister for foreign affairs, announcing the arrival of the mission. On the following day, an interpreter came on board, who asked among the first questions if there were any presents for the king, but received no satisfactory answer. A vast number of questions were also put to Mr. Morrison[4] by the governor. A Cochin-Chinese ambassador arrived at Packnam on the same day, with several small filthy junks laden with merchandise. It was said to be only an annual mission sent by the emperor, while others stated that it was to honour the ceremony of burning the body of the "second king" who died some months since at the capital. On the twentieth, the captain of the port came on board, who said he was sent by the praklang[5] or prime minister, by order of the king, to congratulate us on our arrival; that his majesty was much gratified at the good news, and very desirous of having a friendly commercial intercourse with the United States. After making similar inquiries, as the governor of Packnam, he returned. The day following, the praklang sent some fruit as a token of regard, with complimentary message to me.

On Sunday the twenty-fourth, three large boats came to anchor near the ship, under the charge of the captain of the port of Bang-kok, Mr. Josef Piedade,[6] a Christian Portuguese born at Bang-kok. He stated that preparations were made at Packnam by the governor for

---

[4] Mr Morrison, as we are told on the next page, was the Chinese interpreter for Roberts' embassy, which had no one who could speak Siamese.

[5] The *phra khlang*, corruptly known as the *barcalon*, was in charge of trade and foreign affairs; he was not the chief minister, but his importance was always exaggerated by foreigners since he was usually the only minister they met. The various names for officials working under the *phra khlang* are titles and not personal names.

[6] Joseph Piedade was one of the small group of Portuguese descendants from sixteenth

the reception of the mission, that a feast was there prepared by order of the king, that we should be under the necessity of remaining there that night for it was customary for all foreign ministers to stop there, and notice to be given of their arrival; in congressional language, to "report progress." The vessel in which I embarked was from seventy to eighty feet in length, and perhaps eight or nine in breadth, sharp built; having three long brass cannon highly ornamented with silver, inlaid in fanciful devices. One was placed forward, between the bows, the vessel having no bowsprit; one aft, and two long swivels mounted on fixtures, between the fore and main mast, and between the main and mizen mast. She had three fore-and-aft sails made of light canvass, and cordage made of hemp, with good iron anchors, which are rarely seen on board native vessels in the China seas, wooden ones being in general use. The vessel was propelled with forty short oars, manned by as many Burmese slaves, dressed in the king's uniform; being a coarse red cotton long jacket, a cap of the same material, trimmed with white, and a blue waist-cloth. The boat had two rudders, one under each quarter; and from having two helmsmen, it was either "hard up, or hard down," continually; consequently, she "yawed" not a little. There were no less than seven red flags; one to each peak, two to each bow, and two to each quarter. A small house on deck was appropriated solely for the use of the envoy. It was covered with a carpet, and furnished with a pillow to recline on. The boat was neatly built and painted, and the house slightly decorated with carving and gilding. The passengers in the two boats consisted of Capt. Geisinger, Second-Lieut. Purveyance, Lieut. Fowler of the Marine Corps, Acting-Lieut. Brent, Doctor Ticknor, Midshipmen Carrol, Thomas, Crawford and Wells, and Mr. J. R. Morrison of Macao, Secretary and Chinese Interpreter, and four servants. The other was, in all respects, a similar vessel, but manned with thirty-six oars; rowed by Malay slaves dressed in blue, with caps of the same, trimmed with white. The ship lay in five and a half fathoms water, and not less than fifteen miles from Packnam, which is situated about two miles from the mouth of the river Menam: Packnam means the river's mouth or embochure. The shores are every where very low, and as flat as the south side of La Plata, or Arkansas on the Mississippi, and in the rainy season are

---

century immigrants who had become completely Siamese in nearly everything except names, religion, and language, and were often used as English and Portuguese interpreters.

completely submerged. The entrance to the river on the starboard hand is rather more elevated than on the left, which is quite sunken, mangrove and other trees only appearing out of the water. The river takes a sharp turn to the northward, at the entrance; the left bank running parallel, gives it the appearance of being closed at the mouth.

We arrived at Packnam, on the left bank of the river, about eight, and found there, waiting for us, the captain of the port, and a great number of slaves at the landing, with torches in hand, and fastened also to temporary posts, to light us on the way to the government-house, situated just without an extensive fortification. There was a narrow way paved with broad bricks, which led to the governor's. The gentlemen composing the company, the servants on each flank with their numerous flambeaux, with many hundred lookers-on, preserving the utmost decorum, made no small show, and produced, upon the whole, rather an imposing effect, for this was the first envoy ever sent to the "magnificent king of Siam" from the United States.

We were ushered into the best house in the village, enclosed by a bamboo-fence and guarded by soldiers with long wooden poles, pointed with iron. The houses are erected as all the houses are here, from five to seven feet above the ground, on substantial posts; the sides are covered with attap, a species of palm growing abundantly on the banks of the Menam; they have a double roof, one of tile and another of attap to moderate the intensity of the heat. We ascended a stairway and were ushered into "the presence" through lines of *prostrate* slaves,[7] from thence to a raised platform.

The governor was sitting cross-legged on an elevated seat, under a broad canopy, surrounded, a little beneath him, by his sword and silver-stick bearers, and a man holding a long fan made of feathers, which was kept in constant motion to keep him cool and to drive off the myriads of moschetoes. His menials were all prostrate, resting on their knees and elbows, coming in and going out in the same attitude, always keeping their faces turned towards him. He was smoking a long pipe, having before him areca-nut,[8] chunam, ceri (siri) or betel-leaf, and tobacco, all of which were deposited in several large gold cups or

---

[7] Roberts was used to seeing slaves, but not prostrate ones; many of his republican susceptibilities were to be disturbed during his stay.

[8] Areca nut, chunan, siri or betel leaf were the three ingredients needed for betel chewing (tobacco was a recent addition); chunam is a lime-based plaster or cement concoction.

goblets. His dress consisted of a *waist-cloth*—his head was shaved excepting on the crown, "à la Siamese." He received us very graciously, courteously, and hospitably, shaking us heartily by the hand; chairs were prepared for us and the best viands the place could afford, consisting of at least a dozen dishes, were shortly ordered in, well cooked in the Portuguese fashion, clean and neat with porter, cocoanut water, and a square Dutch bottle of gin—there were clean tablecloth, knives, forks, plates and spoons, and the floor was covered with a neat woollen carpet. The usual inquiries were made for our healths, ages, children, &c., &c. He congratulated us on our arrival, and said the mission was not only gratifying to him personally but to the country, as he was informed by the praklang or principal minister.

Supper being ended, bamboo-chairs covered with mats, some mattresses and pillows, were prepared, and the raised canopy or throne was assigned to me. Three fourths of two sides of the room were open to the air, protected from rain only by the long projecting attap roof— we were guarded during the night by soldiers and excessively annoyed

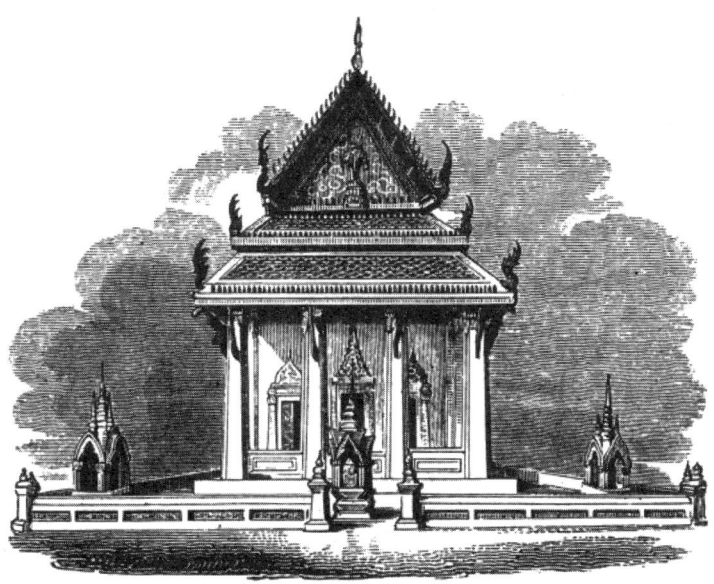

Siamese Temple.

by moschetoes. By daylight, all were upon the "qui vive," glad to escape from the torments of the night. An early ramble carried us to a pagoda, neat in appearance, decorated with carved work and gilding—it was built of brick and neatly plastered—figures of non-descript animals were about it, which were probably intended for lions, cut from granite, and there were small pra-chades or single spires built of brick and plastered, the whole being enclosed by a wall; the doors were shut so that we could not obtain an entrance; the ground every where was very low and swampy, and the houses mean; the people appeared to be wretchedly poor, diseased and dirty, but still cleaner than the Cochin-Chinese. Breakfast ended, we took leave of the hospitable governor and proceeded up the river.

Very extensive fortifications are here to be seen on both sides of the river, having water batteries, apparently of great strength. A great number of soldiers manned the walls in compliment to us, all dressed in the royal red uniform. We proceeded on with the flood tide, cheered by the passing scene. Occasionally, we met a single hut or a group of huts, having a boat at the door, and a ladder to ascend into their only room; this ladder is taken away at night, making their habitations more secure against wild beasts and reptiles, which are in great abundance in the swamps. Their principal neighbours are tigers and leopards, snakes of various sizes from the boa-constrictor and venomous cobra de cappello to the more deadly viper, which they say is black, about four or five inches in length, and has two short legs. Alligators bask in the sun at the foot of the ladder or under their building, and moschetoes bear the palm here over the swamps of Louisiana and Texas, coming in myriads so as partially to obscure the sun.

We passed on to Pack-lac[9] situated on the right bank, where we again found very extensive fortifications; but we were unable to ascertain the number of guns either here or at Packnam, which is probably about ten or twelve miles below. The ebb tide here met us, and the slaves made but slow progress in rowing—a breeze occasionally helped us, but the remainder of the passage was rendered tedious by the great heat of the sun. The river has a great many bends, so that it is nearly double the distance, by water, from Packnam to the capital, being from thirty to thirty-five miles, and only twenty by land. The

---

[9] Paklat, a Mon community, in fact linked with a small canal two wide bends in the river.

PAKLAT BELO.

shores are upon a level with the river at high spring tides, even at Bang-kok, and as I am informed, a long distance above Jutaya, the ancient capital.

Not until we were within a dozen miles of the capital, were there many clusters of huts to be seen; but, from thence, they gradually increased in number till we arrived at the city. The graceful and favourite areca-palm, with its tall slender trunk and brush-like head, and the towering bamboo and cocoa-nut, were to be seen every where along the banks, interspersed with a great variety of fruit and forest trees; and the water's edge was bounded by the attap, or cocos-nypa, which is in universal use as a thatch for their huts. As we approached the capital, we began to see pagodas, some houses with tiled roofs, and a great many large junks, building in dry docks, which consist of a simple excavation made on the banks, the water being drained out by an ordinary barrier of plank, well banked with clay. Many of these junks were upward of a thousand tons. From two to three hundred were lying in the river.

Numerous temples of Budha were now seen, covered with neat coloured tiles, some blue, and others green or yellow. Tall single spires, or prah-chadis, were observed every where. The temples present a very splendid appearance, having highly ornamented carved work in front, and literally blazing in gold. There is something very novel in their style of architecture, which can only be made clear to the understanding by drawings. Fruit and palm-trees overshadow their houses, interspersed with the sacred fig-tree, giving to them a cool and tropicallike appearance. Floating houses, resting on rafts of bamboo secured to piles, line both banks of the river, which seem to be occupied by industrious Chinese, as their long narrow red signs indicate: the latter serve to show the various articles they have for sale, &c. The Chinese are easily distinguished by their complexion, being more yellow than the Siamese; but they have generally *docked* the *entail* to their heads, and dress à la Siamese, with a circle of hair on the *roof*. But few of the "long tails," the distinguishing appendage to a Chinaman's head, are to be seen.

We were upward of nine hours in reaching the landing,* in front of the house assigned to us by the king. We landed, and formed a procession to the house; the officers being dressed in their uniforms, and the servants bringing up the rear. We were ushered in by the pia-visa,[10] or general of artillery, Benedetts de Arguelleria, and some other of the king's officers, to the finest looking house we had seen on the river, having the front view entirely unobstructed. Passing through a neat white gateway, having a well-built stuccoed wall, over a grass-plot, through the inner gate, we found ourselves within an extensive area, between two long rows of buildings, having large trees in the centre; an outside staircase conducted us to a saloon, where we found a table set, and shortly after supper was announced. It was cooked in the European and Indian style, having a variety of curries of fish and fowl. It was well served, and in profusion; and followed by a great variety of sweetmeats, and fruits of the season. Certain king's officers attended,

---

* On the right bank of the river, which is called Bang-kok[11]—the word Bang-kok is derived from ban, a house, and kok, a garden. Most of the fruit used at the old capital came from this place. [Author's note]

[10] Phya Viset was the title of the commander of the artillery, and Sur Beneditto de Arvellegaria a Cambodian Portuguese in the King of Siam's service; Crawfurd gives his name as Pascal Ribeiro de Alvergarias, which seems more probable.

[11] Old Bangkok was indeed the location of modern Thonburi. Si Ayutthaya is later given as the name for Bangkok on the left bank.

THE FLOATING CITY—BANGKOK.

and ordered every thing; bedsteads and beds were brought; and, in a day or two, moscheto-nets, &c., &c. A cook was provided, and a purveyor, who partially supplied us with provisions. There was, also, a superintendent of the household, a Siamese Portuguese by birth, Domingo by name, having four other servants to do the ordinary work of the house; and these, again, are all under the orders of Piedade, the captain of the port, who receives his orders from the praklang, or prime minister for foreign affairs.

Every day or two, presents of sweetmeats, fruit, or more substantial food is sent, by the praklang, served up in glass dishes, and sent on gold and silver salvers. When brought in, the servants kneel down and present them, in a more humble manner than suits our republican notions. Our residence has two ranges of buildings, running back about one hundred and fifty feet, exclusive of the front yard, with a wide area between them. It is built of brick and stuccoed, having a neat tiled roof. A long covered gallery conducts to the dormitories, consisting of eight on each side, which are about twenty feet square, with wooden floors; underneath are magazines, or offices; between the two ranges of buildings, and connected with them by a high wall, is the dining-hall, open so as freely to admit the air, commanding a fine view of the capital and suburbs, on the left bank: underneath the dining-hall, is a private go-down, or magazine. The river at all times has a great number of boats upon it; but in the morning, when the bazar is being made ready, there are many hundreds, probably thousands, going in all directions, from the smallest canoe, scarcely able to contain a single person, to others which are nearly a hundred feet in length, and made from a single teak-tree: they are paddled by a great number of men, having a house in the centre, or a palm-leaf roof; the passengers reclining, on a raised platform, covered with mats, carpets, and pillows.

Water-pedlars, of both sexes, but principally women, are in abundance, carrying tin and brass ware, English, and China, and India goods. Rice, oil, dried and fresh fish, balachang,[12] eggs, fowls, siri-leaf, chunam, pork, fruit, vegetables, &c.; indeed every thing that is wanted, or supposed necessary for the comfort, convenience, or luxury of the inhabitants. Budhist priests, with their yellow waist-cloths, mantles, shaven heads and eyebrows, are seen in great numbers, going their daily rounds among the inhabitants, in canoes, for food and clothing. Women, also, use the oar, in great numbers, and with equal dexterity as the men.

Although the Siamese are not a cleanly people, they are far superior to the Cochin-Chinese; they bathe frequently, their skins are clear and free of eruptions, and they do not everlastingly scratch, scratch, and keep scratching, like the people of Vunglam;[13] but their coal-black teeth are excessively disgusting, and the saliva created by chewing areca, siri-leaf, and tobacco, is constantly issuing in a red stream from their mouths. Fishing being farmed out, there are not the same lively scenes exhibited here as on the Pasig.[14] I have seen but a very few occupied in that way since my arrival. Every floating house has necessarily a boat to go visiting from place to place, or to transact business. The front parts of all these houses are shops, having their

---

[12] *Blachang* is the Malay term for the Thai *kapi*, fermented shrimp paste.

[13] Vunglam was a harbour in the Cochin-Chinese province of Fuyan before proceeding southwards to Tourane; it is used here as a synonym for Vietnam.

[14] The Pasig River flows through Manila.

wares neatly arranged on shelves and terraces. These buildings are of one story only, and are used as a bedroom at night, or to take a siesta when the heat of the day, low water, and want of customers, give to their inmates a temporary respite.

The river here is about fifteen hundred feet wide, and very deep, probably fifty or sixty feet, and the stream rapid on the flood and ebb; the water is, notwithstanding, fresh, and is used for all domestic purposes, filthy as it is. The upper stratum of the banks of the river is alluvial, and the under, where exposed, shows a stiff strong clay. The houses on the land, with very few exceptions, are of one story, built on high piles, made of plank or bamboo, and roofed with tile or attap.

Having expressed a desire to the praklang, through the interpreter, to enter as early as possible on the subject of the mission, I received an invitation early the next morning, from the minister of foreign affairs, to meet him the same afternoon at five. He sent me word at the same time, that it was always customary for foreign ministers to pay him the first visit. Suitable boats were sent in due time, and Captain Geisinger and his officers, and Mr. Morrison, accompanied me, dressed in their uniforms. A few minutes brought us to his house. Numerous people were present to attend our landing, a large portion of whom came, probably, from motives of curiosity only. The house being but a short distance from the river, we were soon within his gates, and entered by a flight of steps into the audience hall. In the centre was a raised seat, on which the minister reclined. He is a very heavy, unwieldy man, weighing, probably, nearly three hundred pounds, and about fifty-five years of age; his only dress was a waistcloth of silk; he was resting on a new crimson velvet cushion, supported on the back by one of triangular shape. In front, on the seat, were utensils of gold, handsomely wrought, containing areca, chunam, betel-leaf, &c., the gift of the king. The front of the hall was entirely open, the room decorated with a great number of very ordinary oval gilt looking-glasses, placed near to the ceiling, on the pillars which supported the roof; common English prints of battles, rural scenery, &c., were closely placed along the walls. Instead of wooden panels, painted Chinese glass was placed in compartments of about four feet in height, with a profusion of blue and gold, and outré figures of Chinese men, animals, &c. Brass chandeliers and common glass lamps were suspended from the roof. On the left of the praklang, being the seat of honour in the East, and at the distance of a dozen feet, were placed two chairs for Captain Geisinger and myself. I was requested to occupy the one nearest to the minister. A short distance from us, parallel with the praklang's seat, chairs were placed for the officers of the Peacock and Mr. Morrison. On the right, on a raised platform, but lower than the minister's or our seat, and fronting Captain Geisinger and myself, were Mr. Piedade and other interpreters, secretaries, &c., to the number of six or seven, closely wedged together; they were all crouching, in a brute-like attitude, on their knees and elbows. On the left, between me and the minister, were two of his younger sons, decorated with a profusion of golden necklaces, set with large stones, having beautiful golden coronets around the tuft of hair on the top of the head, and a large golden bodkin secured the hair on their crown; a silken waist-cloth covered their loins, and silver bangles or rings decorated their wrists and ankles. Their skins were stained with turmerick, sandal-wood, or saffron. A sword-bearer, resting on his shoulder a sword, having a rich and highly-finished and ornamented gold sheath; another slave, with a long feathered fan, to keep his excellency cool, if possible, with others, were all prostrate on the floor, like the interpreters; without, in the court-yard, were a great number of people, all in this humiliating posture. His sons, when called, crawled as well as the others, and went backward in the same attitude, always facing their lord and master. One of them was ordered to bring us palm-leaf cigars; he came crawling on, poor fellow, bowed his head to the ground, and presented them; he then went to the officers, but stood up, after leaving Captain Geisinger and myself; he afterward crawled back to his station, on the left of his father. We all made a bow in the usual style of our country, on entering and retiring, and were presented with tea, sweetmeats, and fruit.

The minister congratulated us on our arrival, inquired, as is customary here, as to our ages, children, &c., what ports we had been to, the object of the mission, all of which he previously knew by a letter received from me, dated on the day of our arrival off the mouth of the Menam. Having got through with this interview, and appointed the next evening for a conference, we took leave. I observe that the greater chiefs within sight of our habitation, have high poles erected close to their houses, on which small flags are displayed, and at night large lanterns are hoisted at the top, as a distinguishing mark over their less fortunate neighbours. Every sort of humiliation is practised by the lower to the higher classes, according to their rank: from that of making a simple obeisance by uniting their hands, raising them to the forehead, and bowing the head low, to kneeling, and the entire prostration of the body.

We went by invitation, on the sixth of March, to the house of the praklang's brother, to attend the celebration of the feats given, in consequence of cutting the tuft of hair on his son's head, which is done between the ages of ten and fifteen. The principal part of this evening's entertainment was comic acting and posture dancing, which consists in graceful attitudes of the body, and in slow movements of the arms and legs, particularly of the former, even to the distinct motions of the hands and fingers. The actors consisted of a king and queen, and male and female attendants, amounting to a dozen, all glittering in gold and tinsel, barefooted and barelegged, their faces painted white, and having silver guards to their nails, not less than six inches long, pointed at the end, and recurvated: singing in rather a melancholy strain, not altogether unmusical. There were about a hundred beating sticks on a long board, which were changed occasionally for another stick, which, when struck, sounded like castanets: two drums beaten by the hands, trumpets, small horns, and an instrument called a ranat: it is made in Lao or Laos, of graduated pieces of bamboo, which give a sweet sound when struck with a sort of wooden hammer covered with pieces of coarse cotton thread: it has eighteen keys or bars, each fifteen inches long, two inches broad, strung together, and suspended over a wooden boat-shaped box; the top part being left open. There was another instrument also, the khong-nong; being a series of small cymbals in a bamboo-frame, forming a large segment of a circle.

During the posture-dances, and through a considerable part of the divertisement, the principal singer to all splendid entertainments, the prima donna, squalled to the very top of her voice various ditties in a melancholy strain, until I thought she would have swooned from exhaustion: but I was mistaken, for she was made of tougher materials than ever fell to the lot of any other female. She was seated on the ground, and dressed in a dingy cotton waist and breast cloth, and her hair arranged "à la Siamese ;" it being all shaved off excepting on the crown, which was combed perpendicularly, standing "like quills upon the fretful porcupine." Her teeth were as black as ebony, and her lips and gums were of a livid red: out of the corners of her mouth issued a stream of dark coloured saliva, which, ever and anon, she wiped off with the back of her hand, and which was finally deposited on the waist-cloth behind: the saliva was produced by masticating areca, siri, chunam and tobacco; the latter projecting from the right corner of her mouth, according to the disgusting practice of the Javanese and Siamese. A Catalani, a Sontag or a Garcia,[15] could not feel much flattered by this addition to their sisterhood. When the actors enter on the floor, it is in a crouching or kneeling position, till they come in front of the master of the feast; then all kneel, bow their heads, and at the same time touch their foreheads with their united hands, and then slowly lower them to the waist. The second night's entertainment consisted mostly of representations of gladiators engaged in combat, fighting with swords and sticks, while numerous Chinese crackers were let off in imitation of musketry: there were pugilistic contests also with the fists, and slapping with the flat of the hand; but there was no real "set-to". There was also a most excellent company of vaulters and tumblers; some of the feats were truly surprising, as the following description will show: it was a feat of strength, which surpassed every thing of the kind that I ever witnessed. Four men placed themselves in a solid square, two others then got up and stood upon their shoulders, and another man again upon theirs; a very athletic young man, apparently about sixteen years of age, by the assistance of a ladder, placed himself in a similar position, on the shoulders of the last man, standing however only on one foot, occasionally shifted; a boy of about twelve then mounting a ladder high enough for the top

---

[15] Angelica Catalani (b. Sinigaglia 1780, d. Paris 1849) made her debut aged 17 in Venice, and sang before Napoleon in Saint Cloud in 1806. In 1804 she married a French officer who became her manager, and after a great success in London, moved to Paris in 1814; she was noted for her beauty as well as her voice. Henriette Gertrude Walpurgis Sontag (b. Coblenz 1801, d. Mexico City 1854), a German soprano, had an international career from her appearance in Paris in 1826. She ended her stage career in 1830 but continued to sing in concerts, specializing in Rossini and Donizetti. In 1828 she secretly married Count Carlo Rossi, a Sardinian diplomat; she was given a patent of nobility by the King of Prussia and thereafter lived openly with her husband until they encountered financial difficulties; she died of cholera in Mexico. Maria Malibran Garcia (b. Paris 1808, d. Manchester 1836) was the daughter of a Spanish tenor and composer who took his family to New York in 1825, forming the first Italian opera company to visit the New World. Maria Garcia returned to Europe in 1827. Her feverish stage performances were dramatically and musically very varied; she became a bitter rival of Henriette Sontag, but died when only 28.

man to seize him by a belt round the waist, he was raised at arms' length with perfect ease, standing on one leg, and occasionally shifting it to the other. After balancing him for a minute or two he threw his burden from him, who descending turned a somerset and came without harm on his feet, being pitched from an elevation of about twenty-four feet. There were a great many hundred spectators all sitting on the floor, excepting the wives and relations of the master of the feast, who sat in a narrow gallery. Chairs were used only by our party, consisting of eleven.

A handsome entertainment was served up to us, in a very neat large room, to which we ascended by a flight of four stairs, leading from a court open on two sides. The supper consisted of a great variety of sweetmeats and fruit, served up in a very neat pretty style, on silver salvers, placed on half a dozen tables—the chairs being borrowed expressly for our use; the head of the table was assigned to me; cocoanut water was the only drink, which was taken from the shell. The room was decorated at one end with an elegant canopy, rich in gold and silk, under which were displayed elegant glass, China ware, and gold and silver utensils, arranged on a wooden-terraced frame, highly gilt, painted, and varnished, flowers being interspersed here and there. The canopy was brilliantly lighted with coloured lamps, and made a handsome, rich, unique, but rather tawdry appearance. As I cannot tell a Siamese man from a woman when numbers are seated together, so it is out of my power to say whether any females were present, excepting the young actresses, who were all barefooted young girls. The hair of the Siamese women is cut like that of the men; their countenances are, in fact, more masculine than those of the males: they are generally very fat, having very stout lower limbs and arms; are excessively ugly; and when they open their mouths, truly hideous; resembling the inside of a black painted sepulchre.

On the eleventh, a large fire took place in the Christian Portuguese company of Santa Cruz,[16] immediately in our neighbourhood, which stopped at our premises. It blazed with great fury, the houses being roofed with attap, and the bamboo-frames being covered with the same combustible material: it produced great distress among the poor

---

[16] Santa Cruz, the quarter inhabited by Portuguese descendants, centred round their church of the same name, on the right bank of the river.

people: their houses were probably all their property, their beds being only a mat, and their cooking utensils, small earthen pots and a water jar; a waist-cloth or two, and a few trifles, were easily saved; but plunderers, in great numbers, stole their few miserable trifles as fast as they were conveyed to the rear. About one hundred and fifty huts were burnt, and some fifty or sixty of the sufferers took shelter in and about our house, and some of the unoccupied rooms; and, for many days, we supplied most of them with food. The king and the praklang ordered them to be assisted with bamboo, &c., to rebuild their houses; and rice, and, other small articles, were sent to them by their more fortunate neighbours. As soon as the fire commenced, every person who could use a long-handled scoop, made of closely woven basketwork, began throwing water on their houses, even on the opposite side of the river. The floating houses moored along the shore near the fire were cast off, and it being the first of the ebb, they moved down the river in great numbers. As many of them were on fire, they exhibited a very novel but painful scene: four, unfortunately, were consumed, with all their goods, and two China-men were burnt to death. On the next flood, the river was filled with the floating houses returning. It was predicted, by a superstitious Siamese, some days previously, that a fire would take place, as a vulture was seen to alight on the house of the port-captain. This officer's house, situated close to the Roman Catholic church, was burnt—the latter building receiving no injury, as the walls only are up; and, I suppose, from the great poverty of the Catholic Christians, it will take many years to finish it. The old Catholic church, in the rear, built of wood and attap, is in a very dilapidated condition. There are four other churches at Bang-kok and the suburbs, and only one at Jutia—the rest have fallen into ruins.

We landed, on the thirteenth, near the walls of the city, at the point where one of the white elephants is confined: he was in a large, airy stable, and had a great number of attendants. His colour is dusky, or rather yellowish white, and he was far from being clean; his skin was scurfy, and his eye very small, and of a bluish or light-gray tinge. On account of his unruly temper, he is secured by a cable around his right fore leg; the two fore feet are also well secured. One tusk is entirely broken, and the other partly destroyed. He is annually confined, for about three months, during the rutting season. We entered the city, and saw part of the king's elephants. In one place were six noble animals, males and females; two of the largest sized males had several massive silver rings on their tusks; they were kept clean, and were in fine order. There were many other elephant-stables, bordering on two streets, which we visited.

The streets, through which we passed, were from sixty to eighty feet in breadth; the houses, generally, ordinary in appearance, built of boards or brick, stuccoed, with tile roofs, or with bamboo with attap roofs. Most of them are raised on posts, and stand five or six feet from the ground. The streets are paved with very large-sized bricks. Stalls are kept in front of most of the buildings, where are sold fowls and pork, fruit and vegetables. The China, and Indian, and European goods are sold mostly in the floating bazars. There were few people to be seen.

Our object in visiting the left bank of the river, was to see an immense edifice, in the form of a temple, which was erecting for the purpose of burning the wang-na[17], generally called the second king, who died about six months since; and whose body has been embalmed, according to the imperfect knowledge of the Siamese in this art. The body is first washed, and then a large quantity of crude mercury or honey is poured into the mouth; it is then placed in a kneeling posture, and the hands are brought together before the face in the attitude of devotion; strips of cloth are then bound tightly round the extremities, and the body is compressed in a similar manner, for the purpose of squeezing out the moisture. It is then put into an air-tight vessel, more or less expensive, according to the rank of the deceased; (some of the vessels are even made of gold;) a hollow tube is inserted into the mouth, passes through the upper part of the box and the roof of the house, to convey away the effluvia; a similar tube is placed in the bottom, which communicates with a vessel, placed there to receive the draining from the body. The sordes thus collected, if they belong to a prince, are conveyed, with many ceremonies, below the city, and there emptied into the river. Should they belong to the king, they are boiled until an oil separates, and this is used on certain occasions (as when his family or his descendants pay their devotions to his departed spirit) to anoint the singular image, called Seina,[18] which is generally placed in a temple after his death. By the process, named above, the

---

[17] *Wang-na* is correctly the name of the palace of the second king.

[18] *Seina* may be a misreading of *sema*, the temple boundary stones, though Roberts seems misinformed here.

body, in a few weeks, becomes quite dry and shrivelled.

I am fully sensible that any description I can give of the building to which I have alluded, will fall far short of the reality; in fact no language can convey an adequate description of it. The "*tout ensemble*," when viewed at a distance, glittering in gold and flowers, recalls to our recollection the brilliant and splendid castles of fairy-land, so bewitchingly set forth in many an idle work of former days. Many hundreds of people have been employed in its erection ever since his death; the centre building is a large open dome, and probably reaches to the height of eighty or ninety feet; it is supported by immense wooden pillars of teak all in one piece—the roof is of various indescribable forms, and differs from any I have ever seen—the parts rise one above another till it comes to a point; from the centre rises a high slender spire, and from the base to its apex cannot be less than one hundred and fifty feet; the roof is covered with brass leaf, which gives it a splendid appearance at a distance: it has a great number of projections with various singular ornaments on their edges and the inside of the roof is dome-shaped: beneath it was erected a small temple, in the same form, having in the centre a high platform, to which we ascended by a flight of steps, over which was a small spire: it is supported upon four pillars and cannot be less than thirty-five feet high—the roof is ornamented with neat carved work and richly gilt—on the platform, the body is to be burnt. The whole inside of the building was painted to resemble flowers, profusely gilded, and otherwise richly decorated with gold and silver leaf—the walls were made of matting covered with paper and secured to bamboo-frames, as well as the outer covering, which was painted brown, decorated with large flowers made of brass or copper leaf and pasted on, which gave it a brilliant appearance. Eight temples, one fourth of the size of the great temple, stand about one hundred feet from it, so that the whole forms a complete square, of rather less than five hundred feet on each side; these are similarly gilt and painted, and are connected with each other by a corridor inside; the covering outside is similar to the great centre temple, being painted brown and overlaid with flowers. Around the base of all these buildings are projections of about three feet, like the base of a column, having imitation mouldings: these are overlaid again with sheets of brass leaf, as well as the cornices and architraves. The entrances to all the doors have a profusion of gilt and painted ornaments as well as the base, shaft, capital, and architrave of all the columns. The great building was surrounded at proper intervals (so as not to appear crowded) with small temples or sheds standing on four columns, and neatly gilt and ornamented. A wide space on the east side was left open, on which were erected very high narrow stages, neatly built, for the use of musicians, for the exhibition of rope dancers, tumblers, and gladiators, or sword fighters, pugilists, &c. At regular intervals were raised conical umbrellas or a series of canopies, the lower one being about six feet in diameter and each covering gradually lessening to the top, which terminated in a point—they were about thirty feet in height and alternately were of silver-leaf and brass-leaf, gilt, and ornamented with flowers. The whole ground and passages were covered in with bamboo framework, as well as the passage leading to the king's palace; the latter had a covered walk or roof of the same material extending the whole distance to the entrance within the enclosure. There were four entrances through long passages to the temple-altar or place of burning, and the whole building was surrounded with hideous images of men about a foot high, low dwarf-trees being interspersed between them, protected again by a low neat network railing of iron.

On the fourteenth, we went to partake of a feast at the praklang's, in company with Mr. Silveiro, the Portuguese consul,[19] and Captain Geisinger and the officers. This invitation was given about ten days since, and renewed from time to time. It was conveniently arranged by the praklang, as this day was set apart for shaving the heads of two of his sons and a nephew. The feast could not have taken place without our assistance, for they borrowed one of our cooks, the tables, tumblers, wine-glasses, tureens, ladle, spoons, &c. We were informed they had no wine, and, therefore, requested me to furnish the requisite quantity. At three, covered barges were in waiting for us, and in a few minutes, we found ourselves seated in the hall of audience; the praklang was sitting in all his majesty, on a raised seat. The dinner was already on the table. As soon as the usual compliments were over,

---

[19] "Mr de Silveiro, whom we frequently saw during our residence in Siam, was a native of the Brazils. He spoke French and English with facility and made many communications to us" (Crawfurd, *Journal of an Embassy to the Courts of Siam and Cochin China*, London, 1828, p.105). He was not technically a consul, but a foreign resident handling Portuguese trade and other matters, and had been in Bangkok since about 1820.

PORTUGUESE CONSULATE AND MISSIONARY HOUSES, BANGKOK.

and we had sat down to dinner, music struck up within the house, accompanied by female voices, which were good and natural, and the songs were not unmusical, being rather of a plaintive cast. The court-yard, during the feast, was thronged with people, who came, I suppose, "to see us eat," and to see the officers in their uniforms; they were very orderly and quiet, crouching to the ground. I have seen no instance, thus far, of the slightest degree of rudeness, which was much and justly complained of by Mr. Crawford [sic] and others, but quite the contrary: every mark of respect has been shown.

The dinner was dressed "à la Siamese and Portuguese." A stage was erected in the court-yard for vaulters and tumblers; when the dessert was produced, which consisted of some thirty dishes of confectionary and fruit, they commenced their surprising feats. They consisted of about a dozen, belong to the step-brother of the king, the prince Cha-fa-Nooi, or Mum-fa-Nooi,[20] and are the same that were exhibited at

---

[20] 'Chao-Fa Noi' was Prince Chudamani, Prince Mongkut's younger brother, and future second king.

the praklang's brother's a few nights since. After the cloth was removed, the king of Siam was given, as a toast by me, all standing; and in return, the praklang proposed the President of the United States, which was drunk likewise, all standing up. Two or three complimentary toasts then followed. The tumblers continued their sports for two hours, until sunset; then twelve young actors and actresses, very richly clad, made their appearance, and performed pantomimes and posture-dances till past nine, when our party, being heartily tired of the performances, begged leave to retire. Their sports, we understood, were continued till after midnight; the music was the same we had before. The three curtains, which conceal the entrances into the interior of the house, were raised; when the players began, each door appeared to be full of the minister's numerous wives, and in front some dozens of his children, all bedecked with necklaces, bangles, &c.; their skins being coloured with saffron or turmeric, for it is considered here a great desideratum to have the skin of a light yellow. The women were not generally so masculine in appearance as those we saw abroad, and were of a lighter complexion, being less exposed. Some of them appeared but a shade or two less than white. They were clad in sombre-coloured silk waist and breast cloths, but wore no jewels; the teeth of even the youngest were black as jet, and their lips and gums of a livid hue.

On the cutting of the hair from the crown of the male children, a display is made by every person, however humble, from the firing of two or three muskets to feasting, fireworks, dancing, music, and acting, in all their varieties; presents are expected from all relatives, acquaintances, and friends, which constitute a fund for the boy. A similar amount of gifts is expected in return, upon a like occasion; but a man high in office always has the best of the bargain.

To show the extreme indelicacy, in truth, grossness, of these people, even among the higher classes, the captain of the port, Piedade, was sent to me from the praklang, to say that the envoy from the United States would of course make a present, as Mr. Crawford and the Portuguese consul had done on a similar occasion; being placed in rather a delicate situation, in regard to the treaty, having two troublesome points unsettled, I complied with this piece of spunging, and gave a hundred silver dollars, which were presented to the praklang in the course of the afternoon, in a gold vase, by the general of artillery,

Benedito,[21] with a complimentary message from me, wishing that his children might be useful members of society, virtuous and happy, &c. It was highly ludicrous, yet most disgusting, to see the general of the eleven ranks of nobility, who stands second in order, viz.: a *phaya*, crawling like a dog on all fours, dressed in a striped silk cloak, bound round with heavy gold lace, of the fashion of the fifteenth century, shoving the vase before him, till he came to the praklang, and delivering it, making his obeisance to the ground with hands united; then *backing out* of "the presence," in the same degrading position, till he reached me, to return the great man's thanks. The vase was then taken just beyond our table (one step below, for every step, in fact, has its appropriate rank) and delivered to two persons, one of whom, I suppose, was the treasurer, the other the Moorish or Chuliah[22] secretary, who always makes his appearance, crawling on all fours, with his black paper, slate, and pencil, whenever there is any business to be transacted. The money was counted within our sight, and reported to the praklang to be *all right!* ! ! It was but a few days previous to this, that an elegant gold watch, set in pearls, two cases of silks, and four elegant fillagreed silver baskets, edged with gold, and ornamented with enamelled figures, had been presented by me to the praklang, which I intended to deliver at the conclusion of the treaty; but he having obtained information, by some means, that I had a present for him, sent Piedade to inquire of what it consisted, *and the cost*; the next day he returned, with the eldest son of the praklang, who is one of the four household officers of the king, being the second in rank, and called "Luang-nai-Sit," requesting to have them examined and an inventory taken, which was done; a hint was then thrown out by the captain of the port, that it would facilitate my business, if the praklang had his presents. It was evidently improper to give them, until those intended for the king were presented; but I complied with it, satisfied in my own mind it was done *by command*. They were presented the same afternoon, on gold vases, when I went to discuss certain points in the treaty.

The king's presents, consisting of silks, elegant watches set in pearls,

---

[21] Beneditto; see note 10.

[22] Chuliah was a term given to a particular class of Muslims from the Malabar Coast and Ceylon.

and very superior silver fillagreed baskets, with gold rims, and enamelled with birds and flowers, were shown at the same time, at their request, and an inventory of them taken also; again they inquired the cost of them, made some remarks respecting the colour of the silk, and said that some other colour would have suited the king better; that the reason why they were ordered to examine the articles was to know if they were *suitable* presents to give the king. Having expressed some slight degree of indignation at their gross conduct, they said, such were their orders from the praklang, and that Major Burney[23]—who succeeded Mr. Crawford, in finally making a better treaty with them than was ever made before, although it was effected after a long negotiation, by the sacrifice of the personal liberty of the king of Quedah, and their great fear of the English government, who possess the key of their country, in holding possession of most of the strongholds of the Burman empire, as well as Malacca and Singapore, and their possessions at Pulo Penang—brought, among other articles, a parcel of painted boxes, &c., which they rejected. After a slight personal knowledge of three weeks only with this people, I infer that they are extremely disingenuous and fickle-minded, because many articles of the treaty, passed and agreed upon in the evening, have the following day been subverted, or the strength of the language so materially weakened, as to take away nearly its whole force. That they are great intriguers, past history will confirm: the present king, the illegitimate son[24] of the late monarch, by the sudden death of his father, aided by bribes, placed himself on the throne, to the exclusion of the eldest legitimate son,[25] who, on the death of his father, fled the place, and became a Talapoy[26] to save his life. Cha-fa-Nooi, the next in succession, has a small stipend allowed him, and lives in what is called the Portuguese fort, opposite the city: his life is safe, as long as his eldest brother lives.

---

[23] Major Burney was a well-connected East India Company servant who spoke Siamese and Malay. His mission to Siam took place in 1826 and he later was sent on a mission to Ava.

[24] Rama III was the son of Rama II by a concubine, not a queen; he gained the throne legitimately, being much older and more experienced in statecraft than Prince Mongkut.

[25] Mongkut was already in the monkhood when his father, Rama II, died, and decided, perhaps out of prudence, to remain there.

[26] Talapoy, usually Talapoin, was a term used by Westerners for Buddhist monks. The etymology of the word is disputed.

That these people are highly superstitious, is shown by their constant watching for the flight of vultures, and the worshipping of idols; and the ten thousand follies attached to the Budhist religion, is sufficient evidence. That they are servile, is a necessary consequence, arising out of their despotic government. Subordination of rank is carried to a most degrading and revolting point; true politeness therefore is destroyed; they are abject in the extreme to superiors, and most insolent and disdainful to inferiors. It appears to be impossible for an inferior, to stand erect and manly, in presence of a superior: they are sluggish, ignoble and crouching. A people who are habitually crawling upon their knees and elbows, and performing "the knock-head ceremony," cannot be otherwise than ungraceful and inelegant in their manners. If they were allowed to carry arms, they would be constrained to be civil and polite to each other; but custom sanctions the right of avenging private wrongs. They are a most extravagantly vain people; are reputed to be very deficient in courage; excessively lascivious and immoral; of which proofs are presented at every step. Temporary marriages are so notorious, that to sell a daughter wholly to a stranger, or for a stipulated term of time, is as common among the middling and lower classes of people, as to sell any common commodity, usually to be found in a bazar. Custom has also fixed a certain price for a certain rank. It is said by Mr. Gutzlaff,[27] that they are in expectation of the coming of the Saviour of mankind, and that the people who are to effect a change in their religion, are to come from the West, (meaning Europe and America.)

If the overturn of an idle, superstitious and debauched priesthood like the Talapoys, (or Talapoins,) who are said to amount to upward of ten thousand generally, in Bang-kok and its neighbourhood, can be effected, what a glorious field will there be opened, to enlighten a nation who are not blood-thirsty or revengeful, but naturally mild and tractable, and exceedingly charitable to distressed objects. They are willing to be instructed, and gladly accept of any books in their own language, which are presented to them. A better form of government would of course make them a better people, but they are now bowed down by oppression, and their highly productive soil is

---

[27] Gutzlaff was an intolerant Prussian Protestant missionary who stayed a short while in Bangkok in the 1830s working chiefly among the Chinese.

almost untilled, because the hard earnings of the labourer are wrung from him by the rapacious cruelty of his rulers. I omitted to say, that during the evening's entertainment at the praklang's, a brown, highly varnished, and gilt seat, was brought in and covered with carpets, cushions, &c., and placed on the floor a short distance from where we were sitting, and shortly after, (preceded by crawling slaves,) a swordbearer, others carrying highly wrought gold vases, containing areca and a water goblet, a small tea apparatus, &c.; then followed the prince Cha-fa-Nooi, or Mom-fa Nooi, and, without any ceremony whatever, took possession of the seat without noticing in any degree the praklang: when the prince entered, the praklang left his usual seat, which was of the same height as the prince's, and seated himself on the floor, with his feet resting on a broad landing, leading to the upper floor: this is an acknowledgment of inferiority in rank. On this landing, at his feet, reposed the praklang's son and brother, and a step below, were his chubah,[28] secretary, &c., &c.: actors beneath the last, and a host of crawlers. The prince retired after sitting a short time, but without noticing his host, who immediately returned to the upper or highest seat.

During the afternoon of the feast of the entertainment, the supercargo, a Chuliah, belonging to the English brig Highland Chief, Captain Henry, from Madras, came crawling in on all fours from the inner gate, and presented, on salvers, some coarse Indian calicoes and lawns. They were received with a sullen air, and I could not perceive that the slightest notice was taken of them, when the praklang was informed of the present. This same supercargo was one of the crouchers, placed on the seat with the captain of the port, when we paid the introductory visit to the minister.

I went to visit the great resort of the fox-bats, on a branch of the river leading to the sea. We found them in immense numbers within the grounds owned by mendicant Talapoys, whereon were many temples in a state of ruin. These birds were hanging by their claws, head downward, where they remain during the day, occupying the limbs of many hundreds of large trees. Having procured some, we measured one, and found it was forty-three inches in length, measuring from one extremity of its wings to the other: it has the head of a fox; the

---

[28] 'Chubah' is probably a mistranscription of *chuliah*; see note 22, and five lines below.

body is covered with long hair, and it has a most unsavoury, strong, foxy smell; it uses its teeth when fighting, but its main defence is in a hooked claw, placed at the middle joint of the wings, by which it occasionally suspends itself. In walking about the grounds of the pagodas, we observed hundreds of small conical mounds, which had been moulded by a form made of plantain stock, and surmounted by small paper flags fastened to a slender rod; these were said to be offerings made by some votaries of Budhistical nonsense.

In passing up the river a day or two since, we saw a snake of about twelve feet in length, and about eight inches in circumference; he was swimming about close to our boat, and did not appear to notice us, excepting when we struck at him with a paddle. Crows, vultures, and sparrows, abound every where, and we find the former very annoying to us, occupying the trees in the area of our house, pouncing upon the cooks' premises, continually, and carrying off large pieces of meat or fish. The most common reptiles about our premises are lizards; several beautiful species are found every where. We have, among others, the tokay or ghecko in great numbers. This name is given to it here from its singular harsh and monotonous cry, which sounds like its name, to-kay. Throughout the night, these noises are made at intervals, probably of half an hour, commencing with a loud cry, and gradually growing weaker, making pauses of perhaps five or six seconds, between the cries; they are repeated from three to nine or ten times before exhaustion takes place. These reptiles are frequently seen eighteen inches in length, having red and light-green spots, with many tubercles. Fish are abundant in the Menam, and the Siamese, notwithstanding their pretended aversion to taking animal life, do not hesitate to eat fish, flesh, or fowl, if it is killed for them. All these articles are sold daily. Beef is not to be had but there is plenty of pork. Fruit is by no means abundant here at this season, although this is said to be the greatest fruit country in all Asia. A few small mangoes have made their appearance, but the stones are so large that little fruit is to be found on them. We have seen no oranges excepting those brought by China junks—a few poor watermelons and guavas, which are a tasteless fruit, and plantains, bananas, and cocoa-nuts: the latter are in abundance, and the water from the young ones is very refreshing.

Here, for the first time, I tasted the water of a certain delicious kind of cocoa-nut, which was frequently sent by his majesty; it was highly flavoured, and tasted like burnt almonds. Oil is made in large quantities, and is used, when fresh, for cooking, burning, and for anointing the skin, and nourishing the hair. A little later, and the delicious mangosteen will be ripe, the orange, the durian, the pineapple, and lichi, will be in abundance, besides all the other tropical fruits common to this climate. The only vegetables we have yet seen on our table are the sweet potatoe, yam, garlic, onion, Indian corn, beans, peas, and *celery*, which latter is used in soups only.

The valley of the Menam produces marsh-rice, of various qualities, and in the greatest abundance; it is often exported in large quantities, by license from the king. Rice is almost the only article of food used by the inhabitants ; this vegetable is mixed with a little balachang and compound of shrimps, or the spawn of shrimps, or small fish, mixed with salt, and dried in the sun, and then moistened with fish-pickle: it is not only unsavoury to Europeans, but some of it is most offensive to the smell. The inhabitants have but two meals a day, in the morning and evening; the richer add tea, which is drunk in great quantities, without sugar or milk, during the day. Chewing areca and smoking cigars, are common to all, even among small children, and both are constantly used during their waking hours.

[2]

# CHAPTER XVII

PRESENTATION AT THE PALACE OF BANG-KOK—DESCRIPTION—ROYAL ELEPHANT—WHITE ELEPHANTS—KING OF SIAM—GREAT TEMPLE OF GUATAMA—CITY OF BANG-KOK—TEMPLE OF WAT-CHAN-TONG, AND FIGURE OF BUDHA—BANYAN TREE—FIRE-FEEDERS—MISSIONARIES.

ON Monday, the eighteenth, arrangements having been previously made, three large boats were sent by the praklang, to convey us to the palace, for the purpose of being presented to his majesty. On the previous evening, the second praklang, or the phaya-phiphat kossa, with a long train of attendants, came to visit us, with the ostensible object of talking farther respecting certain articles, which the praklang wished to have altered in the treaty. After a few minutes' conversation upon this subject, the audience of the king was spoken of, and he said that certain ceremonies, according to court etiquette, must be observed on our visit. I replied, that every proper respect would, of course, be shown to his majesty; but that nothing mean or servile must be expected. He then said, on our entrance into the hall of audience, on passing the screen, three bows were expected in the European style; that, on sitting down, in the Asiatic style, (as no chairs are there ever used,) our feet must be placed behind us, that three bows were then to be made, by uniting the hands and touching the forehead, and lowering them to the breast. Seeing nothing unreasonable or degrading in this formality, it was agreed to, excepting that we refused to bow the head, like the Siamese. On the king's naming us personally, we were to bow in the usual style of recognisance with us; and when the curtain was drawn on his appearance, we were to make three such bows, as might suit us. This was all very well; and I was glad to find the taking off the shoes was not spoken of, and entering in a stooping position, which could not have been complied with, as it was by Mr. Crawford, when on a mission a few years since, who, to effect his purpose, (in which he totally failed,) complied with their insulting demands. The Siamese amuse themselves with talking upon this subject even now, and say, that the gentlemen belonging to the mission, were obliged to walk ankle deep in mud and water; that some of them lost their shoes,[29] they being thrown away purposely by the Siamese servants; of course, by order of their masters. Once or twice, the subject was named to me, and I severely reproved them for their disgraceful conduct. Major Burney, it seems, on a more recent mission, agreed to comply with the demand of taking off his shoes, but on the condition that he kept on his hat: they, however, preferred he should keep on his shoes, and take off his hat.

Our mode of conveyance from the water-side to the palace, was agreed upon previously, viz.: A palanquin, with eight bearers, dressed in red uniforms, and caps to correspond, was to be provided for myself, and ten horses for the other gentlemen, properly caparisoned, according to rank. We embarked at nine o'clock, and were, in a few minutes, at the palace-stairs. Spectators were numerous, in the floating houses and boats, on our way; and. on landing, the place was thronged with them, leaving sufficient space, however, for the procession, there being officers in attendance to keep the multitude in order. However, every thing was well conducted, and without noise. Excellent horses, handsomely caparisoned, with elegant saddles and silk bridles, breastp late and head-stall, ornamented with various-coloured gems, decked in rich embroidery, were provided: each horse was led by one of the king's servants.

The procession moved on, the envoy being placed in front, through two long streets, passing a gate of the city, and finally arrived at one of the gates to the palace-yard, where we found a guard, dressed in red broadcloth coats, and waist-cloths of every colour, with and without hats and caps, bearing muskets with black barrels and red stocks. We proceeded to the hall of justice, where we dismounted.

Fronting the building, were ten large elephants, well caparisoned, having a guide on their necks, with his hook and spear fixed to a staff, while another sat on the rump with a similar weapon; and in the centre, a standard-bearer, having a spear, to which was attached a long tassel of elephant's hair: these men wore red turbans and neat parti-coloured dresses, well fitted to the shape. We ascended two or three steps to a landing, which was crowded with people of various

---

[29] Some of them did indeed lose their shoes; the episode is recorded by both Crawfurd and Finlayson.

A WAR ELEPHANT

descriptions: from this we advanced one step, which led to the floor, being escorted by the officers in waiting, by Col. Pasqual,[30] and others. We were desired to wait a short time, till his majesty had arrived in the hall, which was at a short distance. The floor was covered with a good Persian carpet, apparently made for the place. Among others present, were ten Pequan[31] officers of rank, sitting on the landing, outside the pillars which supported the roof, for none were permitted to be on the floor where we were but the interpreters, and these, according to etiquette, sat on the floor. The Pequan officers were dressed in gold-flowered crimson silk, and long jackets, reaching below the knee, and turbans of silk of the same colour, trimmed with gold fringe: all were sitting in the Asiatic style. Having waited some time, we were told the king was ready to receive us. In proceeding to the hall, through a very spacious and extensive yard, we saw, on our right, drawn out, standing on a grass-plot, under high canopies, eight other elephants, richly caparisoned, having no riders, but plenty of attendants. We passed on—preceded by a number of Chuliahs, or Moors, having elegant silk dresses, reaching to the feet, and turbans, some of flowered crimson, others with white silk having gold flowers,

---

[30] Colonel Pasqual was presumably a Sino-Portuguese.

[31] Pequan is a repeated misspelling for Peguan, meaning Mon.

# Part I: Treaty Mission of 1833

and turbans of the same—through several hundred musicians, in red coats and caps. In the rear were soldiers, placed in pens, in a crouching posture, armed with spears and shields, with the interpreters and peace-officers. The music, consisting of drums, brass horns, trumpets, &c., &c., struck up a most deafening noise, on our entering within their lines, which ceased when we arrived within the walls of the hall.

Every thing was conducted with the utmost decorum. Just before reaching the hall, we passed a most noble spotted elephant—he had four massive gold rings, which must have weighed several pounds each, studded with jewels, secured around each tusk: a raised seat, a foot or two above the ground, was fixed for him to stand on, because he was a royal elephant, and could only be mounted by the king: a servant was feeding him with fresh cut grass and bananas. Facing us was part of the king's stud of fine Arabian horses, placed under a high shed, richly, and in fact, superbly dressed, attended by their keepers, which we were requested to admire. The spectacle thus far was quite imposing, and it seems every thing had been arranged to make a favourable

Front of the main Building of the King of Siam's Palace.

impression. The elephants were placed in those positions, where they would show to the greatest advantage—as well as the king's stud of horses, the immense number of military with a vast many officers richly clad, many of them being most splendidly dressed—the singular unique style of architecture of the king's palace—a large number of cannon placed under open sided sheds, the hall of audience, &c., &c., illumined by a brilliant sun and an unclouded sky, gave to every thing an Asiatic and novel appearance.

We entered at length the vestibule through a line of soldiers, and passed to the right of a Chinese screen of painted glass, into the presence of his majesty. There lay prostrate, or rather on all fours resting on their knees and elbows, with hands united and head bowed low, all the princes and nobility of the land: it was an impressive but an abasing sight, such as no freeman could look on, with any other feelings than those of indignation and disgust. We halted in front of the presents which were delivered the day previous, being piles of silks, rich fillagreed silver baskets, elegant gold watches studded with large pearls: they were well disposed to make a show. Having gone through the first ceremony of bowing, we sat down on a carpet: on our being seated the prostrate slaves around us (being the great men of the land) bowed simultaneously three times to the ground, in a slow solemn manner, and we joined in the ceremony as had been previously agreed upon. The king was seated under a canopy, in the Asiatic style, on a cushion of red silk velvet, on the lower and more advanced of the two thrones, which occupied the upper end of the apartment: this was a square seat raised some half dozen feet from the floor. Every thing was blazing in gold, in and about the two thrones: the larger and unoccupied one was of an hexagonal shape, and resembled a church pulpit, so that the king's person when seated in it, can be visible only through the open spaces, in the form of Gothic windows, about four feet in height by one and a half and two in width. One of these windows is in front, and one on each side of the throne. A pair of curtains of gold cloth formed a partition between him and several individuals of the royal family, who lay crouching just without, on separate carpets, leaving a wide open space between the throne and the two interpreters, who were midway of the hall. Before the curtain and on either side, were eight or ten umbrellas of various sizes: these consist of a series of canopies eight or ten tiers, decreasing in size upward.

His majesty is a very stout fleshy man, apparently about forty-five years of age, of a pleasing countenance. He was dressed in a cloth of gold tissue around the waist, while a mantle was thrown gracefully over the left shoulder. Four noblemen's sons were seated at the base of the throne, at the rear and sides, having long-handled pear-shaped fans, richly gilt, which they kept in constant motion. A few questions were addressed by the king in an audible voice: they were repeated in a lower tone by the phaya phiphat, or second praklang, to the phaya churat, or chief of the Chuliahs, by whom they were whispered to the captain of the port, who interpreted them to us in the same low tone—the answers were returned through the same channels by us; inquiring, in the first place, as to the health of the President and all the great men in our country—our own healths—those of the officers and crew—how long we had been from America—where we had been, and whence bound—desiring me to acquaint the praklang with all my wants, that they might be supplied, &c., &c., &c. The curtain was now drawn and his majesty disappeared; the court made three solemn kotows, and we our three salams, and then retired. The hall is probably one hundred and twenty feet in length by sixty in breadth, and has seven or eight stout square pillars on each side, probably built of brick and stuccoed, which support the roof; the highest part of the ceiling must be thirty-five or forty feet, is painted vermillion, having gilt starlike ornaments: the pillars and sides of the wall were painted so as to resemble paper hangings, and were altogether in bad taste: common looking-glasses, and ordinary European paintings of men with frizzled and powdered hair, were placed against the wall. The floor was covered with a new kidderminster carpet, such as may be bought in the United States for about a dollar and a quarter a yard; in fact there was no richness or elegance displayed; excepting about the throne there were neither jewels nor costly workmanship: the dress of the king himself was by no means extraordinary.

We were surrounded by Siamese, Cambojans, Burmese, Pequans, Malays, Chinese, Cochin-Chinese, Moors, and people of Lao, dressed all in the costumes of their respective countries, but all of them at the disposal of the "master of lives," as the king of Siam is styled. It was before observed, that the princes were nearest the throne, on a separate carpet; behind them, on another carpet, were the praklang and the higher officers of state, as precedence is decided here by relative vicinity to the throne: the lowest officers admitted, are those at the very entrance of the hall. When the courtiers enter, they crawl in on all fours, and, when dismissed, crawl out again backward, "à la crab," or "à la lobster;" and when the numbers are great, their appearance is most ludicrous. During the audience the utmost silence was observed by the courtiers; not an eye was even cast toward us until it was ended. One would suppose that all who were there present, were assembled before the throne of Him who is to *sit* in judgment at the latter day, rather than before a temporal monarch; there were such a stillness and solemnity at times, that the scene was quite oppressive. The audience, which lasted about half an hour, being ended, his majesty ordered us to be shown the white and other elephants, the temples, &c., within the palace-walls.

On our exit from the building, the music again struck up and ended when we passed the lines. We were first conducted by the interpreters and some half dozen officers, to the stables of the more valuable elephants, kept within the enclosure. The first shown to us was the sacred white elephant, a more gentle and peaceable character than the one secured without the walls, near the river; he was much whiter also, but this might be owing to his being kept cleaner, his eyes were larger, sound, and healthy in appearance, and the skin free from scurf. I was particularly requested to feed him with bananas and sugar-cane, which he received from my hands most gently, rubbing his long proboscis once over the back of my hand and then made three salams with his trunk. Fresh cut grass was placed in small bundles before him, and when annoyed by the flies and moschetoes, he would take a wisp and brush his legs, throwing it afterward on his back. In this stall was a white monkey, of the size of a small dog, a perfect Albino, the iris, pink, &c., &c.; he was kept in a cage, and appeared never to be quiet for a single second. We passed on to four other stalls, which contained spotted elephants; they are noble animals, and I consider them more worthy of notice than the white ones. We passed on to the great temple of the palace,[32] which was repairing, where Budha sat enthroned on high, of a gigantic size, shining with gold and yellow cloths, and protected with a yellow umbrella. The walls were covered with historical paintings, relative to the wanderings of Rama: and the

---

[32] Wat Phra Keo.

outer courts were filled with descript and non-descript animals of all sorts, in plaster, stone, and marble. Within the columns, plates of artificial fruits were placed; the favourite lotus was growing in large ornamented stone and porcelain vases, and there were artificial ones in stone. Two warriors,[33] of immense size, guarded the entrance as usual. The doors were splendidly adorned with mother-of-pearl, inlaid so as to represent flowers and fruit of various elegant devices. The thermometer being at nearly a hundred, we remained but a short time, being much exhausted by fatigue and the intense heat of the sun. We returned in the same order in which we came, being much gratified with our reception, and rejoiced that it was at an end.

I have frequently asked the question, How many priests there are belonging to the different pagodas? The answer has been always, sometimes ten, and sometimes twenty thousand; there is no particular number. Pray, what is the cause of this great difference in numbers, at different times? Oh! it depends altogether upon the price of rice; if rice is abundant, priests are fewer in number than when it is scarce; for a great number of them enter the priesthood for a short time only, when they have nothing to eat: this is the reason, why there are so many small boys dressed in yellow, because their parents have no food for them. During the great inundation of 1831, the number of priests doubled, in consequence of the scarcity of provisions. This vicinity was, until that time, remarkable for the great abundance and variety of its excellent fruit. In the course of three months, during which the country was so submerged, it was almost totally destroyed, as well as the crops of rice and cane. In speaking one day of the extreme servility of the lower classes to the higher, I was informed, that the praklang, in coming out of his house during the overflow of the river, always had the usual homage paid to him by the people, of kneeling or stooping when he passed them; and that they have been frequently seen so deeply immersed in water, as to be obliged to rise a little to prevent its entering their mouths, and suffocating them. This degrading homage, I have seen frequently paid him by his eldest son, Luang-nai-Sit, crawling on all fours into his father's presence, and bowing his head to the ground, with united hands. He is about twenty-five years of age—has several wives and many children; he is of an inquiring mind,

---

[33] The guardian *yaksa* or giants.

but said to be very intriguing and cringing to those who can promote his interests. He says, "his father frequently sends for him to breakfast, and the constrained position in which he is placed (on all fours) prevents his eating much, he, therefore, unfortunately suffers before he can obtain his dinner."

Among the queer articles of export from this place to China, are snake-skins, which are there used for musical instruments principally, and also for medicinal purposes. Many of the reptiles, from which these are taken, are of large size; and it is said are upward of thirty feet in length, and wide in proportion. The floating houses on the river, when sunk nearly to the water's edge, by the decaying of the bamboos on which they rest, are frequently annoyed with them, for they are always in search of poultry. Among other methods of taking them, is this: a chicken is placed at the further end of a bamboo coop, near the door, over-night; a hole is made in this coop of a sufficient size to admit the entrance of a snake of fifteen or twenty feet in length; if the reptile enter, after having gorged himself with his prey, he is unable to get out, and is then easily killed. The skin is then dried, and rolls of it are found suspended from the ceiling of the floating shops. The entire carcasses of tigers are also exported to China, for the people of that country ignorantly suppose them to possess great medicinal qualities. Last year, sixty carcasses paid duties on exportation, besides a large number smuggled; they are generally in a very putrid state long before they are shipped.

The thick hide of the rhinoceros is also another article of export to the same country, and by a peculiar process, it is made into, and used as a nutritious jelly.

*March twenty-seventh.* Reconnoitring in my boat yesterday evening, on the left bank of the river, up one of the numerous canals, we saw under a common shed, a short distance from a wat or temple, a number of idols. We stepped on shore to examine them, and at the feet of the great idol, lay a poor wretch, dying with the confluent small-pox; his bloated features and his person, covered with pustules, made him a disgusting object; he had crawled thither that morning, and had brought half a dozen saucers of sweetmeats, cooked rice, and fruit, and placed them on the lap of Budha, praying no doubt most fervently, that he would be pleased to cure him of his foul disease: but his cries were of no avail to this gilded block of wood, although they lasted from morning until eventide; for he died that night, at the feet of Budha.

*March twenty-eighth.* This morning, it being very high water, we entered on the canal which runs near to the southern wall of the city; passing along it, about a mile and a quarter, we turned to the left, and proceeding along about the same distance, we again shot out into the main river: thus taking a complete circuit of the city. The wall is about twenty feet in height; not a piece of cannon was seen, nor even a solitary sentry taking his weary round but a number of canals passed under the wall, and were filled with market-boats: there are no portcullises ready to drop, in case of a rebellion, or the invasion of an enemy; these canals, therefore, offer a ready and easy entrance. The houses in the suburbs in many places, are built immediately against the walls. No defence could be made, against even a small disciplined force, for there is no regular military force in the kingdom; the soldiers are never drilled with muskets, the government being unwilling to trust them with arms in their hands: their mode of warfare is altogether desultory. Many parts of the canal which surrounds the city, were much crowded with pedlars' boats, containing coarse cloth, paper, brass, and iron utensils, &c.; others with salt, sapan-wood, cotton in small baskets, areca-nut, siri-leaf, chunam, coloured with turmeric, dried fish, oil, sugar, balachang, fresh pork, fish, fruit, and vegetables.

The back of the city bore, altogether, a rural appearance; the banks were thickly settled, people of all ages were bathing, washing at the same time their simple dresses; children were seen asleep in short square-net hammocks, and the mother lying at full length on a mat, chewing areca-nut, or smoking a cigar, propelling with her foot the hanging cradle; the cat and dog lay stretched also at full length on the platform, overcome with the intense heat of the day; the banks were, however, well shaded by the many trees which occupied every vacant place. The mango, now fully laden with its oblong green fruit; the religious fig-tree with its broad and pointed leaf; the plantain bending beneath the weight of its fruit; the areca-palm with its slender and regular stem, and brush-like head; and the useful cocoa-nut and bamboo, were seen towering in every direction. We visited a number of the king's boat-houses, and saw a canoe one hundred and five feet long, made from a single teak-tree, excepting the high curved stem and stern; we saw also, hundreds of useless boats, most of them intended for war, while others were for pleasure, being neatly gilded about each

VIEW OF A WATT, OR TEMPLE.

quarter. The war-boats would be altogether useless in a sea-fight.

*March thirtieth.* Yesterday we visited a wat or pagoda, built by the present king, when he was prince Chroma Chiat; it is called wat-chan-tong[34] or "the temple of the golden sandal tree;" it is situated about six or seven miles from the outlet of Bang-kok Yai, into the Menam. The company consisted of the Rev. Mr. Jones, and Doctor Ticknor; a boat and rowers were sent to us by the praklang. The buildings are more substantial, and in better order, than any I have heretofore seen; hewn granite steps and pillars were about the principal entrances; the floors of the temples were of marble tessellated; the walls leading to the temples, and the dwellings of the Talapoys, were of square pieces of split granite; and there was a greater air of neatness about them, than any we have yet viewed. Noble banyan, and the religious fig-tree, shaded the walks; large porcelain figures of men, and non-descript beasts, embellished the fronts of churches, the entrances into the outer courts.

There are two islets near to the landing place, having on them miniature temples, and small images, overshadowed by noble banyan trees, which are to be found in great abundance every where in the vicinity of Bang-kok. It is one of the most curious of nature's productions: each full-sized tree is a grove; for every branch, on reaching the ground, vegetates and increases to a large trunk, and these again send forth others, till, from old age and exhaustion, the parent dies, and the progeny gradually decay for want of sustenance,

---

[34] Wat Chan Tong on Bangkok Yai is now known as Wat Raja Orot.

leaving a forest in ruins. It affords most beautiful walks, vistas, and cool recesses; and bears a small fig, which is scarlet when ripe, and affords a luxuriant repast to monkeys and peacocks, and other birds, which inhabit this father of trees, that shades and protects their young, in cool recesses, from a burning sun, where they sport and idle their leisure hours away, free from cares, excepting from the mischievous monkey, which robs them of their eggs, or the wily serpent, that beguiles them of their tender progeny.

The principal wat is occupied by a colossal figure of Budha, lying on his right side, supported by the elbow and hand, and seven square and triangular pillows, with ornamented ends of coloured glass. It is of the enormous length of *sixty-three* feet, having on its head a high peaked cap. The "phra-bat," or "holy feet," are each six feet nine inches in length, having five toes, all of equal length, being one less than the Budha of the Burmese. It is made of brick and stuccoed; but overlaid with heavy gilding, highly burnished. It was covered, on its exposed or left side, with yellow, or talapoy cloth, and canopied by an enormous yellow umbrella. Many priests and young students of the monastery accompanied us. They were asked why the idol was protected with cloths, and the umbrella? They replied, that the great Budha would be offended if neglected, and he ought to be kept warm. As the

THE TEMPLE OF THE SLEEPING IDOL

thermometer was little short of one hundred, and we were panting for breath, with the perspiration running from us in streams, they were told that all clothing was oppressive; but they said, they dared not neglect him. They were also asked, how long he was to lie? They said, about three thousand years, when Budha would be annihilated, or his authority rather would cease.

The ceiling of the wat was painted of a rich vermillion, and "thickly inlaid with patines of bright gold." The walls, and inside of the doors and window-shutters, were entirely covered with rural and aquatic scenes, birds, flowers, &c., &c.; all rich with gold and beautiful colours, highly varnished, displaying a cultivated taste. The doors, at the entrance, were most splendidly inlaid with mother-of-pearl, wrought into various and elegant devices. Surrounding the wall of the courtyard, was an extensive corridor, containing eighty Budhas, of about four feet high, in a sitting posture generally, while others were standing. At the feet of each were two smaller sized devotees, kneeling and facing them, with their hands spread out and united in the attitude of prayer. These, together with a group of eight in one corner, made, altogether, two hundred and forty-six images, being all highly burnished with gold. Other images, of women,[35] are scattered about the court; and the two gigantic warriors, as usual, placed as guards at its common entrance. The Indian lotus was growing in handsome vases of granite, porcelain, and marble. There was also a large gilt image in a sitting posture, made of a composition of copper, tin, and zinc. The ceiling, walls, &c., were nearly similarly painted to the other, having a tessellated marble pavement; but the doors were painted black, with borders of richly gilded flowers. A devotee had taken up his lodging within the temple, near one of the doors, and was then praying at the feet of the image. He passed his days there, and at night watered his couch with his tears, in the vain expectation that, at his death, Budha would cause his soul to be transmigrated into a higher and holier state of existence.

There were about one hundred and fifty Talapoys generally at this monastery. Here, also, was a small deep bathing place, having in it a number of small alligators—they are common. We passed a great number of temples, and counted twenty-five on this route. The banks

---

[35] Presumably mythical half-bird, half-human *kinnaree*.

were thickly inhabited, having a low but rich country; and the various fruit and flowering forest trees, by which it was overshadowed, contributed greatly to its beautiful scenery. Boats were continually passing in great numbers, variously laden. The fronts of the cottages being open, all the domestic operations were fully seen. At the foot of the ladder, childhood and old age were seen, bathing in the turbid waters of this tributary of the Menam, all seemingly happy, although living under one of the most despotic governments in the world.

On our return, observing an artificial mound[36] near a small wat with a gilded front, we were induced to stop and examine it; it was in height about twenty feet, built of brick and overlaid with rough pieces of rock. We entered by a flight of steps into some dark winding passages in imitation of caverns—on the step was a small temple court and a relic of Gautama, which we were unable to see owing to the Talapoy who had charge of it being asleep. The thermometer being at ninety-five, with a dead oven-like heat, we were glad to retreat to some cooler place. Proceeding on by another route, we saw a number of Talapoys, collected near to a place for the burning of the dead, under a high pyramidal shed placed amid a grove of the religious fig-tree: we landed and proceeded to the spot. In the centre of the building, on a brick platform, was placed a bier of seven or eight feet in height—the sides which concealed the body were covered with white muslin and the top, &c., ornamented with yellow tinsel; the bier, I suppose, was of wood, but it was neatly covered with plantain stock, and being fresh cut resembled ivory with a slight tinge of yellow: fanciful devices were cut in the sides and red paper inserted; which gave it a very neat and finished appearance. In each corner were raised platforms, and on one of them sat fifteen or twenty Talapoys, having before them a feast of nice things, such as rice cooked in various ways, sweetmeats and fruits, and a pile of yellow cloth, all of which were presents, from the parents of a dead daughter, lying before these senseless worshippers of idols. They were talking aloud and laughing, apparently insensible to the solemn occasion for which they were assembled: being disgusted with their conduct, and finding that the ceremony would not take place until three in the afternoon, we left the place intending to return in due time.

---

[36] Phu Kao Tong and the temple there.

At the appointed hour, we were again there, but the burning had commenced half an hour previously: a part of the scull was remaining, the head having separated from the body: the back bone was nearly entire as well as part of the limbs; two grim looking fellows were replenishing and stirring the fire with three-pronged forks, smoking cigars, and laughing as though they were attending a baker's oven. They were constantly employed in going from this funeral pile to another, situated in the open air, a short distance off, where was consuming the body of a dead slave.

Besides the "fire-feeders," there was assembled a party of young females, acquaintances of the deceased girl, waiting to collect the unconsumed bones, that they might be conveyed to the mourning parents: they were decent in their behaviour, but there were no visible signs of grief on their countenances at this sad spectacle; they were seated on one of the raised platforms, chewing areca-nut, and talking with considerable earnestness—but the instant they saw us, they started on their feet, and exhibited very strong symptoms of curiosity; probably, many of them had never seen a white person before, and our dress, of course, appeared strange to those who were only accustomed to the sight of a waist-cloth. They inquired of a gentleman who spoke Siamese and English, if we came to see a body burnt, or what was the object of our visit: we told them it was to see a body burnt, and to view the temple near by. They asked us to look at the remains, on the funeral pile, and see if we could tell whether it was a male or female, (for the natives are under the impression that Europeans know every thing, and all the European race even if born in America, are called Europeans.) They were told after taking a view of them, that they were those of a female. At this answer, they held up their hands, and appeared to be exceedingly astonished, for they were not aware that we had ascertained this fact in the morning. We immediately left them, not wishing to be questioned farther, and they are under the delusion without doubt, that we do, indeed, "know every thing."

The poor slave who has just been mentioned, must have had a friend who was willing to pay the expenses of the burning to the Talapoys, or *alias* the phratais or phra-bo-coots[37] as they are called in Siamese,

---

[37] 'Phratais' is presumably *phra thai*, meaning Thai monks; 'phra-bo-coots' may be a corruption of *phra putta rup*', referring to the Buddha.

otherwise he would have been thrown without ceremony into the Menam and become food for fish or alligators. A worthless priesthood, who *daily* spunge the most abject in society of their scanty pittance of rice, clothing, or fruit, refuse even a few sticks of wood to consume the dead bodies of their poor benefactors, and to recite a few heathenish prayers without being amply paid for their trouble; but the priests of Budha are not the only ones who exact payment for what is obviously their bounden duty. Some of the Christian churches, even in this vicinity, as well as those of other countries, will be paid for burying their dead, and saying mass for the repose of departed souls.

The ceremony of burning the dead may be witnessed almost daily, between noon and three o'clock, within the precincts of the temples. During the ceremony, music of a most discordant kind is frequently introduced. The instruments are noisy and consist of gongs, drums, &c., &c. Prayers, written in the Pali language on slips of palm-leaf, are first read by a priest from a pulpit; females and males set beneath it each holding a taper: the language is probably unintelligible to every one present, for most of the priests can barely read it, and few of them understand it.

These places are generally thronged with idle persons, who take no part in the ceremonies, and walk in and out talking and smoking cigars, &c., &c. At the head of the coffin is a piece of white cloth; a number of priests take hold of it on each side, reciting certain prayers— this being ended, the coffin and bier are dismantled, the body is washed by one of the servants of the pagoda, who is always paid a small fee for this most disgusting piece of service. Bodies are frequently kept for days in this sultry climate, and then the office is no sinecure—it is truly loathsome. The ablution being concluded, a layer of wet earth is laid on the bier and dry wood is piled upon it—the body is then replaced in the coffin, and carried three successive times around the altar by the nearest male relatives, and afterward deposited upon the pile; tapers and incense rods are distributed to all who will receive them; a priest delivers a final prayer, then sets fire to the funeral pile, and is followed by all who receive tapers and rods for that purpose. The scull is always broken with a heavy bar of iron, to prevent, as they say, an explosion and scattering of the bones and brains. Small pieces of money are now distributed to objects of charity, who are always in waiting at these places at the usual hours, and are disappointed if there are no rich victims ready for the funeral pile; sometimes the male relatives throw bundles of cloth over the pile—those on the opposite side carefully catch them, and in other cases it is dispensed with.

No explanation of this singular piece of ceremony could ever be obtained. I ought to have mentioned, previously, a horrible custom which occasionally prevails here: many Siamese give directions that their dead bodies shall be stripped of the flesh and given to dogs, and carniverous birds, which infest the neighbourhood of the altars, and the bones only are burnt. This is considered to be both laudable and charitable. The unconsumed bones are carefully collected, prayers are recited over them, and various ceremonies are performed by the priests. They are then burnt to ashes, reduced into a paste with water, and then formed into a small figure of Budha, and gilded; the latter is then placed among the household gods, or deposited in a temple of Budha. If any important branch of the family die, it is carried in procession, and this is called "the procession of the bones of their ancestors." But as the priests are very exorbitant in their demands for this small piece of service, none but the richer class can afford the expense.

I omitted to mention the arrival, some days since, from Singapore, of the English schooner Reliance, commanded by an American, Captain Burgess of Maine, and owned by Robert Hunter,[38] a Scotch gentleman, who has been trading for eight or nine years past between Singapore and some of the ports on the eastern side of the Malay peninsula, but more particularly with this place. In this vessel came an American Baptist missionary, the Reverend John Taylor Jones—wife, child, and servants: he has been residing for about two years past at Maulmein, in Burmah, but latterly at Rangoon. He had been expected for some months, and a house was preparing for him by the very respectable Mr. Silveiro, the Portuguese consul at Cokai,[39] near a campong of Burmese. I immediately wrote a note and sent it to the roads, about forty or fifty miles distant, offering them every accommodation in our extensive house, until they should be able to take possession of their own. Two days afterward, the family arrived

---

[38] Robert Hunter was a British merchant settled in Bangkok, at first in favour with the court, which gave him a title, but was later accused of smuggling opium into the country.

[39] Cockai is an unidentified quarter of Bangkok on the right bank.

with the exception of Mr. Jones, who came the following day, and remained with us till every thing was arranged. Their house is a tolerably comfortable one for the climate; they appear to be well satisfied with it, and their contiguity to Mr. Silveiro, who speaks French, English, and Siamese, and is able to give every sort of information relative to the people and the country, having resided here about thirteen years. The house is situated a short distance back from the river, amidst palm and other trees, and is surrounded by a dense population. The house formerly occupied by the Reverend Mr. Tompkin, an Englishman, Mr. Gutzlaff, a Prussian, and Mr. Abeel an American, all missionaries, residing here within the last few years, is a short distance from it, and immediately on the banks of the Menam; it is a very small cottage, fit only for humble dwellers, and the very appearance of it, with the very respectable men who occupied it, will convince any one, that a life of luxury and indolence was not their object in leaving their country and their homes, and all that was dear to them; but to go about doing good in the cause of Christ, according to their best abilities.

These worthy men did much good when they were here, by administering medicines to the sick, and in many instances, no doubt, in distributing useful and religious tracts in the Siamese and Chinese languages; but the injudicious though well-meant zeal of Mr. Gutzlaff in the very outset, within the first two days of his arrival, gave great cause of offence to the government; for he immediately threw many thousands of tracts into every floating house, boat and junk, as well as into cottages. An order was issued for his immediate expulsion from the country, and that his tracts shouid be collected and burnt; and had it not been for the friendly interference and good management of Mr. Hunter, who was a favourite with the praklang, the order would have been executed.

The king ordered a translation of the tracts to be made, which was done very fairly; he read them and said candidly and openly that there was nothing objectionable in them, but he preferred his own religion. The government raise no objections to Christian missionaries residing in the country, and it is as favourably disposed toward them as can be expected, considering the great influence of the Budha priests; but missionaries must never suffer their zeal to transport them beyond the bounds of common prudence. A certain sect of Christians here are very inimical to Protestant missionaries, much more so, I am credibly informed, than the Talapoys, who believe themselves so firmly seated that they do not trouble themselves about the Protestant preachers. As a convincing proof that the government is far from being unfriendly to missionaries, the praklang sent down a good covered boat, expressly to convey Mr. Jones and his family to their new residence, at Cokai, two miles distant from our house. Mr. Jones was introduced by Mr. Hunter to the praklang, who received him with apparent kindness.

It it said, by some, that this favourable reception is owing, to his being an American citizen, and because of the friendly terms existing between the government of Siam and the United States. It is true, without doubt, that the king openly expressed much gratification, that an American man-of-war had arrived with an envoy, for the purpose of forming a treaty of amity and commerce. This fact was named to me repeatedly, by the praklang and by others, who daily attend the court. His Siamese majesty immediately ordered his best unoccupied building to be prepared for us, (and it certainly is the best on the river;) two of his best war-boats to be sent to bring us to the city, and a feast to be prepared by the governor of Packnam; and on our arrival at the house, every comfort and every luxury were spread on the table; and cook, purveyor, servants, interpreters, and guards, at our service. The praklang was ordered to facilitate the speedy execution of the treaty, &c.

All this was very gratifying; but, under the frequent delays and obstructions thrown in the way of the treaty by the praklang, influenced, probably, by the preference which the government people of Siam were said to have for my countrymen, it is said by Mr. S.[40] and by many others, to have been the most extraordinary instance of despatch ever known in the history of diplomacy in this country, even when an enemy was at their door. Their friendly disposition towards us was confirmed by Major Burney, who was sent to Siam, by the governor-general of India, about six years since, now ambassador at the court of Ava. He informed Mr. Jones, that the Americans were decidedly preferred to any other foreigners. He was detained here about seven months, and met with a thousand vexations. He was not more successful in his negotiations than we were, although aided by the sacrifice of the king of Quedah, and the fears the Siamese have of

---

[40] Silveiro, the Portuguese consul.

their English neighbours in Burmah, and the Malay peninsula. Mr. Crawford, his predecessor, likewise, who came here for a similar purpose, in 1812,[41] was detained several months, treated with insult, and dismissed without obtaining a single commercial advantage. I omitted to mention that Mr. Abeel is held here in the highest estimation, by those who have the pleasure of his acquaintance. He possesses talents of a very superior order, and acquirements that do great credit to his industry; is mild and conciliating in his manners, forcible in his arguments, yet possessing a sufficient degree of zeal, never giving offence to the government, nor creating dislike by being over-zealous, and thereby disgusting the natives; but the bad state of his health would not permit him to remain on this good missionary ground, which may be made, in a few years, ready for the harvest. Missionary stations should never be left vacant, and several teachers should be on the spot at the same time, so as to be able to relieve each other occasionally. The language of the country must first be learned, and at least a partial knowledge obtained of the Mandarin and Fokien languages of China. Missionaries should also be well acquainted with the peculiar doctrines of the Budhists, which they are labouring to subvert: free schools should be established; a printing-press put in operation, and those children should be preferred who have never attended the schools of the Talapoys. Although a good wife contributes in a thousand ways to the comfort and convenience of the missionary, yet the prejudices of the people they visit should be consulted, at least for the present; for the Siamese are firm in their opinion, that the vow of perpetual celibacy should be observed by all who bear the title of priests, of Christians as well as worshippers of Budha. All missionaries should also have some knowledge of medicine and surgery.

---

[41] An error: Crawfurd was in Siam in 1822, not 1812.

# [3]

# CHAPTER XVIII

CHINESE JUNKS—MECHANIC ARTS OF SIAM—AMUSEMENTS—
DANCING SNAKES—ANNUAL OATH OF ALLEGIANCE—DESCRIP-
TION OF THE CAPITAL—EMBASSY FROM COCHIN-CHINA—EDUCA-
TION IN SIAM—PALACE.

THE climate of Siam is more healthy than that of Batavia. Notwithstanding the great heat of the climate, and the vast quantity of uncleaned and undrained land, epidemics do not often prevail; yet the spasmodic cholera, a few years since, swept off upward of sixty thousand inhabitants.

During our stay, the weather has been clear and serene, a breeze visiting us about the middle of the day; yet the thermometer has ranged 93°, and has frequently been 94° and 95°.[42] No one has been sick, excepting of complaints in the bowels, occasioned by a change of diet.

The profuse perspiration under which we suffered, day and night considerably exhausted our strength. Those pests of all swampy countries, moschetoes and other insects, have not appeared in such vast quantities as they do in the rainy season, nor reptiles, which then abound every where; nor is the heat so great as it will be within the next four or five months, when the thermometer will rise from 100° to 103°; yet, it is said, the climate then is not more unhealthy than it is at present. Where the ship lies, the thermometer has not risen above 84°, and prevailing winds have been from the southward, blowing fresh the most part of the time, with a considerable sea. During the heat of the day, notwithstanding bathing is resorted to, and the natives are often seen with a wet cloth on their shoulders, to keep them cool and mitigate the effects of a scorching sun; yet it is a rare circumstance to see any of them with a covering on the head, excepting the women-pedlars on the river, who wear a palm-leaf hat, the exact shape of a milk-pan reversed; this is kept on the head by means of a framework, made of split rattan; their dress also is different from other

---

[42] 93 degrees F = 33.9 degrees C; 95 degrees F = 35 degrees C; 100-103 degrees F (mentioned below) = 37.7-39.4 degrees C.

women's being a tight cotton jacket, with sleeves, and the usual waistcloth worn by both sexes.

It is surprising how few of the mechanic arts are here practised, excepting those which are connected with the building of junks and boats; and in this case, strickly speaking, there are but two or three employed. The carpenter, who builds the vessel, makes the masts and wooden anchors, and the very few blocks that are used; pumps are not known, for the water is bailed out from vessels of one thousand tons burden. They go to market and buy their mats to make sails, which are spread out on the ground within certain pegs, which give the proper dimensions and shape; the bolt-rope is then sowed on, being made of a species of very coarse strong grass, abounding every where; and the sailmakers, being the sailors of the vessel, make the cordage generally, and assist in making the immense cables. Blacksmiths are necessarily employed to make bolts, and calkers are indispensable.

A true Chinese junk is a great curiosity; the model must have been taken originally from a bread-trough, being broad and square at both ends—when light, (I speak of a large one,) it is full thirty feet from the surface of the water to the tafferel, or the highest part of the poop. Forward, a wide clear space intervenes, where the cable is worked, there being a stage erected, some twelve or fifteen feet above the forecastle, on which they help to work and keep a lookout for sail. The mainmast is a most enormous stick of teak or other hard wood, big enough for a line-of-battle ship, on which they hoist an enormous sail, which generally takes all the crew, consisting of at least a hundred or a hundred and fifty men; when they wish to lower it, it is necessary to send a number of men on the bamboo poles, which stretch from side to side, to assist in its descent. A small mast, the after or mizen mast, is placed on one side, not in the centre as in other vessels, but stepped or secured on the deck. The enormous cable is hove up by a common windlass, without the assistance of pauls, stretching from side to side of the vessel, through the bulwarks. The centre of the vessel is at least fifteen or twenty feet lower than the tafferel, open for the most part amidships, planks being placed here and there to step on. There is tier upon tier of cabins aft. The hold is divided into compartments and made water proof; these are hired or owned by the shippers, so that each one keeps his goods separately; and in case the vessel spring a leak, in any particular part, it is more easily repaired.

The caboose[43] is on one side; and their meals, as at home, are made of rice and salt or fresh vegetables, and perhaps a little fish, and of every cheap article, however unsavoury, served up in a great number of small saucers.

The vessels are kept in a most filthy condition, and can be scented a long way off. Scenes of the grossest debauchery are practised on board these junks; and gambling is carried on to a great extent. They are called either male or female, according to the shape—the former being sharp aft, if not forward; but these are considered to be illegitimate upstarts of modern date, and are not the true Chinese junk. The female has an enormous broad convex stern, there being a hollow or cavity, where the broad, clumsy, grating-like rudder is placed; it probably recedes two feet from the quarters to the sternpost. They are generally painted white and red, perhaps blue, and the two enormous eyes of vigilance are ever to be seen on each bow. On the stern, all the art of the painter is exhausted by a profusion of meretricious ornaments—an eagle, or what is intended for one, occupies the centre of the stern, surrounded by all sorts of non-descript figures, and on one side of the counter is a Josh, or god of wealth, resembling in shape Toby Filpot,[44] besides a great variety of indescribable nothings.

The boat is exceedingly stout and clumsy, and an exact counterpart of the junk, being of an oblong square, nearly flat, and propelled by a long oar, placed on a swivel.

Another kind of mechanics, are tin and leather-dressers, which, strange to say, are always to be found in the same shop. The makers of qualtahs,[45] or iron pots and pans, which are a very neat, light article, and little liable to be broken, owing to the ductility or toughness of the iron. These pots are sold at a cheap rate, and are preferred to all cast-iron vessels imported from Europe. Some iron is also made into small bars or pieces. There are also makers of sandals, which articles are worn only by the Chinese. The tin-ware is very neatly made, and the patterns show a good deal of taste; but it is useless to put on the

---

[43] A caboose is a kitchen on a ship's deck.

[44] Toby Filpot, a Toby jug, a squat, fat figure from which one drinks.

[45] Qualtahs, later given as kwaltahs, are defined here; the origin of the word has not been traced.

CHINESE COOK ON THE MENAM.

fire, as there is no alloy mixed with it. The leather is died a common red, made of deer-skin, and smoothed by a black stone, the size of a brick; it is used for mattresses, pillows, &c. House-carpenters, canoe, and boat builders, and a few makers of musical instruments, with a little coarse pottery, and a few ordinary knives and locks, comprise all the mechanic arts that have fallen within my knowledge. Gold and silversmiths, I have nowhere seen; if there were any, who possessed such ingenuity, they would be seized upon by the king or his officers, and employed in their service. The gold vessels, containing areca, cigars, &c., &c., are carried to every place they visit, by the princes and higher officers of government, are made at the palace, and can only be used by the king's favourites. I have seen a few rude hand-looms in operation; but the fabrics, both of silk and cotton, were very ordinary.

They import their brass ware and silk stuffs from China and Surat,[46] and their cotton and woollen goods, cutlery, &c., principally from Singapore. Even the Talapoys' razors for shaving their heads, are imported from Canton: they are made of thin brass, of a curved shape, about two inches wide throughout, and six inches long, fixed into a coarse wooden handle. The mechanic arts are carried on almost wholly by the industrious Chinese. The common houses are of bamboo, with attap roofs; some are built of wood, and few of brick; but with few exceptions, they all stand upon high piles. They are thus raised, in consequence of the inundation of the river, to make them more secure,

---

[46] Surat, in north-west India, was from the seventeenth century an emporium for Western goods.

against depredations, to keep them dry, and to avoid the numerous reptiles. The bridges which cross the canals, are generally a single plank; some few have timbers laid on apartments of wood or brick, planked, and about six feet wide, but an arched bridge is nowhere to be seen. Roads there are none; and the only carriages are those owned by the king which are brought out only on some great occasions, and are never seen beyond the walls of the city; of course, there is scarcely any use for horses or elephants. The Menam with its thousands of boats, and the numerous canals and branches of the river, make the communication every where cheap and easy, and compensate in a great measure, for the want of roads.

The principal amusement of the inhabitants, within their houses, is singing and playing on musical instruments, of various kinds: their singing is of a plaintive and melancholy cast, and they display considerable taste in its execution: but there is too much monotony, too much sameness in it; still they have got beyond the point of being pleased with mere sound, like the Chinese. Their musical instruments are very numerous: I have been able to describe but few; the music produced by them is very different from the vocal, being cheerful and lively. Playing chess is also a pastime. Dancing girls are kept for the amusement of the women of the higher classes. Tumblers, rope-dancers and actors, are considered necessary appendages for a complete establishment. Gambling is carried to great excess by the Siamese and Chinese; and the revenue derived from it, as will be seen in a statement of the revenue, is of considerable importance to the government. Flying kites is a favourite amusement with all, especially with the Talapoys, and a great number of them may be seen employed, in this way, at all hours of the day. Playing shuttlecock with their feet, three on a side, is much practised by them, as well as the laity; and in their houses, and even within their temples, they spend a large portion of their time at chess. These amusements, together with chewing areca, smoking cigars, begging, and sleeping, leave but little time for devotion and study.

A few days since, a Siamese came into the yard, and desired to exhibit some dancing snakes; he uncovered a basket, and drew out with his naked hand several of a large size, and of the most venomous kind known in India, the cobra de capello—they were full six feet in length, and large in proportion; he had eight in the basket, and took out three or four at a time, and suffered them to run about: he would then touch one slightly on the body, as he was retreating, which caused him instantly to turn his head backward toward the tail. The head, from being round and small in proportion to the body, was quickly expanded to the width of full three, and probably five inches in length, showing a crown or circle, in the centre; the head was nearly flat, his forked tongue was thrust out with great rapidity, and he kept vibrating from side to side, and his keen fiery eye shot forth most terrific glances; but he made a most noble and graceful, although frightful appearance.

The exhibitor kept a cloth moving, a short distance in front of his eyes, and the snake, in endeavouring to elude it, so that he might spring upon his adversary, kept in a dancing motion. Having tied two or three of the largest round his neck, and put the head of one of them in his mouth, the exhibition ended. Being satisfied that the fangs were extracted, or otherwise they could not be handled with impunity, I suffered two of them to run between my feet, but they did not offer to molest me or any one else.

The water used for domestic purposes is taken, with all its impurities, from the river, in water-tight buckets, neatly and strongly woven; it is put into unglazed earthen jars of thirty or forty gallons, and is suffered to settle in the best way it can, without any foreign aid. The filth of half a million of people, which is all emptied into the river, renders it most impure, and dead bodies are frequently thrown in to save the expense of burning. In a family, where no garments are made or mended—in which there is no baking or ironing of clothes; no stockings nor shoes worn, and the washing and drying of their simple garments, done at the river, does not occupy a month in a year—no books read, and no writing done—a large portion of the time of the females must, of course, be spent in sleep and idleness. This is the life led by the Siamese women of a good condition, they having in fact no occupation—this must be the true "dolce farniente"[47] of the Italians, and a sorry one it is.

They wear no jewels, these being used altogether by the children, their dress consisting only of a waist and breast cloth of dark silk. A little music, the dancing girls, actors, and tumblers, occasionally exhibited, chess, colouring their skin yellow with turmeric; and

---

[47] (Italian): sweet idleness.

anointing the tuft of unshorn hair on the top of their head; scandal, with frequent dissensions, the natural consequence of a plurality of wives; no riding out, seldom paying visits, and, rarely diverting themselves with shopping, the almost unvaried repetition, from day to day, of the same dull round of occupations and amusements, cause their lives to drag on wearily, heavily, and listlessly. Long nails being considered a sort of patent of nobility by the Siamese, as well as the Chinese and Cochin-Chinese, draw a certain line of distinction between the vulgar, who are obliged to wear short ones and work for their living, and the higher orders. Those of the latter are carefully preserved from being broken, but not quite so much pains being taken to keep them clean, they are generally disgusting in their appearance—some of them are full two inches in length, and are put into cases of bamboo or metal on retiring to rest. The female actresses wear silver-pointed cases to them, which curve backward with a high sweep, nearly touching the wrist.

The higher orders of nobility, in fact, all who are allowed to crawl as far as the lowest place within the palace, and all the officers of state, must pay a morning and an evening visit to the "Lord of the White Elephant," to his "*golden-footed majesty*," "the master of all men's lives." Not to attend regularly, is considered a mark of disrespect and disaffection to the king: sickness, or some great calamity, only, is good cause for excuse.

Regularly, at half past eight in the morning, the praklang passed the mission house, having about a dozen paddles to his long canoe, sitting cross-legged or sidewise under the palm-leaf awning, or reclining on a carpet and cushions, a slave crouching on all fours in front of him, administering to his comforts in lighting a cigar, or helping him to areca. His palanquin (or rather a lacquered handbarrow) protected from the rays of the sun by a large umbrella, was carried in the same boat, so as to be in readiness, on landing, to carry his unwieldy person to the palace. About noon, he returned. Between six and seven, he again regularly passed, and returned again usually about midnight. The paddlers on the numerous boats crouched low when he passed, as they all do when passing by the king's bathing-house on the river: he never notices, in the slightest degree, their obeisance, but wo [sic] to them if they omit it. The bath-house is of great length, painted red, and decorated in front with numerous dwarf-trees and shrubs, and is used, it is said, daily, by his hundreds of (some say, eight hundred) wives and many scores of children, with their countless attendants.

Annually, every public officer renews his oath of allegiance to his majesty, in the most horrid and revolting terms, calling down upon himself every curse and punishment in the present and future world, should he prove disloyal. At the commencement of the Chinese year, every governor, or other important officer, even of the most distant province, is obliged, on pain of death, to present himself at the krong, or capital, for this purpose.

A few days after our arrival, the venerable bishop of the Roman Catholic church sent a deputation to wait upon me, consisting of a young French priest, who has been in the country about two years, and a native Portuguese priest. The bishop sent an excuse for not paying a visit in person,[48] owing to his advanced age and great infirmities, and requested me to call upon him, which I accordingly did in a few days thereafter, in company with Mr. Silveira and Doctor Ticknor. He made but few inquiries respecting his own country, which he had apparently almost forgotten. He said he was born at Avignon, in 1760, left France in the year 1786, and, with the exception of the time occupied by a tedious passage, three months passed at Macao, and six months at Hué, the capital of Cochin-China, he had been ever since in Siam. He was very infirm, and in his second childhood: sans teeth, sight dim, sans every thing. The house he lived in was very old and far from being clean. The church was built of brick and stuccoed, having a very gaudy and ordinary altar-piece, and destitute of images. It has been finished but a few years and is called Santa Assomption.[49]

A college, erected within a few years since the church, and neatly built of wood, stands near it, having about twenty students. It is erected on high posts, and is one story high. This Christian campong stands in the midst of palm and forest trees; and the situation is altogether very rural and pleasant. It will bear no comparison with its neigbours, the rich and gorgeous temples of Budha. The Catholic churches in this country, since the first bishop arrived, in 1662, have scarcely made

---

[48] Crawfurd also remarks on the circumspection of the elderly French Bishop of Sozopolis in Bangkok.
[49] It was unfinished at the time of Crawfurd's visit in 1822.

any progress: the descendants of the Portuguese constitute, I may say, with propriety, all the Christians in the kingdom; so say the Catholics themselves. All that can now be found here, and in the vicinity, do not exceed, according to the most zealous of that sect, thirteen hundred; but, according to a Protestant, Christian missionary, who resided here nearly three years, and numbered them with considerable accuracy, they do not exceed four hundred. There are four churches in this vicinity; three of them are merely long sheds, in a wretched condition. In the campong of Santa Cruz, the walls of a brick one are erected, near to the old shed of that name; but the building will never be finished, for there are, already, evident signs of dilapidation in many parts of it.

Of the splendid churches that once adorned the old capital of Jutaya, there is but a small one now remaining,[50] built out of the ruins of the others; and in Camboja, where the Catholics once had a strong foothold, they have dwindled to a mere name. The descendants of the Portuguese, in whose veins courses the blood of the courageous adventurers with the bold and fearless Vasco de Gama, who had the temerity first to double the cape of Good Hope, and the cruel Albuquerque, are now crouching slaves before the nobles of the country; and are employed only in menial offices, with the exception of two, which give them a bare subsistence.

The number of temples erected in the city and vicinity, I was unable to ascertain: that they amount to several hundreds, (some report from four to five hundred,) there cannot be a doubt. They occupy the most conspicuous and beautiful spots on the bank of the Menam, on its tributaries and numerous canals: you never lose sight of them; frequently eight or ten are in view at the same moment. In the most sequestered rural spots, they are always to be found; and wherever a brick pathway leads into the depths of the forest, it is a sure indication that there is a temple to be found. They are erected by pious individuals generally, believing that it will be the means of their souls being transmigrated into a higher and holier state of existence, than they would otherwise enjoy; but most of them are built from ostentatious motives.

They are of brick, and plastered; are one story in height, having neither arch nor dome; of a square form, and the roof is covered with

---

[50] St Joseph's in Ayutthaya.

neat coloured tiles, which gives them a gay appearance. At a first view, one is deceived, by supposing that there are three or four roofs to every building, as there are a series of them, which gradually diminish in size, to the main roof. The fronts, or gable ends, are laboriously and elegantly carved, with fanciful devices, and richly gilded. The eaves, doors, and window-frames, are, more or less, carved and gilt, painted and varnished. The doors and windows greatly resemble the pointed, or Gothic style of architecture. A figure of Budha, generally in a sitting posture, wearing the peaked crown, and having the soles of his holy feet turned upward, occupies nearly one entire end of the building, and is usually surrounded by votaries of a small size. He is partially covered with yellow cloths, having a high umbrella suspended over his head. Incense is occasionally burnt before him. The ceiling of the roof, which is flat, is painted with vermillion, ornamented with gilded stars. The entire sides, doors, and window-shutters, are covered with figures, fruit, and fancy work of various kinds—painted, varnished, and gilt. The floors of most of the buildings are of cement, having neither galleries, benches, nor seats of any kind, and scarcely a mat to kneel on. There are but few public temples. The front and rear of all have a portico. China plates, saucers, and common English crockery, stuck into plaster, intended as ornaments, are seen on many of them; bits of coloured glass, also, make up part of the ornaments around the doors and windows. The images are either of brass or iron—brick plastered, and wood; but all richly gilt and burnished. Two temples, of a lesser size, stand on either side of the principal: they are generally not so highly ornamented. Small pyramidal pagodas, of six or seven feet in height, and open at the sides, surround these buildings, and contain two stones, or rather slabs, standing about six inches apart; they are of the exact shape of a bishop's mitre.[51] I repeatedly asked the use of them, or what they were intended to resemble; but all professed their ignorance of their origin. In them were generally found palm-leaves, containing characters, written in the sacred or Bali and Siamese languages, strung together in the centre, at a proper distance.

Small temples, or rather buildings, for various purposes, occupy the

---

[51] These are the *bai sema*, the temple boundary stones; a double stone indicates a royal foundation.

fronts and sides, among which, in a distinct building, is the belfry, which is ascended by a flight of steps, containing generally five or six bells, having no tongues, but being sounded by means of a heavy stick, or piece of metal.

Early in the morning, "when dying clouds contend with growing light;"[52] when the fox-bat is returning from his nightly wanderings, to suspend himself on the holy fig trees, which lie scattered about the temples of Budha, and like the midnight marauder, shrinks from the sacred light of day; the tokay has ceased to send forth his harsh, loud, and monotonous cry; the prowling tiger has retired to his lair; the tuneful birds have chanted forth their first matins, or the labourer has returned to his daily task; when every thing is hushed in the solemnity of night, in the stillness of a temporary death, you are suddenly aroused by the din of the pagan bells, sounding far and wide through the depths of the surrounding palm-forests, summoning the worshippers of Gautama to early prayers. In the confusion of the moment, between slumbering and waking, you are transported, in imagination, to far distant lands, where the Sabbath bell calls forth its votaries. But how great the contrast! One summons to the worship of an imaginary god; the other to the worship of the everlasting and true God, the Lord of all things—of light and life.

Pra-chadis, or thin tall spires, from twenty to sixty feet in height, are in great numbers; and there is one at the krong or capital, which towers to the height, probably, of a hundred and fifty feet. The houses of the Talapoys are contiguous to the temples, and are generally shaded by fruit and forest trees. Small temples, having a high roof, and four wide avenues leading to the centre, for the burning of the richer sort, and a raised platform in the open air, for those who can only pay small fees, are placed at the most convenient spot near the water. A long bath, or small pond, containing young alligators, seems to be a necessary appendage to all temples. The grounds about the front of many of the richer temples, are neatly and prettily laid out with avenues, clumps of trees, shrubbery, &c. The priests derive a considerable revenue by making small images, either of the unconsumed bones of certain deceased persons, or else of common

---

[52] "When dying clouds contend with growing light": the source of the quotation has not been traced.

clay, gilt; and also by writing on palm-trees, certain moral or religious sentences, in the sacred language. The Indian lotus, with its broad leaf, is nowhere neglected, but is found about every temple, growing from large porcelain or stone vases, neatly, and sometimes elaborately wrought. Every Siamese temple is not only a place for worship, but it is likewise a monastery: females are in them, old and worn out, and their characters are far from being respected. They only do menial offices, dress in white, and have nothing to do with the worship in the temples. As rice, their chief support, is abundant, it is but just that the Talapoys should support them in their old age.

The spot on which the present capital stands, and the country in its vicinity, on both banks of the river for a considerable distance, were formerly, before the removal of the court to its present situation, called Bang-kok; but since that time, and for nearly sixty years past, it has been named Sia yuthia, (pronounced See-ah you-tè-ah, and by the natives, Krung, that is, the capital;)[53] it is called by both names here, but never Bang-kok; and they always correct foreigners when the latter make this mistake. The villages which occupy the right hand of the river, opposite to the capital, pass under the general name of Bang-kok.

A Cochin-Chinese ambassador, with several junks, arrived here from Longuar (alias Saigon) a few days before our arrival, being the same mentioned previously. Ambassadors' junks of both nations, whenever they visit each other's country, or pay their annual tribute to China, are always well laden with goods, out and home, on account of the king or his ministers; it is in part a trading expedition, and the secret is, they are allowed to go duty free, as I have before stated.

The object of the emperor of Cochin-China, in this case, is blended with a more serious piece of business; it is no less than to demand the delivery, to them, of the person of the first minister of state, and superintendant of Pegu, and the principalities of Laos and Camboja, whose title is "Chan-phaya-bodin-desha;"[54] he is a "meh-tap,"[55] or commander of the Siamese force now in Camboja. It seems, in 1827, the Siamese government oppressed the subjects of one of the Laos

---

[53] Si Ayutthaya, as with the former capital, is indeed one of the many names forming the official appellation of Bangkok.

[54] Chao Phaya Bodindecha, Sing Singhaseni.

[55] *Mae-tap* does indeed mean commander.

tributary princes, Chow-vin-chan,[56] to such a degree, that he was obliged to take up arms in defence of his rights, against the neighbouring Siamese government; this was the point to which the Siamese government wished to force him, for the purpose of taking into possession his territory. Hordes of soldiers were sent among them under the command of the said Chan-phaya-bodin-desha, and they committed all sorts of enormities; the country was stripped of its riches, and the inhabitants, fleeing from the enemy, were shot down indiscriminately like wild beasts; this process being found too tedious, thousands were packed into houses and blown up with gunpowder; the younger women be came the prey of a licentious soldiery, and the smoking ruins of a peaceable people marked the track of a band of savages, whose knives were steeped to the hilt in the blood of their fathers and mothers, husbands, wives, and children. Those who escaped were sent to the capital and sold as slaves ; thousands and thousands died on the rafts which floated them down the Menam, with wounds, sickness, and starvation. In fact, the country was made desolate, was in ruins: "He made a solitude and called it peace."[57] The survivors were never more to see their country; their soil was given to their savage invaders. In the midst of these horrible excesses, an ambassador from the emperor of Cochin-China was sent to the general in command, with the ostensible object of interposing in behalf of Chow-vin-chan and his family, who had fled into their territory—not from motives of compassion, I conceive, for the present emperor of Cochin-China[58] is an ignorant, blood-thirsty savage, and pursues his enemy, where he dares, with an unrelenting hand. The object was, in truth, to prevent the conquest of the kingdom of Laos by Siam, which would give the Siamese a better chance of obtaining a larger slice at a future day, which they had long contemplated with eager and with gloating eyes. The Siamese commander, smarting with all his wounds, and red-hot from the bloody battle-field, or to speak less hyperbolically, not having filled a heavy purse from the spoils of the conquered, anticipating a golden harvest from the onward march, and feeling deeply indignant at the insidious policy of his wily neighbours, ordered an instantaneous massacre of the

---

[56] Chao Anu of Vientiane, who died in 1829 in Bangkok after being captured and exhibited in a cage.

[57] Byron, *Bride of Abydon*, Canto II, Stanza 20. The quote should read "He makes..."

[58] Minh-Mang (reigned 1820-1841), a strict Confucian, persecuted the Christians in his realm.

envoy and his suite of a hundred men, with the exception of one, who was sent back to say, "I alone am left out of all my brethren." Highly enraged as was the emperor at the fell swoop of the embassy, and the gross violation of the law of nations, he dissembled, not daring to wage a war or revenge cruelty by cruelty; for his crazy, disjointed, and puny government would probably crumble into atoms, the moment a large force should quit the kingdom.

The Cochin-Chinese government are aware that the Tung-kinese, on the north, are watching keenly for the first possible chance which offers of freeing themselves from their despotic oppressors; the Cambojans on the south are desirous also of measuring the length of their swords with their hard task-masters, and the lower class of Cochin-Chinese, which comprise nine hundred and ninety-nine of the thousand, are ripe for a revolt; being ground to the earth by the higher orders. They are ragged, filthy, and starving, from the gulf of Tung-king to the gulf of Siam, and from the coast washed by the China sea, to the boundaries of his "golden-footed majesty." Year after year this demand has been made and evaded, and so far from his Siamese majesty ever intending to comply with it, he has lately sent this same "Meh-tap" into that part of Camboja which fell to his majesty's share in the division of that kingdom with Cochin-China, to receive, and to protect from capture, the many thousands of Cambojans, who have recently fled into the Siamese territory. The ambassador paid his first visit a few days after his arrival, to the chow-pia-praklang, and was treated with bare civility; he was told, by order of his majesty, that a copy of the same letter which was sent to his majesty the last year, was all the answer which would be returned to the letter received from the emperor through his hands. His audience with the king, which took place a few days previously to ours, was marked by no distinguished honours; the pomp and parade exhibited to us were dispensed with upon that occasion. It is said by Mr. Silveira, and all others, that no embassy from a foreign country ever had so favourable and honourable a reception as ours, marked at the same time with the most extraordinary despatch ever known.

This same emperor of Cochin-China, this deep sympathizer in the wrongs of the people of Lao[s], has lately persecuted to death a handful of poor Roman Catholics, all who would not trample on the cross and renounce Christianity. To conclude, the Chow-vin-chan and family were betrayed into the hands of the Siamese. Sickness, distress of mind, and long exposure to the elements, fortunately put an end to the prince. He died in a cage, a few days before his cruel oppressors intended to put him and his family to the most excruciating tortures; the heir apparent escaped, but committed suicide by throwing himself from the roof of a temple to the ground, rather than fall into the hands of his blood-thirsty pursuers. The female part of the family receive a scanty subsistance from the government and remain in the capital. Thus ended the dynasty of Chow-vin-chan, adding another victim to the millions that have heretofore perished, from the effect of inordinate ambition.

The barbarous conduct of the Siamese last year, in the Malay peninsula, in sending hordes of soldiers, or rather common coolies, under the command of the chow-pia praklang, which destroyed Patani, Singora, &c., plundering them of their property, and sending nearly five thousand prisoners as slaves to this place, which had been given away, or "sold in lots to suit purchasers;" the thousands that died from wounds, bad treatment, and starvation—deserve the bitter execration of every friend of humanity.

Education is carried to a very limited extent; a mere smattering only is generally diffused among the Siamese, in reading, writing, and arithmetic. The suan-pawn[59] is in general use as an assistant in making calculations. Those who wish to attain to a greater degree of knowledge, more particularly in the Pali or sacred language, resort to the monasteries of the Talapoys. In their composition, (if I may be allowed to judge from the various articles of the treaty, being again and again altered to make them clear and perspicuous,) they are fond of being ambiguous in all their forms of expression. There was always a disposition evinced to hint obscurely at things, like the Chinese, rather than express their full meaning.

A plain unmasked style, in speaking or writing, is totally unknown to a cringing people, born under a despotic government; but they are rapidly becoming wiser. Their intercourse with the English and Americans is gradually bringing about a more honest, manly, and open mode of expressing themselves, both in speaking and writing; but it can never be thoroughly effected under such a form of government as

---

[59] By 'suan-pawn' the abacus is presumably intended.

the present. The lower classes of the people are obliged to make use of gross flattery and adulation to their superiors, who again treat them as slaves, using high authoritative language. Subordination in rank is so strongly marked, that not the slightest appearance of equality is to be seen. They attach a ridiculous importance to mere form and ceremony. A Siamese, in the presence of a superior, either crouches to the ground, or walks with his body bent. It seems utterly impossible for him to sit or walk in an upright posture. Women are allowed more freedom here, than in any other country where polygamy is tolerated. They wear no veils, and almost hourly boat-loads of the wives of the nobility were seen to pass; the curtains were drawn aside to satisfy their curiosity, which always appeared to be more ardent than ours. The lower orders of women, apparently, do most of the labours of the field, and are employed in the boats on the river in great numbers. They are the principal traders, and are said to be very shrewd and cunning.

The most conspicuous objects which strike the eye of the traveller on the Menam, besides the splendid wats, are the new palace, a large watch-tower, and a prachade or tall thin spire, which is many feet higher than any other building; all are situated within the walls of the city. The palace itself, with its pagodas, and many other buildings, is surrounded by a high wall, having strong gates, and a guard of a miserable and undisciplined militia. The palace is a handsome and extensive building of brick, and stuccoed; the doors and windows are similar in style, taste, and outward decorations to the better class of temples, and bear a strong resemblance to the Gothic style of architecture. It has a high cupola, formed by a series of roofs, or it rather resembles a conical umbrella diminishing in size to the spire, which is without decorations, and rises to the height, perhaps, of one hundred and sixty feet. The roof of the building has also a diminishing series of roofs like the pagodas, and it is covered with very neat coloured tiles. The cupola appears to be gilded upon copper, or more probably slabs of tin.

The watchtower is of the height of the palace, and is an oblong square building; the base is probably one hundred feet square, built of brick and plastered, having a guard-house and strong gates; fifty feet from the base commences the first look-out room, and there are two others above it. In them are gongs and bells, which give notice of an enemy, or a fire, or an insurrection of the people. The inhabitants are at once informed by the sound of one of these instruments, of the calamity which assails them, each one being appropriated to one of these particular objects. A few days before the procession of the wang-na took place, there arrived the governor of Ligor, whose title is chow-phay-a-lakhow[60] alias Ligor; he commands one of the most important provinces belonging to the Siamese, in the Malay peninsula, is a Siamese by birth, a man of powerful talents, fond of Europeans, and adopts all their improvements in the mechanic arts. His boats are handsomely modelled, carrying two or three fore and aft sails; they are coppered, carry a suitable number of cannon, and every thing about them is in excellent order. The model is superior to that of the king's, having a greater breadth of beam, and they are of a greater length. The soldiers are well and uniformly clothed, and well drilled with the musket and the use of the bayonet, according to the tactics of the Europeans. There is some trade from the port of Ligor, in what is generally called the Malayan produce, viz:—tins, black pepper, rattans, rice, sapan-woods, &c., and several small cargoes of cotton are taken away annually by Chinese junks. Four of his sons govern other provinces in the peninsula; the eldest is governor of Quedah, the former king of which now remains at Pulo Penang, or Prince of Wales island.

Although the British agreed by treaty, on the cession to the Pulo Penang, to protect him and his kingdom against any invasion by the Siamese, yet the latter were suffered to capture Quedah, and the British violated their treaty, for they offered no assistance. The king fled to Penang for protection, demanded to be reinstated, and was refused. Major Burney, in order to obtain a favourable commercial treaty with the Siamese, agreed to keep him a prisoner, and he is now in durance, living upon a small salary, under British protection. The cause of the failure of Mr. Crawford's mission, was his refusal to deliver him to the Siamese, or confine him as a close prisoner.

The governor of Ligor was ordered here to attend the procession and burning of the wang-na; and it was also necessary he should be here at the commencement of the new year, to renew his oath of allegiance. He is a powerful chief; the government is alarmed at the

---

[60] Ligor is modern Nakhon Sithammarat; Robert's rendition of the title of its traditional governor should be Chao Phaya Ligor, but Lakhon was an alternative name for Ligor.

extent of his power, but they dare not dispossess him of his government, or do his person any violence, for his sons would most certainly avenge his cause, and the king's possessions in the Malay peninsula, would probably be lost to him.

The Chinese, who are noted every where for their villanous tricks, import large quantities of ordinary goods here, as well as those of a good quality—among other articles is tea. A story I heard almost daily in Canton, respecting the gross imposition practised upon foreigners in this article, here proved to be true. It is a well-known fact, that all the tea used in China, particularly about Canton, is bought up again, "*fired anew*," as it is termed, and coloured green; even black teas, it is said, are thus coloured, by the use of smalts, and then exported to various countries. Tea of a good quality is exceedingly scarce here, and at a high price, notwithstanding the proximity to China, and the great number of junks which enter here from all the maritime provinces of that empire.

Until the ascension of the present king to the throne, it was a custom with the sovereigns of the country to hold the plough at the commencement of the rains, which generally take place at the latter end of April or beginning of May; this is now dispensed with, and one of the nobility is appointed instead of the monarch.

The rains continue till September, when the lower part of the Menam begins to rise, and it is at its utmost height in November and December: it then begins to subside. Its rise is generally from twelve to sixteen feet, but two years since it rose to the height of twenty-one feet.

The thermometer is occasionally as low as 73°[61] in the months of December and January, during the height of the northeast monsoon.

Vast numbers of boats and rafts, bringing in the productions of the upper country, visited the capital during the flood above alluded to.

---

[61] 73 degrees F = 22.7 degrees C.

[4]

# CHAPTER XIX

PROCESSION TO THE FUNERAL PILE OF WANG-NA OR SECOND KING—ORIGIN OF BUDHISM IN SIAM—SOMMONA KODOM—ATHEISTICAL PRINCIPLES OF BUDHISM—BUDHIST COMMANDMENTS—HISTORY OF SIAM—GOVERNMENT—TITLES OF THE KING—OFFICERS OF THE GOVERNMENT.

*April second.* Having received an invitation from his majesty through the praklang, some days since, to witness the procession of the re mains of the late second king to the funeral pile, and this day being set apart for that purpose, a suitable boat was sent to us early by the praklang, and soon after seven in the morning, we proceeded across the river to the city.

The party in the praklang's boat consisted of Mr. Hunter, Dr. Ticknor, Lt. Fowler, Mr. Morrison and myself—and in my boat were Midshipmen Rumfort, Weed and Wells, Mr. Robinson, &c., &c., and Raymondo the Portuguese interpreter. We landed near one of the citygates and passed through it to the place assigned us, a great concourse of people being collected in the principal street through which the procession was to pass.

Finding the place by no means convenient to see the procession, owing to the lowness of the roof of the building, and being annoyed in some degree by the concourse of people who came to have a sight of us, (although they were altogether civil in their conduct,) I made known to the interpreter that we must remove from that place to one more commodious. Shortly after we went near to a part of the king's palace: it was an open building standing on columns of about twenty feet square, having a tiled roof; mats were spread on a part of it for our accommodation. The praklang was there and a prince of Lao[s], &c., &c. The former shortly took leave to attend the procession, having seen that we were properly accommodated. At nine, or rather at three, in Siamese time, the procession commenced and continued about an hour and a quarter, in the following order:—

First : several hundred standard bearers (three hundred and eighty four,) dressed in red embroidered cloth, wearing caps of the same

MR HUNTER'S HOUSE

material; the banners were of silk richly embroidered with gold of a triangular shape, bearing devices of dragons, serpents, &c., all neatly embroidered also. A band of music, consisting of drums, harmonicon and small hautboys, accompanied them.

Second : a young rhinoceros of about four feet in height, drawn by a party of soldiers dressed in embroidered blue cloth long jackets, on a sledge or low carriage, having on his back a small gilded castle and containing in the centre a small bundle of Talapoy or yellow cloths.

Third : two horses having two pairs of wings, about five feet in height, bearing similar castles with Talapoy cloths; one of them was spotted with red and the other with blue.

Fourth : two gigantic cocks, with demons' heads, having four wings, castles, &c., of various colours.

Fifth : two four-winged elephants, full size, one white and one green, bearing castles and cloth, followed by a band of music.

Sixth : two gigantic cocks with cocks' heads, four wings, beasts' tails, and partly human bodies, castles, &c., accompanied by a band of music; colours of these nondescripts were various.

Seventh : two more with cocks' bodies and tails, four wings, with elephants' trunks and tusks, gilt castles and cloth.

Eighth : two more cocks with four wings, castles, &c., but a little different from the seventh.

Ninth : two cocks with griffin-legs and human arms, four wings, castle and cloth.

Tenth : two cocks with long snouts, four wings, castle and cloth.

Eleventh : two horses with dragons' tails, four wings, castles, &c. Then came one hundred and twenty men carrying flowers made of yellow or Talapoy cloth, having artificial green leaves: they were of the shape of a sunflower and attached to bamboo-poles ten or twelve feet in length.

Twelfth : two horses' bodies, with elephants' heads and snakes' tails, four wings, castles, &c.

Thirteenth : two cocks' with horses bodies, four wings, castles, &c.

Fourteenth : two lions, with deers' horns, wings, castles, &c.

Fifteenth : two lions, with horses' bodies, long tails, wings, &c.

Sixteenth : two leopards, with elephants' heads and tusks, wings, &c., &c.

Seventeenth : two elephants' bodies, with non-descript heads, wings, &c., &c., colour, a dark ground with white spots.

Eighteenth : two horses, covered with green circles, cocks' crests, lions' tails, wings, &c., &c.

Nineteenth : two striped and spotted leopards, with wings, castles, &c.

All the above animals were from four to six feet in height; they were made of bamboo frame and covered with paper; the different pairs were variously painted and gilt, striped, spotted, in circles, &c., &c. They were drawn on low sledges, sometimes by men alone, dressed in blue or green cloth, embroidered with the figure of a tiger, and caps to correspond, with waist-cloths of all colours; others by men and horses: all the animals were in pairs, and about twenty feet apart: they had four wings each, and bore small gilded towers on their backs, containing on a salver, cloths of yellow, intended as offerings to the Talapoys.

Then followed one hundred and thirty men with tom-toms or drums, which they struck occasionally with a covered stick. They were dressed in coarse red cotton jackets, caps, and drawers reaching to the knee.

These were followed by seven hundred men representing angels, dressed in long white frocks, having white high peaked caps in the style of the royal crown of Siam. These represented celestial messengers, and were to show the soul of the deceased the way to heaven: each one bore the sacred Indian lotus and leaf, artificially made: these were accompanied by a great number of musicians, having trumpets and small brass horns, making a great discord: then sixty-four conical umbrellas, each consisting of five separate pieces: they were about fifteen feet high, the lowest part being about four feet in diameter and were made of cloth of gold and embroidered.

Between each two of these men, was carried what resembled a section of a bishop's mitre, similar in appearance to those placed in front of all the wats. They were fastened to the tops of staves, of about nine or ten feet in length, and were flat, broad, neatly ornamented, and gilt.

Following these, came the san-krat,[62] or Siamese bishop, apparently reciting prayers, in a car about twenty feet high. This carriage was broad at the base, gradually lessening to the seat; neatly carved and gilt, and sparkling with various coloured glass. The carriage was drawn by six horses, and led by servants. Then came, dressed in a robe of gold tissue, one of the youngest sons of the deceased, wearing a royal gilt cap, in a car nearly similar to the last, and drawn in like manner. An immense white umbrella was held over him, conical umbrellas at each corner, and four long gold fans, pear-shaped: these are a sign of royalty. Then came another son of the deceased king, wearing the royal peaked cap, in a carriage like the last, drawn by one hundred men, in embroidered green dresses and red caps, assisted by five horses richly caparisoned, holding in his hand the end of a broad sash of silver tissue, which was connected with the funeral car of his father, being about thirty, forty, or fifty feet distant. This latter car was about twenty-five feet in height. It was elegantly decorated with carved work, superior to its predecessors, and highly gilt. The body was seated in a square gilt tower, having gilt network sides, and was supported by two angels, kneeling, in front and rear. The car was drawn by angels dressed similarly to the former, and also by horses. Many of the high officers of state walked in single files by the side of the carriage, dressed in white muslin, and peaked caps, carrying white wands.

The body was placed in a sitting posture, with the knees drawn up

---

[62] The *sangkarat* or head of the Buddhist clergy.

to the chin, and the hands united in the attitude of prayer: it was said to be embalmed.

Eight hundred angels next followed, in two lines, succeeded by a large carriage, containing Agila,[63] and other odoriferous woods, for consuming the remains of the deceased.

The preceding carriages were all similar in structure, and from eighteen to twenty-five feet in height to the top of the towers, fifteen feet in length, and ten feet in width. The wheels were of a solid piece of wood, and about two feet in diameter, similar to those used in buffalo-carts in Manila, Sumatra, and Java: the carriage being broad at the base, and gradually lessening to the tower, and of an oblong form.

Following the foregoing, came six open carriages, covered with beautifully figured cloth of gold, containing Talapoy cloths.

Fifty-six umbrella towers, of a very large size, being a series of canopies, gradually lessening to the top, covered with rich gold cloth, having tassels of green, red, &c., &c.

One hundred men with green and gilt drums, or tom-toms, wearing red cotton frocks and caps.

One hundred and fifty men bearing artificial yellow flowers, made of Talapoy cloth, similar to those already described. On each flank were men carrying artificial yellow flowers, like those before named. Then followed:—

Three pairs of horses' bodies, with non-descript heads, cocks' crests, lions' tails, &c.

Two pairs, with giants' heads and bodies, cocks' tails and legs, in green and gold.

Two pairs, with cocks' legs and fishes' tails, in white and gold.

Two pairs, with gorgons' heads, human bodies, lions' tails, in white and gold.

Two pairs lions, painted blue.

Two pairs, yellow, with horns.

Two pairs, blue, with horns.

Two pairs, yellow, no horns : All having gilt towers, containing Talapoy cloths.

Fifty men, carrying rich silk embroidered pennants.

---

[63] Aguila, agalloch, aloeswood, eaglewood: the soft resinous odiferous heartwood of the *aquilaria*.

Then followed on horseback, in pairs, four princes, two and two, wearing the gold-peaked crown, and dressed in long robes of silver tissue: following them, eight more, of a lower rank. These were succeeded by a great number of slaves or attendants, dressed in white waist-cloths. The horses were richly caparisoned, with gold housings, bridles, &c., and led by slaves. At every few steps they would stop, and the attendants in front would kneel down, facing their masters, as well as those in the rear.

Preceding every prince, went a man, bearing a bundle of rods, like a Roman lictor. In the rear were open palanquins, having gold, or richly gilt supporters on the sides, and rich velvet cushions. Then followed a vast concourse of people, but all preserving good order.

There was an immense multitude convened to witness this splendid funeral procession. Governors and rajahs from distant provinces of the empire, came, by order of his majesty, each one bringing a gift to assist in paying the enormous expenses attending this idle and useless ceremony. Here were assembled persons of all nations. From the western hemisphere, Americans; from the east, Indians, Arabs, Bengalese, Burmese, Pequans, Malays, Sumatrans, Javanese, Cochin-Chinese, Cambojans, the Chans [Chams], or people of Lao[s], Siamese, &c.; and among the whole of them no serious impression could possibly have been made. It could only be considered a fine farcical scene, a pretty raree show, got up as a benefit for the king and his ministers, (for it is expected that every one, who is able, will contribute something,) to show the public that splendid mausoleums are only fit for the great of the land, and that the vulgar herd must be burnt in the common way, either under a shed, or else on a raised platform in the open air: to impress their minds with the magnificence of majesty, and, at the same time, to strike them with awe and fear, so that they may be more easily ruled by the iron hand of despotism.

This whole assembled multitude (with the exception of our party) crouched to the ground like base slaves, whenever any of the higher ranks passed. Along an extensive street, on one side, were playhouses erected, open to public use, in which were exhibited shows of all kinds, and fireworks might be seen nightly, within the enclosure surrounding the temporary funeral pile. His majesty was desirous we should witness the burning of the body on the funeral pile, which was to take place the seventh day after the procession;* but the ship was in want of provisions; the southwest monsoon was about commencing, which is generally attended with violent squalls and heavy rains, the ship was riding at anchor ten or twelve miles from the mouth of the river, in five and a half fathoms' water, in a very exposed situation; and it was necessary to bring our water some forty miles, near the city, besides which, the only provisions to be obtained, were fowls, pork, and rice.

The Budhist religion of Siam, according to historians, originated in Magadha, the modern Behar, in the sixth century, (or 542,) the founder being Gautama, the son of a prince, called Sudhodana. After many centuries it was introduced into Ceylon; and in the seventh century of the Christian era, first into Camboja, and from thence into Lao; and lastly, into Siam. Sommona Kodom, the cattle stealer, a Singalese, was the missionary who first propagated this religion in those countries.[64] He is described as being benevolent in the *extreme*. He even carried his zeal so far, as to murder his whole family, (considering them as encumbrances upon his country,) so that he might maintain a greater number of priests. He was renowned for the daily mortifications of his body, his fastings, his prayers, his miracles, and the fantastic appearance he could assume— now swelling to the size of a mountain, and again shrinking to a mere atom. But notwithstanding he possessed great supernatural powers, he could not resist the cravings of an unsaint-like appetite; for eating a large quantity of pork one day, he died in a fit of anger, because he had transgressed one of his rules, and thereby set a bad example to his disciples.

All professors of Budhism, whether of Tartary or Magadha origin, are atheists. They do not believe in one God, the creator of the universe. The leading doctrine of this religion, is that of the transmigration of souls.

After being purged of all their sins, by being punished in some one or all of their numerous *hells*, having practised the regular number of virtues, they believe that they will at length reach the highest of all their

---

* One of the sons of the wang-na watches at the temple, near the funeral pile, night and day, till the body is consumed; the ashes of the consumed body are then thrown into the river with many ceremonies; and the unconsumed bones are then delivered to the priests, and made into household gods. [Author's note]

[64] Sommona Kodom is simply another form of the name given to the Buddha. Where Roberts obtained the inaccurate information given here is not known.

more numerous heavens, and then no longer come into existence or die; that then they are emancipated from all the cares and passions which belong to our natures, and sink into annihilation.

Here they will enjoy the company of the blessed Guatama, who occupies the uppermost seat, and that of many worthies who will there be found; yet the existence of the founder of their religion is limited to a term of five thousand years, and nearly one half of that time has actually expired. The Budhists say the world was created by chance; it will be destroyed and reproduced, and destroyed again and again.

The founder of this religion—seeing that all mankind was in a state of gross ignorance and barbarism, ferocious, their feet swift to shed blood, that they were given up to a life of rapine—persuaded them that it was a sin to shed the blood of any living creature; that they must cultivate the soil, and live in peace and harmony with all mankind.

He, therefore, enjoined on his converts the following moral precepts, viz.:—First: Thou shalt not kill any living creature. Second: Steal not. Third: Commit not adultery. Fourth: Thou shalt not lie or prevaricate, Fifth: Thou shalt not be guilty of drunkenness, or use any intoxicating drugs. Sixth: Eat not after noonday. Seventh: Frequent not play-houses, or any place of amusement. Eighth: Use no personal amusements. Ninth: Sleep on a clean mat, and use no costly, soft, rich, or elevated beds. Tenth: Do not borrow or run in debt.

The first commandment is violated in every war that takes place; and how many instances have we on record of blood being poured out in profusion, to make clear the path for the ascension to the throne of a lawful sovereign or a usurper, or for some more trivial object. The clergy and laity also daily partake of fish, flesh, and fowl; but they consider the crime of killing them as attached to the vender only, although they may hire him to commit the act. The second and third are but little attended to. As it regards the fifth, the large revenue, derived from the distilling of arrack, is a convincing proof of its general use; and wine and spirits form a part of the cargo of every English and American vessel, which are sold at a good profit; and the use of opium is likewise rapidly increasing, notwithstanding its use is prohibited by their laws and religion. As for the last five commandments, they are imperative on Talapoys only, and they do, or do not, observe them, as it suits their inclination. As for the fourth, it is considered quite obsolete; I believe, it is observed or not, as it may subserve the interests or convenience of either the clergy or the laity. If there were not so great a number of Talapoys employed in cutting grass for the king's elephants, one would be led to suppose that the third commandment was *orginally* intended to be observed more strictly among them than it now is, but he must first be stripped of his sacerdotal vestments, before he can be punished by the secular arm.

All *spiritual concerns* are delegated to the priests. A strict observance of religious duties is not expected from the laity; if they administer to the daily necessities of the clergy, pay them the customary honours, and strictly attend to the observance of the holy day, &c., they consider that they have fully acquitted themselves of every essential part of their duty. Almost every freeman in Siam is, for a longer or shorter period of time, a priest. If married, he must be divorced, having previously made a suitable provision for his family. If he enters the priesthood a second time, it is for life. There are six grades of priests; they enter as noviciates, and are promoted according to their respective merits. Above all, is the san-krat bishop or high-priest, who receives his appointment from the king.

The sovereign is the pope, or real head of the religion of the country, and the priests depend wholly upon him for promotion, and in a great measure for subsistence; he is always deemed holy, and must have been truly virtuous in a former life, to have attained his present eminence. Eighty-four thousand six hundred ba{h}ts or ticals, equal to the sum of about fifty-three thousand five hundred dollars, are placed down among the items of the expenditures of the government, for the year 1832, as given in alms to the priests by the king. The Talapoys cannot be engaged in any of the temporal concerns of life; they must not trade or do any kind of manual labour, for the sake of a reward; they are not allowed to *insult* the earth by digging it. Having no tie, which unites their interests with those of the people, they are ready, at all times, with spiritual arms, to enforce obedience to the will of the sovereign.

No Talapoy can ordain a layman, without first obtaining a license from the san-krat, and all classes of people pay him unbounded honours. Secular persons must make obeisance to Talapoys—even parents to their children; this mark of homage is considered as their due, and, therefore, they never return the salutation. One strong inducement to enter the priesthood, is an exemption from the conscription law, which bears so heavily upon the people; to avoid paying taxes, and to obtain an easy livelihood.

Their time must be spent in studying the sacred Pali or Bali language, in reading hymns, prayers, and moral discourses, and begging: for they must not lay in a store of food, nor make any arrangement for preparing it for use, but still they employ others for that purpose.

They are forbid to be burdensome to beast or tree; but it seems they may be so to their own species. Twice in the month, the head and eyebrows must be shaved, as a token of mortification, and to render them less captivating to the *fair* Siamese. Attached to all temples are monasteries, slenderly endowed by the government or rich individuals—yet by far the largest part of their support is derived from casual alms and gifts. Early in the morning, they may be seen in great numbers, sallying forth in their yellow dresses, which are either of silk[65] or cotton; some carrying a large bason, and others with their scrip, suspended over the left shoulder by a band of yellow cloth; this is made of a composition of iron and sand, and it is exceedingly brittle. These pots are manufactured just without the walls of the city, on the south side. They are covered with a material more or less rich, according to the ability of the owner. Great numbers of Talapoys are seen rowing their little boats, in search of alms, having then no protection for their closely shaven heads against the heat of a powerful sun. But when they go out for exercise, or to pay a visit, they use a long neat pear-shaped palm-leaf fan, called talapat. When they present themselves at the foot of a ladder, or in front of a floating-house, they never ask for charity, but wait patiently till they are supplied with clothing or food: it is received in silence, and they never return thanks to the donor.

Siam appears to have no place in history, prior to the introduction of the Budhist religion, in the year of Christ, 638, when a sovereign by the name of Krek governed the country. In 1521[66] their first intercourse with Europeans (the Portuguese) took place. There were two revolutions, and the country was conquered by the Burmans, and recovered again its independence between A.D. 1547 and 1596. In the year 1612, the first English ship made her appearance, and ascended the river to Yuthia, the

---

[65] Monks' robes are supposed to be of cheap materials, not silk.
[66] Portuguese first came to Siam in 1511 at the time of the taking of Malacca.

ancient capital, about fifty miles above the present seat of government. In the year 1621, a Portuguese mission was sent to Siam, by the Portuguese viceroy of Goa; and in the same year, some Roman Catholic missionaries first made their appearance.[67] In 1627, another revolution took place, which placed a new dynasty on the throne.[68] In 1684, the son of the usurper was instigated by Constantine Phanlcon [sic], a Greek adventurer, to send an embassy to Louis XIV.[69] In 1685, the Chevalier Chaumont was sent there, at the head of a splendid embassy, which was the cause, in 1687, of sending a second mission, with a squadron of ships and five hundred soldiers. The total destruction of the English took place at Magni,[70] this year, in consequence, it is said, of their overbearing and insolent conduct; and, in the year following, their factory at Yuthia was removed. In 1690,[71] a revolution took place, and the reigning family lost the throne; the minister, Phanlcon, lost his life, and the French were expelled from the country, which destroyed their hopes of establishing a French empire in the East, until the year 1787, when they made that famous treaty with Cochin-China, ceding the peninsula of Haw, the bay of Turam [sic], &c.;[72] but which failed in consequence of the troublesome state of public affairs in France, at that period, followed by the revolution. Since that time, and within the last five years, the French government sent a frigate to Cochin-China, and endeavoured, but without effect, to have the treaty ratified. The dynasty of 1690 reigned till the capture of the capital by the Burmans, under Shembuan, the second son of Alompia,

---

[67] Contacts were established with Siam by the Portuguese even before the fall of Malacca, and in 1514 a Siamese envoy took to Goa a letter from Ramathipodi II to the King of Portugal. Catholic missionaries appeared soon after; two Jesuits were in Ayutthaya by 1555.

[68] King Song Tham died in 1628 to be briefly succeeded by his eldest son Chettha; he was overthrown in August 1629 by Athittayawong, his younger brother, who in turn was overthrown by a usurper, known as King Prasat Tong.

[69] The first embassy to France was sent under French missionary influence in 1680 but it was shipwrecked off Africa at the end of 1681. The mission sent in 1684 was to find out what had become of it. Phaulkon is usually reckoned to have assumed ministerial power by 1683, and the first full Siamese embassy to France reached Europe in 1686.

[70] Mergui, then a Siamese possession on the west coast of the Malay peninsula. The typesetters seem to have had trouble reading Roberts' hand.

[71] The coup d'état in Lopburi which ousted Phaulkon and was followed in two months by the death of King Narai took place in May 1688.

[72] The date is correct: Bishop Pigneau obtained from Nguyen Anh (later known as Gia Long) a treaty of alliance between France and Cochin-China; France received the Bay of Tourane and Pulo Condore in return for promises of ships, men, and arms.

PART I: TREATY MISSION OF 1833    101

which took place in 1767, when the king was killed at the entrance of his palace.[73]

The Burman army retired with great plunder, after destroying vast numbers of the inhabitants, making slaves of others, destroying the temples, and committing every sort of excess. The Siamese immediately rose upon the Burmans who remained, and massacred them and their partisans.

A chief, of Chinese descent, Pla-tah, alias, Phria-metah [sic], in 1767, seized upon the throne, and proclaimed himself king.[74] In the early part of his reign, he behaved with moderation, good sense, and discernment, and his courage was unquestionable. He reconquered Piseluk and Ligor,[75] which had declared themselves independent, during the Burmese invasion: but in the last year of his reign, he ruled in so strange a manner, that it was generally believed he was insane. His tyrannical and capricious conduct, in 1782, was the cause of a formidable rebellion, under the chakri, so called, being the title of a great officer of state: it ended in the dethronement and death of the king, in the same year, at the present capital. The chakri reigned in his stead, until his death, in 1809. His eldest son then mounted the throne, but not without opposition,[76] for there was a large party in favour of his nephew, the prince Chow Fa, (or Chaou Pha.) He commenced his reign by committing an act of great atrocity, ordering, within thirty-six hours after the death of his father, the execution of upward of a hundred persons, supposed to be inimical to his right to the throne, including his nephew.

After the committal of this sanguinary act, he ruled with great moderation. Nothing of much importance occurred. Three abortive attempts at insurrection took place during his reign; one was by the Talapoys, occasioned by an attempt to force a large number of their order into the ranks of the army.

---

[73] King Hsinbyushin (reigned 1763-1776) of Burma, second son of Alaungpaya, attacked Ayutthaya in 1766 and captured the city in 1767. The Siamese king Suriyamarin was said to have fled and starved to death ten days later.

[74] Phya Tak, later known as King Taksin, had to establish Siamese authority in the country; he was not crowned king until December 1768.

[75] Taksin subdued Ligor in 1769 and in 1770 took Phitsanulok (Roberts' 'Piseluk').

[76] Rama II's accession was unopposed: he did change nearly all his father's ministers, but no bloodbath is recorded.

The acquisition of the fertile and extensive province of Batalang, in Camboja,[77] took place the same year he ascended the throne. The year following, their implacable enemy, the Burmese, captured the island Junti Ceylon[78] on the western coast of the Malay peninsula, which was shortly after recaptured by the Siamese, attended with scenes of great barbarity. Since the conquest of the Burman empire by the British, the Siamese have lost all dread of their ancient enemy.

In July, 1824, the father of the present king died *very suddenly*, it was said of stranguary,[79] but not without strong suspicions of his being poisoned; in fact, it is said, by every one, that this was the cause of his death. His eldest, but illegitimate son, Chromas Chit,[80] ascended the throne the same day, without bloodshed, to the exclusion of the rightful heir, prince Chow-Pha-Yai,[81] who immediately embraced the priesthood, in order to save his life, or his liberty, or because he would not do homage to a usurper. His younger brother *Chow-Phoi-Noi*,*[82] otherwise *Mom-fa-Noi*, was the next legitimate heir to the throne. He lives at the Portuguese fort, on the right bank of the river, opposite to the palace, and is now about twenty-five years of age.

Joined to a playful disposition, he possesses considerable abilities; he is a friend to the mechanic arts, and to the sciences; and very friendly disposed, as well as his elder brother, towards foreigners. He seems solicitous to become acquainted with all the Europeans and Americans; and not a day or evening passed, during our stay there, but his boat was sent, desiring the company of some of the gentlemen residing at the mission house. In the night-time, by stealth, he went

---

* He speaks and writes the English language with considerable fluency, and his pronunciation is very correct. [Author's note]

[77] Rama II appointed the Cambodian governor of Battambang; Cambodia was divided between pro-Siamese and pro-Vietnamese factions.

[78] The Burmese captured Junk Ceylon (Phuket) in 1810 but were soon expelled.

[79] Stranguary is a condition in which urine is passed painfully if at all.

[80] Prince Chetsabodin, born 1788, was by far the most senior and experienced son of Rama II; as mentioned in note 24, he was the son of a royal concubine, though not a queen. The accession was without problem, though many Westerners regarded him as the illegitimate successor to his father.

[81] Chao Phaya Yai is Prince Mongkut (note 25), born 1804, who had entered the monkhood before the death of his father 'at an ill-omened time' because a white elephant had just died.

[82] Chao Phaya Noi (see also note 20) is Prince Chudamani, Mongkut's younger brother, was indeed proficent in English and interested in naval matters.

down the river and visited the Peacock, having previously received letters from Captain G.[83] to his first officer. He examined the ship throughout; the men were mustered to quarters, and went through the exercise of the great guns, small arms, &c. Never having seen a man-of-war before, he appeared to be astonished at the neatness of the ship, the order, regularity, and activity, of the men when at quarters; and stated, after his return, he was exceedingly surprised at every thing he saw, and highly gratified with his visit. A strict secresy was enjoined upon every one, not to divulge this visit, or it might cost him his liberty, or perhaps, his life. He made application, afterward, through the praklang, to the king, to pay a visit, which was granted; but there was not time; he was obliged to be present at all the ceremonies attending the burning of the second king.*

The government of Siam is a despotism, subject to no restraint except the apprehension of popular tumult or foreign invasion. The fact of being in high station, is regarded as sufficient evidence of exalted merit in a former state of existence. The king is therefore considered almost, if not altogether, equal to a deity; and is always addressed as such. His most common designations are Chao-cheveet, "the lord of lives," Khun-luang, "the owner of all," Phra-putty-chao-jahooa, "the sacred lord of heads," and numerous others of the same nature. His more formal title, as translated in the treaty with the British, concluded by Captain Burney, is the following: "The great lord who is in possession of every good and every dignity, the God Bood'h, who dwells over every head in the city of the sacred and great kingdom of Sia-yoo-thya, incomprehensible to the head and brain." The Siamese, when they possess titles, cease to be designated by any personal names; hence the king is never spoken of except by the abovementioned or other similar titles.

Next in rank and station to the king, is the wang-na, commonly called, by Europeans, the second king. This high officer is always one of the most exalted of the princes, and is chosen by the king at the

---

* The present king is very desirous of encouraging foreign commerce to enter his ports, and the perplexities and endless changes which formerly annoyed them, are now removed. As long as the present king lives, this wise policy will be pursued. The amount of imports is rapidly rising in importance. A historiographer is regularly employed at the court of Siam, and the recorded events are deposited in the public archives. [Author's note]

[83] Captain Geisinger, commander of the *Peacock*.

time of his accession to the throne. When he survives the king he commonly succeeds him on the throne;[84] but when the wang-na dies first, it is seldom that another is appointed to fill his place, during the reign of the same king. Hence there was no one who held the office at the time of our arrival, the one chosen on the accession of the present king having died about ten months before.

At the head of the Siamese administration is the supreme council, consisting of the following officers:[85]—

First : A president, a prince of high rank. When the mission was in the country, this office was held by the prince Khroma-luang-rah.

Second : Chao-phaya-bodin-deeha or khroma-ha-thai, formerly called Chao-phaya-chakri. He has the general superintendance of the northern provinces adjoining Pegue, and of the principalities of Laos and Camboja.

Third : Chao-phaya-maha-sena, or khroma-ka-la-hom; he is of equal rank with the lastmentioned, and holds the office of commander-in-chief of all the land and sea forces, with the general superintendance of the southwestern provinces, even to the last tributary Malay rajah.

Fourth : Chao-phaya, praklang or khromatha, the minister of commerce and foreign affairs, who also has the superintendance of the southeastern provinces adjoining Cochin-China. This office and the lastmentioned, are at present held by one individual.

Fifth : Chao-phaya-jomarat, or khroma-muang, minister of criminal justice.

Sixth : Chao-phaya-phollathep, or khrom-na, minister of agriculture and produce.

Seventh : Chao-phaya-therama-terat, or chroma-wang, governor of the royal palace.

The mission, during its stay in the country, had intercourse only with the praklang, and the subordinate officers of his department. These were:—

First : Chao-phaya praklang: Chao-phaya is the first in order of the honorary titles. Praklang is said to signify, "lord of the store-houses,"

---

[84] There were in fact very few instances where the crown passed to the *upparat* or second king on the death of the king. Rama III appointed no successor to his uncle, Prince Sakdiphonlasep who, as *upparat*, died in 1832.

[85] Roberts' ministerial stratification and titles have to be treated with caution.

and is the title of the office. This signification corresponds with the title given to him by the Chinese, viz. "Great minister of the treasuries or store-houses."

Second : Phaya-si-piphat. This office is held by one of the brothers of the praklang. Phaya is the second honorary title.

Third : Phaya-piphat-kossa, called by the Portuguese, the second praklang.

The other officers in this department, consisting of four phayas, two pras, (or officers of the third rank) eleven luangs, (of the fourth rank,) &c, were never met with by the mission, except when in the presence, and acting under the orders, of their superiors.

Connected with this department is that of the Farang-khromatha-tha "Frank (or European) commercial board," under the direction of the Luang-sura-sakhon, chief of the Linguists, or captain of the port. This office is at present held by Sur-Jose-da-Piedade.

The commander of the artillery, Phaya-viset, Song-khiam, is also often brought in connexion with foreign missions. This office is held by Sur-Beneditto-de-Arvellegeria, a Cambojan Portuguese, who, with his brother, Sur-Pascoal, has been for many years in the employ of the king of Siam. The governors of all provinces, whether great or small, are of the second rank, or phayas, with one exception, that of the governor of Ligore, called Chao-phaya-lahhon. Their subordinate officers are not known.

[5]

# CHAPTER XX

ANCIENT LAWS OF SIAM—LEGAL OATHS—PUNISHMENT FOR DEBT—DIVORCES—POPULATION OF SIAM—STATURE AND COMPLEXION OF THE SIAMESE—DIVISION OF TIME—BOUNDARIES AND POSSESSIONS OF SIAM—MARINE OF SIAM—IMPORTS—INLAND TRADE—CURRENCY—TREATY OF COMMERCE—TABLE OF EXPORTS.

THE Siamese have written *laws*, which are dated as far back as 561 of Christ; and others are referred to in their courts, to the years of 1053-1614 and 1773.

The higher officers of state are the justices and magistrates, but the final decision rests with the principal local authority within whose district the delinquent resides. Where the government is a perfect despotism, and the channels of justice are polluted by corrupt propounders of the law, equity and justice are but empty names, and good laws a mere mockery. Oaths are administered to witnesses only on formal and solemn occasions: the following being the form used in their courts as translated by Capt. Lowe[86]:—

"I, who have been brought here as an evidence in this matter, do now, in the presence of the divine Prah-Phutthi-rop (Budha,) declare that I am wholly unprejudiced against either party, and uninfluenced in any way by the opinions or advice of others, and that no prospects of pecuniary advantage, or of advancement to office, have been held out to me; I also declare that I have not received any bribe on this occasion. If what I have now spoken be false, or if in my further averments I should colour or pervert the truth, so as to lead the judgment of others astray, may the three Holy Existences, viz.: Budha, the Bali (personified,) and the three priests, before whom I now stand, together with the glorious Dewatas (demigods) of the twenty-two firmaments, punish me.

"If I have not seen, yet shall I say I have seen; if I shall say that I

---

[86] Captain James Low, not Lowe (1791-1852), acquired some proficiency in Siamese and was used on diplomatic missions to the ruler of Ligor by the British. He wrote prolifically, including the first Thai grammar in a Western language.

know that which I do not know, then may I be thus punished. Should innumerable descents of the Deity happen for the regeneration and salvation of mankind, may my erring and migrating soul be found beyond the pale of their mercy—wherever I go, may I be encompassed with dangers, and not escape from them, whether arising from murderers, robbers, spirits of the earth, of the woods, of water, or of air, or from all the divinities who adore Budha, or from the gods of the four elements, and all other spirits.

"May blood flow out of every pore of my body, that my crime may be made manifest to the world; may all or any of these evils overtake me within three days, or may I never stir from the spot on which I now stand, or may the *hatsani*, or lash of the sky, (lightning,) cut me in two, so that I may be exposed to the derision of the people; or if I should be walking abroad, may I be torn to pieces by either of the four supernaturally endowed lions, or destroyed by poisonous herbs or venomous snakes. If when in the waters of the rivers or ocean, may supernatural crocodiles or great fishes devour me, or may the winds and waves overwhelm me; or may the dread of such evils keep me, during life, a prisoner at home, estranged from every pleasure, or may I be afflicted with the intolerable oppressions of my superiors, or may a plague cause my death; after which may I be precipitated into hell, there to go through innumerable stages of torture, among which may I be condemned to carry water over the flaming regions in open wicker baskets, to assuage the heat felt by Than-Wetsuan, when he enters the infernal hall of justice, and thereafter may I fall into the lowest pit of hell; or if these miseries should not ensue, may I after death migrate into the body of a slave, and suffer all the hardships and pains attending the worst state of such a being, during a period of years, measured by the sand of four seas; or may I animate the body of an animal, or beast, during five hundred generations; or be born an hermaphrodite five hundred times, or endure in the body of a deaf, blind, dumb, houseless beggar, every species of loathsome disease during the same number of generations, and then may I be hurried to varah, or hell, and there be crucified by Phria-yam, one of the kings of hell."

The Siamese are extremely capricious, in the standard value of witnesses; the oath of priests and men in office bearing a preference over all others, while there are not less than twenty-eight in number, who are excluded, and declared to be incompetent; they are as follows:

contemners of religion, persons in debt, the slaves of a party to a suit, intimate friends, idiots, those who do not hold in abhorrence the cardinal sins, among which are enumerated, besides theft and murder, drinking spirits, breaking prescribed fasts, and reposing on the mat or couch of a priest or parent, gamblers, vagrants, executioners, quack-doctors, play-actors, hermaphrodites, strolling musicians, prostitutes, blacksmiths, persons labouring under incurable disorders, persons under seven or above seventy, bachelors, insane persons, persons of violent passions, shoemakers, beggars, braziers, midwives, and sorcerers.

Tortures are resorted to in cases of treason or atrocious robbery, and even among debtors where property is supposed to be concealed, as well as the ordeal by water and immersing the hands in boiling oil or melted tin. He who remains the longest under water, and the hand which comes forth unscathed, are pronounced to be innocent. A debtor may be punished by stripes and imprisonment, or dried, as it is termed by the Siamese, that is exsiccated by being exposed to the direct rays of a burning sun, suffering in addition the torments from myriads of noxious insects, and finally to be sold as a slave if he is unable to discharge his debt.

A great number of debtors are seen in irons about the bazars, whose only mode of subsistence is by begging; and they seldom ask in vain of a people who are pre-eminently charitable.

Theft is punished with the bamboo and with imprisonment, and even hard labour for life, in aggravated cases. Murder, counterfeiting coin, and forging the royal signet, with imprisonment for life, and the severest punishment of the bamboo; and in cases of cruel and deliberate murder, with death, by decapitation. A breach of the marriage-vow is not deemed a highly criminal act, and it is easily commuted by paying a fine, according to the rank or standing of the parties, from the sum of two hundred and seventy to ninety dollars. Marriage is a civil contract, and the Talapoins are not considered, in any way, necessary to legalize the contract; but their prayers and benedictions are occasionally bestowed. Insults are punished, from an inferior to a superior, according to the aggravation of the offence, by a fine, and even by corporal punishment, when a priest is the aggrieved party.

If a priest commits a criminal act, he is divested of the sacerdotal habit, and is punished generally with more severity than a layman. Divorces are easily obtained, and each party receives back whatever was contributed to the common stock. The minor male children go to the mother, and the female to the father. Property can only be given to the wife and children, and daughters receive from a half to a whole share more than the sons. Wills must be made in the presence of four witnesses.

Siam appears to be a place of refuge for the surrounding nations, and is composed of a great variety of people, viz.: Siamese, Laos, Cambojans, Malays, Kariangs, Lawas, Kas, Chongs and Semangs, Chinese, Mohammedans, and Hindoos of western India, Peguans, and Portuguese. The population of the whole empire, including their late conquests in the Malay peninsula, does not probably exceed three millions and six hundred thousand, (although many Siamese rate it, in round numbers, at five millions.) Of this number, I am led to believe, from frequent conversations held with men in office, that the Siamese do not exceed one million and six hundred thousand. The native population of Lao[s], about one million and two hundred thousand. The Chinese at not less than half a million, there being nearly three hundred and forty thousand in the capital and the villages which compose Bang-kok. The Malays, probably, amount to three hundred and twenty thousand; and the remainder are natives of western India. Peguans, Cambojans and Portuguese, the latter from pretty correct authority, do not exceed fourteen hundred in the whole Siamese dominions. The Kariangs, the Lawas, the Kas, and the Chongs, are wild and migratory races; the three first inhabit the mountains and fastnesses of Lao, from the Burman dominions to Camboja. The Chongs inhabit the hilly country, bordering on the eastern side of the Siamese gulf. The Semangs are a race of savage negroes, dwelling in the mountainous regions of the Malay peninsula, of which a very curious and particular statement was published by J. Anderson, Esq., included in his account of the "Aboriginal Inhabitants of the Malay Peninsula," which I have subjoined at the end of my Journal on Siam.

By actual admeasurement of a great number of Siamese, it is ascertained that the average height does not exceed five feet and four inches. Their skin is darker than the Chinese, yet they are several shades lighter than the Malays; their complexion is rather a dark shade of yellow or a yellowish brown. All classes delight in heightening it, by using turmeric. A light yellow is considered to be the "ne plus ultra" of all colours and all shades. This taste is derived, probably, from the numerous Chinese who reside there. Owing to their frequent bathing, and daily using a clean waist-cloth, their skin is remarkably smooth, soft, and shining. They are inclined to obesity, have large lower limbs and stout long arms; yet they are by no means a strong or robust people. The *face* is broad and flat—the cheek-bones round, but prominent—the *nose* rather small, round at the point, and rather hollow at the bridge—they have large mouths and rather thick lips—the lower jaw is long and full at the extremities, and the countenance apparently square—the eyes are small and black, the white tinged with a yellow cast—the forehead, although broad in a lateral direction, is generally low—the beard is very scanty. The diameter of the head is remarkably short from the front, backward; the top is unusually flat, and from the crown to the nape of the neck, (in a large proportion of them,) is nearly in a straight line. The hair is always black, thick, coarse, and lank.

The Siamese week consists of seven days; the months, alternately, of twenty-nine and thirty days; and twelve months, or three hundred and fifty-four days, make a year. The year being solar, an intercalary month of thirty days is added every third year after the eighth month. The month is divided into a dark and a bright half, as the moon is upon the increase or the wane. The Siamese new year corresponds with that of the Chinese, which commences *after* the last half of the month of January, or the sun's entrance into Aquarius. It is very certain, that in forming their calendar, they depend upon that constructed at Peking. There is also a greater division of time, consisting of twelve years, each year taking the name of some animal, thus:—

|  |  | *Siamese.* | *English.* |
|---|---|---|---|
| First | year | Chuat | Rat. |
| Second | " | Chabu | Ox or cow. |
| Third | " | Khan | Tiger. |
| Fourth | " | Tho | Hare. |
| Fifth | " | Marong | Dragon, or great snake. |
| Sixth | " | Maseng | Snake, or lesser serpent. |
| Seventh | " | Ma-mia | Horse. |
| Eighth | " | Ma-mee | Goat. |
| Ninth | " | Wock, or Vock | Monkey, or ape. |
| Tenth | " | Ray-ka, or Raka | Cock, or fowl. |
| Eleventh | " | Cho, or Cho-Cho | Dog. |
| Twelfth | " | Khan, or Kun | Pig, or hog. |

The Siamese have two epochs, sacred and popular. The *sacred* era dates from the death of Gautama, and the year 1833 corresponded to the 2376th year. The vulgar era was instituted when the worship of Gautama was first introduced; and the year 1833 corresponded with the year 1194, and was the fifth, or dragon year.

Siam proper extends from about the latitude of 23° north, to the gulf of that name, and is bounded, west by the Burman empire, and east by the Lao (Lau) mountains. This is the valley of the Menam, the "Mother of waters," the country of the true Siamese. The Menam, after watering the low, flat land, by its annual deposits, empties itself, by three channels, into the gulf of Siam. The boundaries of the Siamese dominions on the bay of Bengal, extend from the Burman, (or more correctly speaking, in the present day,) the *English* Burmese dominions, as far south as the boundary line between the petty states of Perak and Quedah, in the straits of Malacca, in about the latitude of 5° north, in which is included the valuable island of Junk Ceylon or Salung, containing a vast body of tin ore. It then extends nearly east, across the Malay peninsula, in about the same latitude, between the provinces of Tungano and Pakhang,[87] the shores of which are bathed by the China sea: it then extends north to the head of the gulf of Siam. The Siamese government, during the year 1832, brought under their immediate subjection, nearly the whole of the tributary states in the Malay peninsula. They possess, also, a large part of the late kingdom of Lao[s], including the former capital of the empire, called Lau-chang,[88] situated on the great river Camboja, in about the sixteenth degree of north latitude, and which is represented to be very populous. They hold also (with the exception of a small portion of the southern part) the province of Batabang,[89] in Camboja. Their eastern boundary line is in about the longitude of 105°, and extends north to the latitude of 15°, being the dividing line between Lao and Camboja, and extending south to the Siamese gulf, the boundary being the island of Kong (alias Ko Kong,) situate in north latitude 10° 43´, and longitude 103° 17´ east. Extending north, on the east coast of the gulf, lies

---

[87] Trengganu and Pahang.

[88] The kingdom of Lanchang's capital was, for much of its existence, at Luang Prabang on the River Mekong.

[89] The Siamese at the time controlled both Battambang and Siem Reap provinces.

Chautabun,[90] once a part of the ancient kingdom of Camboja. It is well known as a rich and valuable possession of Siam.

The Siamese possess no ships of war, but they have an immense number (probably not less than five hundred) of war-canoes; some of them being over a hundred feet in length, and made of a single teak-tree: they have also, probably, fifty or sixty vessels, having two or three masts, using fore and aft sails, and carrying from three to eight brass guns: the largest do not exceed a hundred tons' burden: these are neatly and strongly built, and many of them are even elegant models. The whole number of mariners employed in foreign and coasting voyages, may be fairly estimated as amounting to not less than thirteen thousand.

Siam is a very fertile country, and abounds in productions suited for foreign trade, beyond any other with which I am acquainted to the eastward of the cape of Good Hope. It is no less distinguished for the variety and abundance of its mineral, than it is acknowledged to be for its vegetable productions. I have annexed a statement, showing the exports of 1832, the quantities of each article, the prices, &c., &c.

To the Siamese trade may be added that of ship building, which is carried on very extensively. A great number of Chinese junks are built here annually; the timbers are of a very hard wood called marbao,[91] and the plank is of the finest teak in the world. Many of these vessels are of a thousand tons' burden.

The imports consist of British piece goods, white and printed, with some woollens. India goods, of all descriptions, the coarser from Bengal, and the finer and more expensive, from Surak.[92] From China are brought silks and teas, porcelain, quicksilver, and almost every other article exported from that country. From other sources powder, arms, and cannon; glass ware, and crockery; cutlery; some drugs; arrack; wine, &c., &c. Opium is strictly prohibited; but the Chinese and others introduce, clandestinely, large quantities for sale. There is an immense trade carried on at the capital, called Si-a-Yuthia, (pronounced See-ah-you-té-ah,) and on the opposite, or right bank of the river, at Bang-kok.

---

[90] Chantabun, also known as Chantaburi.
[91] 'Marbao' is possibly iron wood, or *markaa*.
[92] Surat, already mentioned in note 46.

*Cotton twist* is daily increasing in demand, more particularly low numbers, from twenty to thirty. Twist, of a bright red, (not narrow,) from number forty to fifty, always sells well; yellow and green are died in the country, as well as ordinary red. Not more than twenty peculs[93] should be sent by one vessel.

*Siamese dresses* should be of small star patterns, on red, blue, and green grounds, with a few chocolate grounds: the *red* grounds must be *bright*; they should be in the proportion of *four* to *one* of the others. Each case should contain twenty corges, containing four hundred dresses.

*Prints*, generally called seven eighths, find a ready market. They must be all of the star pattern, bright ground and narrow. The proportion is, two pieces of red to one of black or blue, in a case of a hundred pieces. Some on cloth, of thirty-four to thirty-six inches, would also sell.

*Chintz.* Large pattern furniture chintz is saleable. It is used for curtains and screens. Patterns running lengthwise, are preferred.

*Ells.* Long ells[94] find a ready sale. The consumption of red is very great. There should be one hundred pieces of *red* to twenty of green.

*Woollens. Thin* ladies' cloths only are in demand; heavy, thick broadcloths will not sell. From September to December, there is a demand for them. Red and green are the favourite colours. In a bale of twelve pieces, each seventeen and a half to eighteen yards in length, there should be five of red, four of green, one of yellow, one of light blue, one of light purple.

*Steel*, in tubs of a small size, sells readily in small parcels.*

The inland trade is a very important branch, especially with Lau, and the Chinese province of Yunan, &c. This domestic traffic is carried on, on the Menam, in flat-boats, and on bamboo rafts. Boats leave Lau in August and September, when the river is swollen by the periodical rains, and arrive at Bang-kok in November and December. They bring stic-lac, benzoin, raw silk, ivory, beeswax, horns, hides, timber, &c., &c. The articles of merchandise exported into China, through Lau, consist of coarse woollens, broadcloths, cutlery, gold, copper, lead, &c., &c. The Chinese are the principal foreign traders.

---

*Samples of goods should be in readiness, which will save great trouble. [Author's note]

[93] A picul, as we are told later, was 100 cattis or 133 pounds weight.

[94] A long ell was a length of cloth of 45 inches.

The Siamese prosecute a large foreign and coasting trade to China, Camboja, Cochin-China, the Malay peninsula, to Singapore, to the eastern coast of Sumatra, to the bay of Bengal, &c., &c. The traffic between the countries lying on the shores of the straits of Malacca and the bay of Bengal, is generally conducted by three different routes, across the Malay peninsula; and then reshipped, in boats, on the gulf of Siam, to the capital: the imports being British and Indian goods, opium, esculent swallows' nests, &c., &c.

The population of the capital and Bang-kok, with their suburbs, may fairly be rated at four hundred and fifty thousand inhabitants. I deem it best to state this fact, so that it may be seen that, in a commercial point of view, it is a place of great importance.

The Siamese coin no money strictly speaking; they use *bent* bars of silver, made nearly round and stamped with a star. Those of the largest size are called baats, and by Europeans *ticals*. They are of the value of *sixty-one* cents and a small fraction. The halves are denominated two salings,[95] the quarters one saling; there are also eighths, called one tuang. They have a gold currency formed in the same manner and of various values; they have no copper or tin coin: occasionally, some of the latter may be seen brought from Calantin, &c.: cowries or bias are used in their stead.

The *currency* is as follows: one thousand and fifty cowries or bias make one tuang; two tuangs, one saling; four salings, one baat or tical.

Imaginary or money of account: four baats, one tamling; twenty tamlings, one catty or eighty baats; fifty catties, one pecul or one thousand baats.*

The *weights* are the same as in China, being the pecul and catty; one hundred catties making one pecul; one catty, one and a third pounds avoirdupois. The fathom is the measure in most frequent use, being six feet, six inches; also, twelve finger-breadths make one span; two spans, one cubit; four cubits, one fathom; twenty fathoms, one sen; one hundred sens, one yuta or yut.

On the twentieth day of March, 1833, corresponding to Wednesday,

---

* The baat or tical has been assayed in Calcutta and valued at two shillings and six-pence sterling. I have given it the same value as the European traders—viz., sixty-one cents. [Author's note]

[95] Four *salerng* or quarters made one tical or baht.

the last of the fourth month of the year 1194, called *Pi-ma-rong-chat-tava-sok*, (or the year of the dragon,) the final articles of the first commercial treaty between Siam and the United States were concluded after a negotiation of twenty-two days, and on the first day of April they were signed and sealed; but only a single copy of the treaty could be obtained, notwithstanding the promise of the chao-phaya praklang, one of the first ministers of state, that two copies should be furnished me. No other reason was assigned for this breach of promise, than that it was not customary.

It is written in four languages, viz.: Siamese, Chinese, Portuguese, and English, and is of the great length of nine feet and seven inches. Previously to the signing of the treaty, the charges were not defined and fixed; now, all obstacles and impositions are removed, and but a single charge is made of seventeen hundred ticals on every Siamese fathom of seventy-eight inches on the breadth of the vessel, if merchandise is imported, and fifteen hundred if specie only is brought. This charge is in full of all import and export duties either on vessel or cargo. The sixth article of the treaty relates to debtors. As foreigners were equally liable to the penalties with the natives, I deemed it most proper to guard against the barbarity, which gave the creditor in fact the power of life and death over his debtor, and therefore in the early stage of the negotiation, I proposed an article (which was agreed to) which released the American citizen only, from all pains and penalties, by delivering to his creditors all the property he possessed. About a fortnight after its conclusion, the minister inserted an additional clause, making it reciprocal, so that the Siamese debtor might receive the same benefit of the American creditor. He was told it would have an unequal operation, as it would very rarely occur that an American would incur a debt to a Siamese; but he insisted that it should remain as it was, although I proposed nullifying the whole article. But still if any American feels disposed to take advantage of a code of laws written in blood, it will readily suggest to him that a transfer of his debt to a responsible Siamese, will give him a free and unimpeded course to hunt down a prostrate victim.

An attempt was made to reduce the measurement-duty on vessels bringing specie *only*, to eight hundred ticals (instead of fifteen hundred) but it did not prove successful, and a similar failure was the result of another proposition to admit vessels wishing to purchase a part of a cargo only, by paying a proportionate part of the measurement-duty.

The treaty has removed all obstacles to a lucrative and important branch of our commerce; the merchant being left free to sell or purchase where and of whom he pleases. Prior to this period, the American merchant was not allowed to sell to a private individual the cargo he imported, nor purchase a return cargo. The king claimed the exclusive right of purchase and sale in both cases and furthermore, such parts of the imported cargoes as were most saleable, were selected and taken at his own valuation, which was always at prices far below the market value, as *profit* was the sole object in making the purchases.

Secondly : he also fixed the prices of the articles wanted for return cargoes, and no individual dared offer any competition either in buying or selling.

Thirdly : the American merchant not only did not obtain a fair value for his merchandise, but it is notorious that he had to pay from twenty to thirty per cent. more for the produce of the country than he could have purchased it for from private hands.

Fourthly : the vexations occasioned by delay were a matter of serious complaint. It was no uncommon circumstance to be delayed from two to four months beyond the stipulated time. The loss sustained, say for three months' charter, and interest on the capital employed for that time, &c., &c., amounted to several thousand dollars. In addition to all these evils the merchant was frequently obliged to take payment in *inferior* articles, at the *highest* market value for the *best*, and even *unsaleable* merchandise at high prices.

Fifthly : the duties on imports were not permanent ; they varied from eight to fifteen per centum.

Sixthly : the export duty on sugar of the first quality, was one dollar and a half (Spanish) per pecul, which was not less than from 25 to 30 per centum upon the first cost, and other articles were charged in the same proportion.

Seventhly : port-charges and other exactions were not defined and fixed, but they generally amounted to not less than three and a half (Spanish) dollars per ton.

Eighthly : Presents were expected, and in fact exacted, from the king to the lowest custom-house officer, according to the usages of Asiatics; there were but a few vessels that did not pay upward of a thousand dollars, if they had a valuable cargo. The difference, therefore, in exactions and impositions, prior and subsequent to the conclusion of the treaty, may be stated on a vessel of two hundred and fifty tons, having a twenty-five feet beam, as follows: The duties, *formerly*, were from eight to fifteen per cent. on *imports*; the average rate was not less than ten per cent.

| | |
|---|---:|
| Now, on a cargo of $40,000, it would give the sum of | $4,000 |
| *Add* to this $1,50 per pecul on sugar exported, which was equal, at the lowest calculation, to twenty-five per cent., on $40,000, which gives | 10,000 |
| *Also*, $3,50 per ton for charges | 975 |
| And presents, say | 1,000 |
| If there is added the *difference* in the sale of the imported cargo to the king or to individuals, the estimate cannot be less than twenty per cent., and probably twice that amount would not cover the loss, | 8,000 |
| *Add* to this an additional price paid to the king on the produce exported, say it was twenty per cent., is | 8,000 |
| Three months' charter, arising from detention, at $900 per month | 2,700 |
| Three months' loss of interest is | 600 |
| | $35,275 |
| From this amount deduct the *single charge* of 1,700 ticals per each Siamese fathom on the *breadth* of vessels bringing merchandise. If only specie were brought, 1,500 ticals. | |
| Sixty-eight thousand ticals at sixty-one cents, on seventy-five feet beam, is | 4,275 |
| Making a difference of not less than | $31,000 |

The result is, that the treaty has secured to us a valuable branch of commerce which was entirely destroyed, and which will continue to increase vastly, as the Siamese recover from the serious disasters which resulted from the inundation of the valley of the Menam, for upward of three months, during the year 1831.

*Exports from the river Menam (Siam) during the year 1832, showing the quantity and market value of each article.*

| NAMES OF EXPORTS. | QUANTITY. | PRICES. |
|---|---|---|
| Pepper, | 38,000 peculs, | 10 ticals per pecul. |
| Sugar, 96,000 peculs, | 15,000 1 st sort, | 8 do.   do. |
|  | 60,000 2d do. | 7 a. 7 ½ do. do. |
| Sugar, | 20,000  3d sort, | 6 a. 6 ½  ticals per pcl. |
|  | 1,000 Preto or black, | 2 ½ a. 3 ½ do. do. |
| Sugar candy, | 5,000 peculs, | 15   16   do. do. |
| Tin, 1,600,000 lbs., | 1,200 do. | 20    22   do. do. |
| Tobacco, | 3,500 do. | 100 bundles, 4 ticals. |
| Benzoin, | 100    do. | 50 a. 55 peculs. |
| Cardamom, 73,150 lbs., | 550  1st sort, | 100 a. 360 a.   380. |
|  | do. 2d  do. | 150 a. 280     300. |
|  | 3d   do. | 300  200       220. |
| Ivory, 40,000 lbs., | 300 peculs, | 160 a. 180. |
| Bar-iron, 2,260,000 lbs., | 20,000 do.. | 3 ½ a. 4. |
| Kwalahs or iron pans, 60,000, | 1st size, | 4 ticals per peculs. |
|  | 2d  do. | 3   do.       do. |
|  | 3d  do | 2½ do.       do. |
|  | 4th do. | 2   do.       do. |
|  | 5th do. | 2   do.       do. |
|  | 6th do. | 1½ do.       do. |
|  | 7th do. | 1¼ do.       do. |
| Aguils or eagle-wood, | 10 a. 12   do. | 1st sort, 400 ticals. |
|  |  | 2d and 3d, 250 and 200. |
| Cotton, | 30 a. 40,000 | 26 clear, 8 in sced. |
| Swallows' nest, (esculent,) | 10 a. 12 | 1st sort, 10,000. |
|  |  | 2d do 6,000. |
|  |  | 3d do. 4,000. |
| Bichos do Mar or Tripang, | [blank] | [blank] |
| Camphire, Malayan, |  |  |
| Wax, yellow, | 1,800, do. | 55 a. 60. |
| Gamboge, | 250, 6 quantities averaging from 40 to 80 p.p. | |
| Varnish, | 500, | 50 per pecul. |
| Salt, | 8,000 pecul, | 2 ½ a. 3 ½ per pecul. |
| Dried fish, | 60,000, | 3 a. 4   do. do. |
| Hog's lard, |  | 14 or 15  do. do. |
| Sapan-wood, | 200,000, | from 1a. 3½ salings per pec. |
| Teak-timber, | 127,000 logs, |  |
| Rose-wood, | 200,000 peculs, | 3 salings per pecul. |
| Barks, Mangrove, &c., | 200,000 bundles, | 6 ticals per 100 bundles. |
| Leather, Deer, | 100,000, | 20 a. 25 per 100. |
| Iron-wood, (ebony) | 1,500 peculs, | 2 ½ peculs. |
| Dried meat, | 1,600, | 6 per do. |

# Part I: Treaty Mission of 1833

| | | |
|---|---|---|
| Copper | 300, | 50 a. 55. |
| Rhinoceros skins, | not ascertained. | |
| Buffalo do. | 1,500, | 8 a. 10. |
| Ox do. | 300, | 7 a. 8. |
| Elephant do. | not ascertained. | |
| Tiger do. | do. | |
| Leopard do. | do. | |
| Bear do. | do. | |
| Snake do. | do. | |
| Civet-cat do. | do. | |
| " " Drug, | not ascertained. | |
| Dragons' blood, | do. | |
| Sharks' fins, | 65 to 70 peculs, | a. 65 per peculs. |
| Buffalo and ox horns, | 300 do. | 3 a. 4 per do. |
| Deers' antlers, do. soft, | 26,000 pairs, | 1 ½ a. 2 ticals per pair. |
| do. horns, do. | 3,000 peculs, | 8 a. 9 per pecul. |
| Ox and Buffalo bones, | 300, | 1 do. |
| Elephant do. | 450, | 7 do. |
| Rhinoceros do. | do. | |
| do. horns, | do. | |
| Tiger, the entire bodies for China market, | | 56 a. 60. do. |
| Peacock's tails, | 1,200 trains, | 7 a. 8 per pecul. |
| Raw silk, (from Lao) | 200 peculs, | 200 ticals per do. |
| Rough pitch, | 10,000, | 3 to 8 do. do. |
| Wood oil, | 15,000, | 3 to 6 do. do. |
| Takan, an inferior or bastard Cardamom, | 4,000, | 32 to 40 do do. |
| Feathers, | 4,000 pairs of wings, | 65 a. 100 do.do. |
| Large feathers for fans, | 100 to 150 pairs, | 30 ticals per pecul. |
| Fish skins, | 1,800 peculs, | 30 do. do. |
| Jagra or palm-sugar, | 150,000 pots, | 4 to 6 pots 1 tical. |
| Rattans, | 200,000 bundles, | 4 ticals per 100 bundles. |

The foregoing is the quantity ascertained by the government for 1832, to which may be added a considerable quantity for each article smuggled, and principally by the Chinese. The exports, therefore, for the year 1832, taking the foregoing statement to be correct, amount to a sum not less than *four* and a *half millions of dollars*.

# [6]

# CHAPTER XXI

### DEPARTURE FROM BANG-KOK FOR SINGAPORE...

HAVING brought my mission to a close in a very satisfactory manner, I was, on the evening of the third of April, invited to wait upon the praklang. The principal object of the visit was to reiterate his assurances, that every facility should be granted to American commerce, both in selling their cargoes, and in collecting their debts. And, furthermore, to state, that the presents the king and himself desired, should be returned with the ratified treaty.

The following list was then given of the presents desired by the king and the praklang:—

For the king: Five pairs of stone statues of men and women; some of the natural and some of the larger size, *clothed in various costumes of the United States*. Ten pair of vase lamps, of the largest size, plain glass. One pair of swords, with gold hilt and scabbards; the latter of gold, not *gilt*— shape of blade, a little curved.

For the praklang: One mirror, (or pair of mirrors,) three cubits long by two broad, fixed in a stand, so as to form a screen; frame, carved and gilt; back, painted green. Soft, hairy carpeting, of certain dimensions; and some flower and fruit trees, planted, or in seed, with flower-pots.

I then took leave, after many demonstrations of good-will.

Some presents of the productions of the country, were sent to me, of very mean quality,[96] and of inconsiderable value.

On the fourth, the same boats being in readiness, which brought us to the city, in the evening we embarked, reached the ship in the morning, and the day following, made sail down the gulf...

---

[96] The Siamese presents were 'of very mean quality' but it can hardly be said that those presented to the Siamese by Roberts were particularly impressive.

# APPENDIX

*Annual Revenue obtained by the Government of Siam from Farms and Duties*

| Names. | Annual quantity. | Prices in ticals. | Duties. | Revenues. |
|---|---|---|---|---|
| Paddy and rice. | 1,696,424 coyans of 23 picul | 1st sort 16 ticals | | Ticals. |
| " " | " " | 2d " 14 " | | 862,358 |
| " " | " " | 3d " 12 " | | |
| Orchards | 68,235 in No | | | 545,880 |
| Vegetables | 4,251 | | | 17,800 |
| Samsoo or spirit shops | Bang-kok | | | 104,900 |
| " " | Sieuthaja | | | 16,000 |
| " " | Bangxang. | | | 8,000 |
| " " | Suraburi. | | | 4,000 |
| " " | Krungtaphan | | | 4,000 |
| Bazars. | Bang-kok | | | 39,200 |
| " | Sieuthaja | | | 12,800 |
| " | Suraburi. | | | 1,600 |
| " | Bangxang | | | 1,600 |
| Duty on floating houses | | | | 36,000 |
| Chinese gambling | | | | 64,000 |
| Siamese, ditto | | | | 58,000 |
| Teak wood | 127,000 trees | | | 56,000 |
| Sapan wood | 200,000 piculs | 1st sort 3 ½ to 3 | | |
| " " | " " | 2d " 2 ½ to 2 | | 84,000 |
| " " | " " | 3d " 1 ½ to 1 | | |
| Cocoanut oil | 600,000 " | 7 ½ to 8 | 1¼ to 1½ | 56,000 |
| Sugar, 1st | 10,000 " | 8 ½ to 9 | | |
| " 2nd | 60,000 " | 7 to 7 ½ | | |
| " 3rd | 20,000 " | 6 to 6 ½ | 1½ | 40,000 |
| " black | 1,000 " | 2 ½ to 3 | | |
| " candy | 5,000 " | 16 to 17 | ½ | |
| Jaggery | 150,000 jars. | 18 tcls. p.100jrs | 2 ticals | 8,000 |
| Salt | 8,000 coyans | 2 ½ to 3 | 6 | 32,000 |
| Pepper | 38,000 piculs | 10 to 11 | 1½ | 23,200 |
| Bastard cardamums | 4,000 " | 32 to 40. | 6 ticals | 16,000 |
| Cardamums | 1st. 100 " | 360 to 380 | " | |
| " | 2d. 150 " | 280 to 300 | 16 " | 5,400 |
| " | 3d. 300 " | 200 to 220 | " | |
| Sticlac | 8,000 " | 12 13 14 | 1¼ | 9,500 |
| Tin | 1,200 " | 24 26 28 | 3 ticals | 18,200 |

| Names. | Annual Quantity. | Prices in ticals. | Duties. | Revenues. |
|---|---|---|---|---|
| | | | | Ticals. |
| Iron | 20,000 | 4 5 6 | 3 ticals | 54,000 |
| Ivory | 300  "160 170 180 | 12 ditto | 2,500 | |
| Gamboge | 1st.  50 to 60 75 to 80 | | | |
| | "  2d   150  " | 55 to 60 | 6 ditto | 1,200 |
| | "  3d    50  " | 40 to 45 | | |
| Rhinoceros horns | 50 to 60 800 per picul | 32 per picul | 1,600 | |
| Benjamin | 100 "50 to 55 | | 400 | |
| Bird's-nests | 1st. srt. 10,000 | | | |
| | "    "10 to 12 | 2d "  6,000 | 6 ticals | 32,000 |
| | "      " | 3d "  4,000 | | |
| Young deers' | | | | |
| | horns 26,000   pairs | 1 ½ to 2 | 10 per 100 | 3,600 |
| Old, ditto, ditto | 200   piculs | 8 to 9 per pecul | ½ | |
| Buffalo, ditto | 200   piculs | 3 to 4 per picul | ¼ | |
| Deers' nerves | 200    " | 16 to 20 | 1 ½ | |
| Rhinoceros skins | 200    " | 7 to 8 | ½    800 | |
| Tigers' bones | 50 to 60 | 50 to 60 | 3 ticals | |
| Buffalo hides | 500    " | 8 to 10 | ½ | |
| Deers' ditto | 100,000    " | 20, 25, and 30 | 3 ticals | 1,600 |
| White dried fish | 4,000    " | 8 to 9 | ½ | |
| Black, ditto | 15,000    " | 7 to 8 | ½    18,000 | |
| Small dried fish | 60,000    " | 3 to 4 | ¼ | |
| Dried shrimps | 10,000    " | 30 to 35 | 3   " | 4,600 |
| Balachang | 15,000 coyans | 50 to 60 | 12   " | 8,000 |
| Wood oid | 15,000 piculs | 3 to 5 | ½    5,600 | |
| Pitch | 10,000    " | 3 to 4 | ½    6,000 | |
| Torches | 200,000 bundles | 5 ticals per 100 | ½    5,600 | |
| Rattans | 200,000   " | 4  "   " | ½    14,000 | |
| Firewood | | | | |
| Wooden posts | 1st. 500 to 600 in No. | 1 per 4 ticals | 10 per 100 | |
| | "  "2d. 3,000  " | 1 per 2 do. | 5  "8,000 | |
| | "  "3d. 200,000 " | 100 per 25 30 | "   " | |
| | | 40 | 10  " | 8,000 |
| Bamboos | 600,000,000 in No. | 3 ticals per 100 | 15   100 | 3,000 |
| Attaps | 95,000,000,000  " | 3 ticals per 1000 | 20   " | 1,600 |
| Rose wood | 200,000   " | 342 per picul | 10   " | |
| Bark | 200,000 bundles | 100 per 6 ticals | 1,600 | |

|  | Ticals. |
|---|---|

Provinces under the superintendance of the crommahathai or 1st minister 32,000
    Ditto   ditto   ditto   of the croomkallahom,   or 2d ditto   24,000
    Ditto   ditto   ditto   of the crommatha,      or 3d ditto   12,000
Revenue of Justice under the Crammamuang.   4,800
    " of the Tribunal   8,000
        derived from the gold in the province called Bangtaphan, 180 ticals
            weight of gold.
    "   "   "   in the province called Pipri 60 ticals weight of gold.
Tribute which the Malays pay for gold mines, 216 ticals weight of gold.

## EXPENDITURE.

| | |
|---|---|
| Salaries which the king pays to the government officers annually | 618,800 |
| Alms to the Talapoins and the poor | 87,600 |
| Monthly allowances to the sons of the late and present kings, and the second king. | 29,000 |
| Annual salaries of all the princes employed, and the minors | 47,400 |
| Annual pay of the Talapoins | 18,240 |

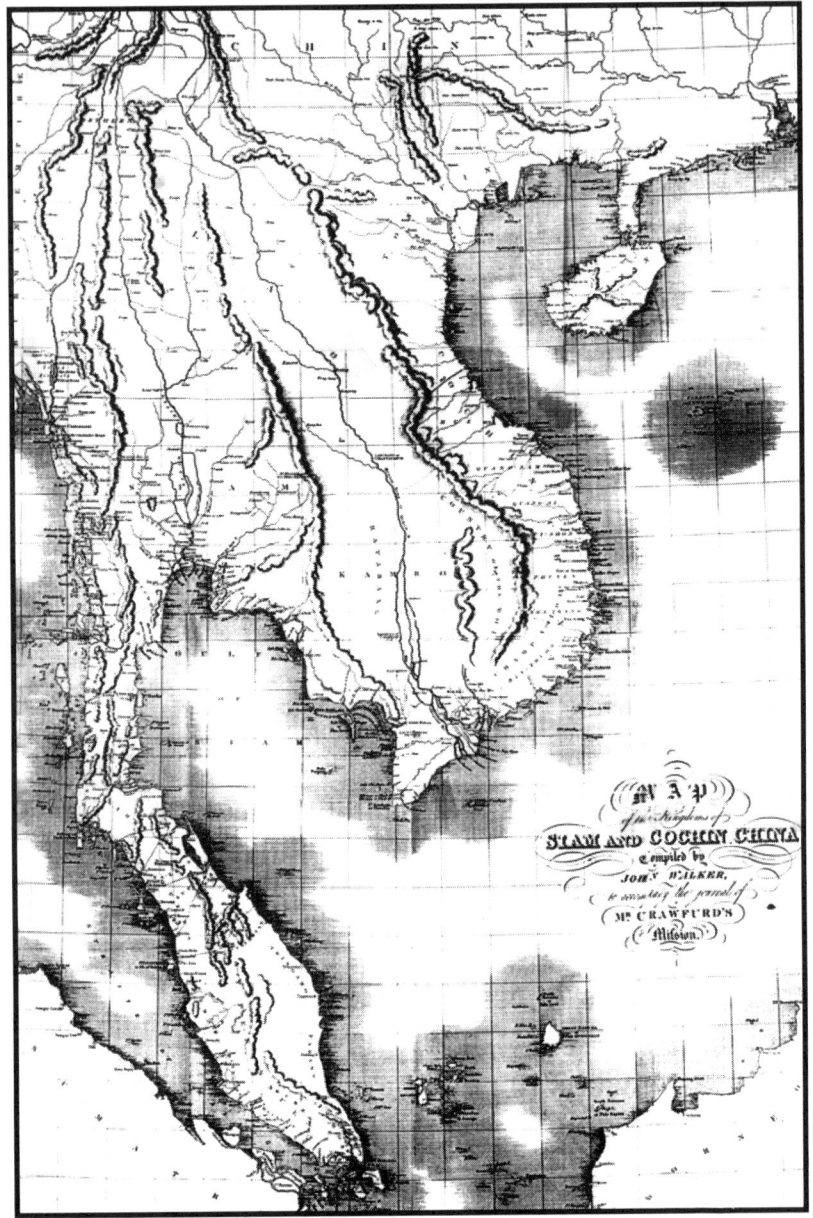

Map by J. Walker showing Siam and Cochin-China

# PART II: THE RATIFICATION MISSION OF 1836

NARRATIVE

OF

A VOYAGE ROUND THE WORLD

DURING THE YEARS 1835, 36, AND 37;

INCLUDING

A NARRATIVE OF
AN EMBASSY TO THE SULTAN OF MUSCAT
AND THE KING OF SIAM.

BY W.S.W. RUSCHENBERGER, M.D,
SURGEON TO THE EXPEDITION

IN TWO VOLUMES.
VOL. 1.

LONDON:

RICHARD BENTLEY, NEW BURLINGTON STREET
(Publisher in Ordinary to Her Majesty.)

1838.

# [RUSCHENBERGER'S]
# INTRODUCTION

VOYAGES of circumnavigation have been so frequent of late years, this being the fourth undertaken within seven years by American vessels of war alone, that much novelty must not be expected in the present Work, though few ships pursued the varied and extensive track of the Peacock. I, therefore, only promise the reader the latest news of the several remote countries visited in relation to their manners, political state, commerce, and religion, upon which topics the best sources of information have been carefully consulted.

In presenting this narrative to the public, it may be proper to state, what were the opportunities enjoyed by the author for obtaining the necessary information.

Mr. Roberts, the special agent of the American Government, frequently expressed a wish that the author would write the account of the voyage, and in order to enable him better to perform this undertaking, he gave him free access to all documents relating to the Embassy, and on every occasion expressed his views and opinions on the several subjects which fell under notice. He, moreover, greatly assisted him in procuring statistical information, which, from his official station, he was often able to obtain, when to others perhaps it might have been denied. To him he feels indebted, and with his many friends deeply regrets his early loss to his country.

In the early part of his life, Edmund Roberts, of Portsmouth, N. H., had visited several of the countries which lie to the eastward of the Cape of Good Hope, and from information then and subsequently obtained, he inferred that those parts of the world offered a wide field to American enterprise. He was convinced, however, that voyages from the United States round the Cape of Good Hope must continue to be limited to a few countries, and uncertain in their results, until treaties of amity and commerce should be formed between the Government of the United States and several powers of Southern and Eastern Asia; in order to open trade with some, and to settle definitely with others the manner in which American merchantmen should be received, and the charges to which they should be subjected. In this latter respect, the practice in many countries is very irregular, depending more upon the notion or whim of the minister at the time, than upon any established law.

Mr. Roberts communicated his views in detail to his friend, the Honourable Levi Woodbury, at that time Secretary of the Navy, who laid the subject before the President. It was determined after proper deliberation, that Mr. Roberts should visit the East in capacity of "Special Agent of the Government," and obtain all the information possible, and negotiate treaties of amity and commerce with such Asiatic potentates as he might find favourably disposed.

Early in the year 1832, Mr. Roberts sailed from the United States on board of the U.S. ship Peacock, then commanded by Captain David Geisinger, and visited Brazil, Buenos Ayres, Java, Manilla, Canton, Singapore, Siam, Muscat, the Red Sea, &c. In May 1834 he returned, bearing with him two Treaties which he had negotiated, one with His Highness the Sultan of Muscat, the other with His Magnificent Majesty, the King of Siam. These Treaties were ratified by the President and Senate of the United States in June, 1834, and Mr. Roberts was appointed to exchange the ratifications. The Peacock was again put in commission to carry him on his distant embassy, the history of which will be found in the following pages.

*January, 1838.*

# VOLUME I, CHAPTER XXIII

...LETTER TO THE FIRST MINISTER OF SIAM—SI-CHANG ISLANDS AND THEIR INHABITANTS—FLYING FOX—RELIGIOUS TEMPLE—A TALAPOIN—SIAM ROADS.

*March, 1836.*

... Early on the 25th of March, we found ourselves within a few hours' sail of the mouth of the river Meinam; and in order to save time, the Enterprise was despatched with the following communication:

"To his Excellency the Chao P'haya Prah Klang, one of the first ministers of state to His Magnificent Majesty the King of Siam:

"Edmund Roberts, Special Envoy from the United States of America, has the honour to inform your Excellency, that he has arrived off the bar of the Meinam, in the United States ship Peacock, commanded by Captain Stribling, accompanied by the United States schooner Enterprise, Captain Campbell, the squadron being under the command of Commodore Kennedy.

"The Envoy begs leave to state, that he has brought back the Treaty, which he had the honour to conclude between His Majesty of Siam and the United States of America on the 20th day of March in the year 1833, and which was ratified on the part of his Government on the 30th day of June, 1834, and which is now returned for the purpose of exchanging it for its counterpart in the possession of Siam, on its being duly ratified by His Majesty, and the royal seal of the kingdom affixed to the articles of the treaty, as well as to the necessary certificate of ratification.

"The Envoy has also the honour to inform your Excellency that he has brought with him the articles, His Majesty of Siam and your Excellency requested should be sent, by the United States Government, with the exception of the stone statues, which could not be obtained, and also the trees and plants and seeds, which were destroyed on the passage, the Peacock having been unfortunately wrecked about six months since on the coast of Arabia; but the deficiency in the statues has been repaired by purchasing an extra number of the most elegant and expensive lamps, together with some other articles.

"Your Excellency is therefore requested to send a suitable vessel to receive the presents before alluded to, with an order directed to me for their delivery. Your Excellency is further requested to furnish the Envoy with convenient and proper vessels, capable of protecting from the inclemencies of the weather, himself, officers, and servants, who may accompany him, to the number of twenty-five persons, with as little delay as possible, as the Envoy has to visit many kingdoms, and has a great many thousands of miles of ocean to traverse; to accomplish which, will necessarily occupy at least twelve months.

"The undersigned has the honour to remain, with the highest consideration of esteem and respect, your Excellency's friend, &c. &c.

EDMUND ROBERTS.

"Dated on board the United States ship of war Peacock, in the Gulf of Siam, the 24th day of March, 1836."

The expression, "your humble servant," &c., commonly used with us, should always be carefully avoided in addressing communications to Asiatics, because they construe it literally, and in their opinion it places the writer in an inferior and inconsiderable position in regard to themselves.

Soon after the Enterprise separated from us, we anchored off the largest of a group of small islands called Si-chang or Dutch islands, situated about twenty miles from the mouth of the Meinam river, and eight from the west coast of Cambodia. The island is not five miles in extent; it is high, rocky, and covered with a thin soil and stunted vegetation.

In the afternoon several parties of officers landed and walked in different directions, to ascertain whether water could be obtained for the ship; but, though it is said to be abundant in the rainy monsoon, we found it to exist in very small quantities at this season. Several white squirrels, a common blue pigeon, and an animal having the general characteristics of a bat, but very much larger, were shot. The flying-fox, as it is called (a species of *pteropus*), is very frequent throughout India. The head resembles that of a dog; the body is about eight inches long, and the spread wings measure nearly four feet. The irides are of an opake yellow. They are often met with in the day, suspended from leafless trees, hanging one from the other, in strings and clusters. They make great depredations on fruit-trees and gardens, but are considered to be harmless in other respects.

In my excursion I came upon a small religious temple, erected near the shore, probably by fishermen to propitiate their patron god. It consisted of a wooden hut, raised on posts two feet above the ground, having three sides closed and the fourth open to the sea. This apartment was about four feet by six, and the height of the thatched roof, perhaps ten. On the back wall were stuck pieces of red paper, marked with black Siamese letters;[1] in each corner leaned a wooden sword and the beak of a saw-fish. In the middle of the floor, standing on a fold of tinsel paper, was a green porcelain bowl, full of earth, planted with dead straws. On either side were some pieces of coral, upon which reposed small boards inscribed with Siamese characters, and the figures of an elephant and a horse, such as we usually see among German toys.

After nightfall we were visited by a Talapoin, or priest, who seemed to be the head man among the very few people on the island. He entered the cabin in a half-bent posture, in token of respect, but very soon assumed an erect position. A robe of dirty yellow cloth hung from his shoulders to the knees; his head and eyebrows were closely shaven, and his arms and legs were bare. He seated himself, and drew from his girdle a small tin box, from which he filled his mouth with areca-nut, betel-leaf and chunam; and, thus

SIAMESE BUDDHIST PRIEST.

---

[1] These were almost certainly Chinese characters. The 'dead straws' mentioned further on are incense sticks.

fortified, he talked, chewed, and gesticulated; but his speech, though it might have been very fine for aught we knew, was to us a rigmarole. In return for it, we offered him bread, tobacco, snuff, and gin; the last he carried to his people; but instead of putting the snuff in his nose, he wrapped it in a piece of paper, and made us understand, if the quantity were increased, the present would be more acceptable. He appeared unwilling to touch a tumbler with his lips, and in place of it, drank out of the top of his own tobacco-box. He carried with him a sheet of slate paper, twenty feet long by fifteen inches broad, folded alternately right and left, so that its dimensions were about two inches thick, four broad, and fifteen long. After making him comprehend, by the aid of a short vocabulary, arranged by Mr. Roberts on his former visit, who we were, and writing with his pencil of talc upon his book, the name of the ship, and whither we were bound, he took leave, seemingly well satisfied with what he had done.

Early the following morning, we went in pursuit of white squirrels; under the protection of the religious prejudices of the inhabitants against taking away animal life, there is nothing to interrupt their increase, and we found them in considerable numbers. Two or three men of Mongol physiognomy attached themselves to our train, and were ever ready to point out the game. With the exception of a sarong about the hips, they were naked, and viewed our clothes and fowlingpieces with apparent wonder and astonishment; and were not content until they had felt every article of our dress, even to our shoes. They all chewed areca-nut and its concomitants; their teeth were consequently black, and their mouths were any thing but agreeable to look upon. It is probably owing to this disgusting habit, that the areca-nut-chewing nations of the East, have never acquired the custom of kissing!

On our return to the boat, we found the inhabitants of the village eating breakfast, consisting of boiled rice and fish, of which they very politely invited us to join, but our prejudices against filthy appearances compelled us to decline. They were squatted round a large dish, from which they supplied their bowls, and then shovelled the mouth-full of rice with chop sticks. The village consists of half a dozen huts of bamboo and boards, raised on posts a foot or two from the ground. They were cheerless, and far from clean. The women, in general, wore only a sarong; some few added a piece of black crape folded diagonally over the chest, so as partially to conceal the bosom, and young girls wandered about in nature's suit, as unsophisticated and shameless as Eve before her fall.

At three o'clock P.M. the ship was got under way, but very soon ran upon a rock in the midchannel, where she remained two hours, until the rising of the tide carried her off without damage. On sounding round, it was found that the rock was not more than one hundred feet in extent, beyond which there was four and five fathoms water. A few hours brought us to the Roads of Siam, where we anchored about eight o'clock P.M. and exchanged signals with the Enterprise.

The next day we looked for land, but without a spy-glass could see none. The anchorage for ships, drawing more than twelve feet water, is ten miles from the mouth of the Meinam, which is deep enough as far as the city; but there is a bar eight miles from its entrance which interrupts large vessels, and may be a serious obstacle to foreign trade.

We were obliged to wait, patiently as we might, a reply to Mr. Roberts's communication, from the authorities, before we could proceed to Bankok. When it was carried from the Enterprise to Paknam, two miles up the river, the old governor was unwilling to forward it to the Phra Klang, until there had been a deal of talk and interpretation.

# [2]

# VOLUME I, CHAPTER XXIV

PRINCE MOMFANOI—DEPARTURE FOR BANKOK—PAKNAM—BAZAAR—GOVERNOR'S HOUSE—RECEPTION BY THE GOVERNOR—THE CAPTAIN OF THE PORT—PADDY-MILL—FEMALE COSTUME—SIAMESE TWINS—UNCOMFORTABLE LODGINGS.

*April, 1836*

ON the 28th of March, the ship was visited by Prince Momfanoi,[2] heir-apparent to the throne of Siam. The boat he came in was not distinguishable from those of the common people; it had a semicylindrical roof of wattled bamboo over the stern, under which he reposed, sheltered from the sun, but suffering from the want of ventilation, though both ends of the oven were open. Unaccustomed to go afloat, he was threatened with sea sickness after being a short time on board, and therefore departed early for the shore.

The Prince was dressed in a jacket of pink damasked crape, closely fitting the body, and reaching from the hips to the throat; a sarong of dark silk, knotted in front, the ends hanging down nearly to the ground, and over it was tied a light sash, upon which two jewelled rings of large size were strung. This costume left the head, arms, and legs bare. He has an active, determined look. His stature is not more than five feet five inches; his limbs are stout and well-proportioned. His complexion is olive, almost as dark as that of the majority of negroes met with in the northern and middle sections of the United States. His hair is coarse and black, and, excepting a tuft, trimmed and standing up like bristles on the top of the head, is cut very close. The general character of his features is that of the Mongol race. The form of the eye is paraboloid, the upper lid extending in a thin fold over the lower one at the side of the nose, which is rather flat; the lips are full, the chin retreating, and, with the exception of a few hairs on the upper lip, he has no beard. The superior lateral parts of the forehead

---

[2] 'Prince Momfanoi' (Chao Fa Noi), Mongkut's younger brother, Chudamani, was not the heir-apparent to the throne, who was, if anyone, Prince Mongkut: Ruschenberger later discusses these points.

CHOU-FAA, THE REIGNING PRINCE OF SIAM.

are a little flattened, while the upper and middle part is prominent; the supra-orbital region is full, and the eyes set well apart. Such is the personal description, which I have thus minutely given, of the most promising individual among the Siamese.

While on board, he displayed considerable knowledge and was very inquisitive about nautical affairs. He made favourable mention of the American missionaries, by whom he was taught English, which he speaks very intelligibly. He was quite at home on board, and when his attention was attracted to any particular part of the ship, he stood with his arms a-kimbo and feet wide apart, with a swaggering air, more characteristic of an old time admiral than a distinguished prince of a royal court.

His several attendants, with the exception of the sarong, were naked; and one named Sap, was distinguished by his master often pointing out to him what appeared worthy of notice. He bore a small gilt salver with a goblet-shaped foot, on which were a gold watch, still in the leathern pouch of the maker; a chunam box; a number of very acute cone-shaped cigars of Siamese cut tobacco rolled in dry plaintain-leaf; a lighted match of cocoa-nut rope in a tube like a Peruvian mechéro, with rolls of cire-leaf, &c. Another carried an enamelled tea-pot and a small porcelain tea-cup. Whenever the Prince passed any of them in his walks about the decks, they at once squatted down; and whenever he took any thing from the salver, the bearer dropped upon his knees.

On the 30th of March I determined to go to Bankok in spite of all formalities, and accordingly set off with a friend. We got the bearings of the mouth of the Meinam, and following the compass course, bounded merrily over the sea till we entered the river. On the bar there are a number of stakes driven into the bottom, and their ends above the surface mark the channel or fishing-grounds, or something else; the stakes were covered with muscles [sic], having clear, apple-green coloured shells. The land is low and thickly wooded to the water's edge. On the muddy margin, exposed by the receding tide, we saw a number of white herons and a crocodile, at least ten feet long.

When fairly within the river, a pretty view presents itself. On the left, all is thickly green, on the right is the village of Paknam with its white fortress, and in the centre is a circular fort with numerous embrasures, over the top of which is seen the tapering spire of a pagoda, a solid mass of masonry without interior apartment. At this point the river is about a mile wide.

We had determined, should we not be hailed, to proceed up the river without stopping; and with this view, steered midway between the fort in the river and that at Paknam. We were not literally hailed, but were gesticulated at, by an individual near the fort on the main, with so much earnestness that it prevailed over our resolution, and we landed. A path through thickly-growing shrubs, ten yards long, brought us to a substantial store-house with a veranda, beneath which several naked Siamese were stretched on the ground, chewing betel, and watching a smouldering fire which had served to prepare their suppers, the evidence of which might be gathered from several earthen pans in the vicinity. Here we were met by one who appeared to be a leader. He nodded his head, pointed towards the village, which was not visible, and, leading the way, we followed. A few yards brought us to a canal over which we passed on a bank of stones, the vilest and roughest bridge I have any where seen. Fortunately we soon trod on a narrow *trottoir*, paved with large bricks, leading between rows of bamboo huts, shaded by trees; some of them were shops having projecting windows, in which were displayed fruit, eggs, &c. We had scarcely got thus far before we were saluted by a host of lank curs, that barked more in fear than threatening. A few yards brought us to the bazaar. The venders, who were all women, were seated among their wares on bamboo platforms about two feet from the ground, shaded by the projecting roofs of the huts before which the stalls were built. They wore only a dark-blue cotton cloth, so disposed about the limbs and hips as to resemble a pair of drawers, and some wore, in addition, a piece of black crape over the shoulders. Their hair was cut close, except a bristling tuft on the top of the head, and all were chewing areca-nut and betel or cire leaf. Here, for the first time in the East, we saw cowries circulating as money; but their value is so extremely small (about 15,000 to the dollar), that bushels of them were seen in many of the stalls, yet there are articles to be purchased for a single one, arecanut-betel leaf, &c. So minute a division of money must be very advantageous to the poor, in a country where produce is plentiful and labour very low.

We soon reached the dwelling of his Excellency the Governor. His mansion, we found on following our guide through a doorway into a considerable enclosure, stood on posts about seven feet from the ground; the walls were of bamboo, pierced with irregular-shaped octangular holes; windows they were not, having neither sash nor shutter. The thatched roof projected at the eaves about five feet, and was supported all round by stout posts, thus forming a sort of veranda. The entrance was by a ladder of five or six steps, which landed in a vestibule or open court, the left side being bounded by the family apartments, and the right by a hall, thirty by fifteen feet, the floor of which was elevated two feet above that of the court. The ceiling of the hall was flat, dark-coloured, twenty feet high, and next to the court, where there was neither partition nor wall, supported by two wooden pillars. This apartment was furnished with chairs and bamboo settees, of Chinese manufacture. In one corner stood a curiously-carved temple of the *Penates*, resembling an old-fashioned bedstead, a use to which, as we afterwards discovered, it was occasionally put. Lamps hung from the ceiling, and many Chinese mirrors with silvered frames were suspended close to the cornice; and in the centre was a chandelier, which consisted of a tarnished brass hoop wrought in an old style, having several tumblers of oil and water in brass rings, suspended by chains from its margin, and a goblet sustained after the same fashion in the middle.

When we came into the presence, His Excellency was only girdled with a scanty silk sarong, reclining on the hall floor, his back reposing on a leathern pillow of prismatic shape, which touched the base of one of the pillars above mentioned. He rested on the right elbow, and with the hand of the same side, supported a long wooden pipe, from which he inhaled the fumes of opium. The right leg was extended, parallel with the terminating edge of the floor, while the left one was drawn up to enable him to scratch the toes with his unoccupied hand.

The floor of the vestibule was crowded by slaves or people of inferior rank—hence their inferior place—resting on their knees and elbows, the body retreating a little, chewing betel as quietly as cows do the cud, and looking up into His Excellency's face as they listened to his conversation, the intonation of which in our ears was maudlin and unpleasant.

All this was revealed to us at a glance. As we entered His Excellency rose, and taking us by the hand with a hearty grasp, fairly raised us upon the floor, where he had been just reclining, and motioned us to a seat. Cigars and tea, in very small cups, without sugar, were immediately served; and in a few moments afterwards an interpreter arrived, whose office we might not have suspected, had he not contrived to make us understand that such was his vocation. He assumed the attitude of other inferiors present, and before speaking, made a salam in the Siamese fashion, by opposing the palms and carrying the hands to the forehead, and again letting them fall. His name was Ramòn, a Portuguese Christian, whose skin was nearly as dark as that of the governor; his costume differed in nothing from that of the Siamese who were present.

We informed His Excellency, we were on our way to Bankok, to procure water and provisions for the ship, which we had in vain endeavoured to obtain at Paknam. He replied that we could not go—that his authority did not extend so far as to enable him to give us permission; and, if we had gone up, his head would have been forfeited—that he would send for the water and provisions.

Such was the substance of our conversation. We next visited Piadadè,[3] the captain of the port, who is also a Portuguese born in Siam. We found him in a mean bamboo hut, chewing areca-nut. He told us, he had just arrived from the city with a letter for Mr. Roberts. He affected much surprise when informed that we proposed to go to Bankok.

---

[3] The Siamese-Portuguese Piedade was already mentioned in Roberts' text.

"Very sorry—but no can go!"

"Who will prevent us?"

"Nobody prevent you suppose you go, I tell you certain,—you break friendship—you get me flog, and that poor old governor get his head cut off."

He offered to accompany us back to the governor's, and there discuss the matter farther. On our return, a large brass salver, with a goblet-shaped foot, was brought, loaded with boiled duck-eggs, fish, sugar-cane, and plantains. This was placed on a chair, and on another beside it, a brass basin of water with a small cup of the same metal, floating on its surface. Some of his visitors from the Enterprise had presented his Excellency with a bottle of gin, which was also produced on the occasion. We were invited to eat, but did not taste any thing except a plantain.

We now urged the necessity of proceeding to the city, but were answered as before. The captain of the port sat upon the floor, wearing the sarong and a piece of black crape over the shoulders. He repeated what would be the consequences to the governor and himself, if we persisted in going to Bankok. He was evidently anxious, and proposed to despatch a letter to Mr. R. Hunter[4] who, he said, would send us whatever we might require. He urged, that the King was now well disposed towards us, and our going to the city at this time would "break friendship." We remarked, that it was any thing but friendly to keep us so long from the city, without water or stock; for want of which, we must be in a short time suffering. He replied, that different nations had different customs, "In the presence of your King, that you call President, you stand up and pull off your hat; in the presence of the King of Siam, you sit down and pull off your shoes. I am your friend. Mr. Roberts can tell you. Your laws are different from those of Siam, all the same as between heaven and—" looking significantly, and at the same time pointing downwards. I thought the comparison was just, and I suspect might be extended to the inhabitants of the two places, without any great departure from justice!

Finding that we still persisted in going to the city, he proposed that the governor should write to the P'hra Klang for permission for us to proceed. To this we at last acceded, telling him at the same time that we did so solely in consideration of the governor's head and both of

---

[4] Robert Hunter, the British merchant settled in Bangkok (see note 38 to Roberts' text).

their skins. Both were evidently much relieved. Our baggage was brought up from the boat and my companion wrote to Mr. Hunter.

In the mean time I looked around the premises. Twenty yards from the house were several huts, occupied by some of the governor's slaves. Several women were walking about, and one was "hulling paddy" in a mill, similar to those used four thousand years ago. It consisted of two circular stones two feet in diameter, resting one on the other; a bamboo basket was wrought around the upper one so as to form the hopper. A peg was firmly set into the face of the upper stone, halfway between its periphery and centre, having tied to it by one end a stick three feet long, extended horizontally and attached by the other to another stick pending from the roof of the shed under which the mill was placed. This forms a crank by which the upper stone is made to revolve on the other, set firmly on the ground. The motion throws the rice through the centre of the stone, and causes it to escape between the edges of the two.

Beneath the governor's mansion were several canoes, one not less than forty feet long, dug out of a single tree. Among the riches of Siam, its quantities of fine timber cannot be reckoned the least.

As soon as it was dark all the lamps were lighted. His Excellency still occupied his place, smoking his pipe or cigars and chewing areca-nut, which was reduced to powder in an iron tube, because, having lost all his teeth, he is unable to masticate it in any other form. His mouth is very large, and when he gapes, which he does very frequently, one almost fancies that he is about to lose his head. He passes his time in sipping tea, chewing and spitting in a porcelain spittoon, kept constantly beside him. He inquired our respective ages, and wondered that we were so young; telling us, at the same time, he was sixty-four years old.

Several of his female grandchildren came in, the eldest twelve years of age; and in feminine existence, years are longer in the torrid than in the temperate zone. They were all in mother Eve's costume after she eat [sic] the apple, except that their fig-leaf was of gold, wrought in filligree, and sustained by a rich chain of the same metal, worn about the hips. The eldest asked for a cigar, which she smoked like one who is a veteran in the vice. I afterwards saw much younger children smoking, and I have good authority for stating that infants not yet weaned smoke tobacco.

We sat on the floor smoking and sipping tea for an hour or two with Piadadè, whom we found to be a mild good-hearted old man. The famous Siamese Twins[5] were a theme of conversation. They have been probably of as much service as any pair of patriots in their country, first, by generally calling the attention of the Christian world towards it, and, secondly, by causing some of the Siamese interested in them, to hear of countries of the existence of which they were ignorant before the brothers set out on their travels. "Where are the twins?" was asked of every one who visited the shore. Piadadè shook his head: "Their poor mother cry plenty about those boys. They say, they make plenty money—no send never any to their poor mother." In fact, they have in Siam the character of being dissipated and unfilial. Nevertheless, they still attract attention.

Strictly speaking, they are not Siamese, though born in Siam: their parents, as I was told, are Chinese.

Straw mats were placed in the middle of the floor, and upon them two mattresses, much patched with velvet. In the mean time the governor had dictated a despatch which was written on a slate book (formerly described) by a secretary squatting on the floor of the vestibule. This state affair concluded, His Excellency retired, and we stretched ourselves out in the middle of the room, and half a dozen slaves of the governor's household occupied the settees. We soon found that sleep was out of the question. The lamps were all burning; the servants were talking, and ever and anon walking across the floor, which, being of slips of bamboo, sprang to their steps like a spring board, communicating no very pleasant motion to our beds. The novelty of our circumstances, suspicious of the cleanliness of our couches, the doubtful honesty of our room-mates were sufficient in themselves to keep us awake; but added to these annoyances were

---

[5] The original Siamese twins, Chang and Eng, were born in Meklong in May 1811 of a half-Chinese mother and a Chinese father; they shared no organs but were congenitally joined at the sides. They were exhibited as a curiosity, were received in audience by the Siamese king, and the enterprising Hunter in 1829 sent them on a tour to the United States, Canada, Cuba, and Europe, exhibiting them. When they were twenty-one years old, they arranged their own tours and made a fortune. They settled in North Carolina, bought a farm, and became naturalized American citizens, taking the name Bunker. In 1843 they married two sisters, and lived some 2 km apart in different homes, alternating three day visits in each household, and fathering several children. They died in 1874 within a few hours of each other.

stealing about in the afternoon, found a bone of contention, and sought to settle their quarrel under the house. The angry growls of the victors and the yelping of those put to flight had scarcely died away, before a party of melancholy ge-kôs assembled on the roof, and set up a lugubrious song in a stacatto movement. Then some poetic youth of Paknam serenaded us for an hour, by the light of the stars, with a screeching hautboy, occasionally relieved by the wooings and mewings of half a dozen cracked-voiced feline Romeos and Juliets, immediately beneath our beds. We bore it for a long time, but at last were forced to laugh outright and get up in self-defence. We sat down near a window, and, at the same time, enjoyed the pleasant air and a cigar. It was long past midnight, yet two or three women were seen at different times, stealing across the enclosure with torches in their hands, and one came out of His Excellency's room and retired with noiseless step. Fairly wearied, we tried "once more to win her into morning;" but we scarcely attained to dreamy forgetfulness before a great ge-kô pursued several lizards in full run over the floor. The attempt was vain. Rather than risk passing such another night, at four o'clock A.M. I took leave of my companion, and returned with the officer of the boat on board ship, convinced that Paknam is the vilest, the dirtiest, the most inhospitable and detestable spot I have ever set foot in.

That afternoon permission was received, and my companion ascended to the city in a canoe; and the day after his arrival, the King, according to the usage of the Siamese, sent him a present of eight ticâls to defray the expense of his table.

I reached the ship about one o'clock P.M. after a tedious beat under a burning sun, and the next day, Piadadè, who set off before us, came alongside with some articles which had been sent for, several days previously.

On further reflection, I think I did the governor injustice; for he treated us as he treated himself, and imagined when he gave us tea, cigars, food, and a bed, that it was our own fault if we were not comfortable and contented. But I doubt whether he was philosopher enough to discover that a total want of accordance of habit and sympathy of feeling rendered his simple efforts to please unavailing.

## VOLUME I, CHAPTER XXV

SIAMESE ETIQUETTE—JUNK OF CEREMONY—GAUDY CREW—POR-
TUGUESE OFFICERS—ARRIVAL IN BANKOK—FEAST OF PAKNAM—
VOYAGE UP THE MEINAM—MISSION-HOUSE AT BANKOK.

*April, 1836.*

WE waited for the boats to carry the mission to the city, until the 5th of April, not in the most patient mood; for we were almost reduced to salt dinners, and had a near prospect of a short allowance of water, under sultry skies. The circumstance of seeing an American brig, which we had passed in the Strait of Banka, arrive four or five days after us (having spent two weeks at Singapore in the mean time), and obtain permission to proceed at once to the city, was not calculated to sooth our impatience, nor change the unfavourable opinion we had already formed of Siamese etiquette. Piadadè insisted that it would ill assort with our dignity, and the friendship existing between the two nations, for us, whom he styled "King's men in King's ship," to go to Bankok in a hurry, before measures had been taken to receive us properly. The longer the delay the more should we feel complimented, because, we might be sure, the time was consumed in preparing for our reception. However unanswerable and honey-like this argument might be to full-fed, ambitious Christians, most of us were ready to sell out his right to Siamese consideration for a roasted capon or a speedy departure for Bankok.

In these waiting days we had no other diversion than to watch the mouth of the Meinam, and speculate on the destination of all boats which appeared from that quarter. Occasionally a clumsy Chinese junk was seen to come out or enter the river, with all the deliberate speed their mould and the elements would permit.

At last the junk or boat of ceremony, bearing a present of fruit and some hundreds of gallons of water, hove in sight. This vessel had three masts and ten staves with red banners waving over the stern. The bows and stern were square, and there were two brass pieces mounted at each, from which, before getting alongside, a salute of thirteen guns was fired in honour of the envoy. In the middle of the vessel was a platform, raised several inches above the deck, furnished with chairs,

# Part II: The Ratification Mission of 1836

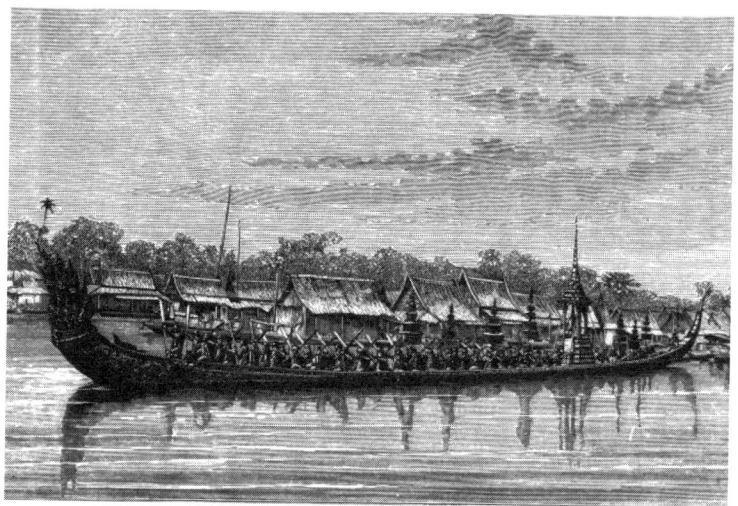

THE KING OF SIAM'S STATE BARGE

and protected from the sun by a canvass awning. The rigging was of cordage, made entirely of rattan, and as pliant as any rope I have seen. The shrouds had no rattlings. From not wearing shoes habitually, the Arabs, the Hindoos, Singhalese, Malays, Siamese, and other Asiatics, have the great toe separated further from that next to it than seems natural to us boot-and-shoe-wearing people. The great toe serves them in prehension almost as well as the thumb; and, for this reason, their sailors are able to mount aloft with as much rapidity and ease without as ours do with rattlings. I first observed this at Muscat, in one of the Sultan's ships of war.

The approach of this piece of nautical architecture was showy. Her crew, consisting of two-and-thirty soldiers and as many sailors, the latter blazing in scarlet uniforms and the former in green. The sailors looked more like mutes at a theatre than sons of river or ocean. Their jackets, which had bell-muzzle sleeves reaching to the elbow, were turned up with white, and buttoned from the hips to the throat, and their breeches were embroidered at the knee. Their caps of green cloth were fashioned like helmets and trimmed with gilt stripes; a band of red cloth, the top edge cut in points, surrounded the head. The legs and feet were bare. The officers in command of this gaudy crew were not less oddly equipped. We were impressed with the notion that old

Albuquerque[6] and his followers had risen from their graves, and were now stalking upon earth as they were wont to do some three hundred years ago, and we could not help remarking that there had been a great change of colour, and seemingly, if not really, a wonderful declension in courage. These worthy gentlemen could boast a Portuguese ancestry, and claim nativity in Siam. As other descendants of the Portuguese in every part of India, while their bones have changed little in form, the colour of the skin has become so like that of the natives of the countries in which they are found, that they are not readily distinguished. Their stature is much diminished, but these changes are not altogether attributable to climate. It is remarkable that these Lusitan-Asiatics are so degraded, they are employed almost entirely as menials, or in very subordinate situations. We could not have expected, *a priori*, that the descendants of the conquerors would have so fallen; their blood has lost its richness, and they only preserve the bony configuration and religion of their fathers.

The chief of the three officers, toothless and sixty, appeared over the gangway, "the observed of all observers," under a green three-cornered cocked-hat, a black satin coat, *chargé* with gold embroidery and white pearl buttons, full pantaloons of red striped silk, sustained by a sash round the waist, but without shirt, vest, or shoes. The second wore a round hat of white felt, a light blue velvet coat, embroidered in gold, red silk pantaloons, shoes, stockings, and shirt. The third was in similar attire, except that he had a white satin vest, and, though he could show no shirt, his neck was buried in a black stock of large dimensions. On reaching the quarter-deck, they bowed awkwardly, and spoke almost unintelligibly in a language intended to be Portuguese. Where did they get all this costume?

These people were full of curiosity, and begged what they could. One of the soldiers addressed me in very intelligible Latin—" Inquis Latinum, Domine?" [Do you understand Latin, master?] I learned from him that the whole corps on board the King's junk were Christians, and had been educated by the Portuguese missionaries. He said all of them might have spoken Latin, had they been studious—their ignorance, as is generally the case, was their own fault, and I suspect it is not their only one. All the hundred jaws were employed

---

[6] Afonso de Albuquerque, the Portuguese commander who captured Goa in 1510 and Malacca in 1511.

masticating arecanut, betel, and tobacco.

The sun had set when we all embarked, or rather transhipped ourselves and baggage to the junk of ceremony. Her sails were hoisted slowly, and we were at last creeping towards the shore. The salute fired by the junk was now returned by the ship, and we went off full of spirits and agreeable excitement. We numbered twenty officers, several servants, and the band, and found ourselves packed pretty closely together. We had scarcely got off from the ship when our officers of Albuquerque memory doffed their finery and appeared in white jackets. The night was dark. A paper lantern was suspended among us, and two or three torches dappled the company with their flickering light, imparting to the picture something of the romantic. The wind being against us, it was nine o'clock when we got near Paknam, and then we encountered the ebb-tide. The junk was brought to anchor, and though it rained, the officer in command opposed our landing, insisting that it would be contrary to etiquette, and would besides endanger him to experience the application of the bamboo. Nevertheless, the commodore set his objections at defiance, and, taking two of us in his gig, pulled on shore. We had scarcely crossed the rough bank of stones, lighted by several torches, before the rain fell in torrents, and we sought shelter until it abated.

We found His Excellency prepared to receive us. A loose robe enveloped his whole person, bearing no slight resemblance to the costume represented in biblical pictures, and his apartment was furbished and dusted into a more respectable appearance than it had worn on our last visit. He received us cordially, and regretted that the whole party was not with us. In about a half-hour the others arrived, in company with Mr. Roberts. In the mean time the governor had changed his dress to a heavy purple silk sarong, and a dirty orange-coloured cashmere shawl; and his badges of office were placed on a table, consisting of a small salver, cups for holding arecanut, tobacco, &c., a small box containing a paste for cleansing the mouth, a sort of quiver for cigars, a bowl-shaped spittoon, all of fine gold, and a silver tea-kettle, beautifully enamelled, together with a gold-hilted sword, in a red velvet scabbard. He gave Mr. Roberts a hearty welcome, and then sat himself in the old-fashioned temple before mentioned, and began smoking his long pipe; meanwhile a long table was prepared for supper, or, as they said, for a feast. It proved to be mean in the extreme.

The cloth was of coarse muslin, the plates were of different sorts and sizes, the glass of the commonest kind. The knives, forks, and spoons were all of iron, and few in number for our party. The materials of the feast were boiled chickens, rice, duck-eggs, and roasted pork, all cold. On sitting down to eat of this sumptuous fare (of which Siamese etiquette requires all distinguished strangers to partake, before visiting the capital), we found the table almost as high as the chin, and it required a keen appetite to sustain our wish to comply with the custom. Some were compelled to cut their meat with spoons, and others with their pocket-knives. We had scarcely taken our places, before the hall was crowded with naked Siamese, to gratify their curiosity with a sight of us. We compared our situation to that of beasts in a menagerie, and one suggested that "His Excellency ought to charge more when the animals were fed."

Immediately after the feast was cleared away, the governor demanded a list of the presents intended for His Magnificent Majesty, but it was refused. The names of all the officers in the party were then recorded on a slate-book by a secretary, to be forwarded to the city by an *avant courier*.

The Commodore and Mr. Roberts, by way of distinction, were lodged in the temples of the *Penates*, and the rest of us sought accommodation on the settees and on the floor, as we best could. The night passed more quietly than on my former visit, the serenade of dogs, cats, and ge-kôs was not wanting.

We arose at early dawn the following day, and, as there were neither towels nor napkins provided, the morning ablutions were finished by a general application to the table-cloth. A breakfast, composed chiefly of the remains of the last night's feast, was quickly despatched, and we marched to the place of embarkation. I observed, when passing through the bazaar, that the sailors and soldiers of the boats of ceremony unhesitatingly helped themselves to fruit and cigars, without offering remuneration or meeting with resistance. On reaching the river bank, we found a native band playing, and a crowd of people assembled to see us embark. Three long, narrow canoes, each pulling forty oars, and decorated with red banners, tufts of white hair, and peacock's feathers, conveyed us to the junk of ceremony, which we thought to be very much more comfortable than even the governor's residence itself. After we were on board, the canoes were arranged ahead, in a line abreast, and, as it was perfectly calm, began towing us up the river. The oarsmen, all in red uniforms, stand behind

## PART II: THE RATIFICATION MISSION OF 1836     147

their oars, and perform by pushing, and keep stroke, stamping the right foot in time and in unison with a leader who stood in the bows, striking together two pieces of hard wood. The rowers were all slaves; they occasionally encouraged each other by a sort of chant or song. Thus led, the procession moved up the river, the banks of which are low and green, cheered from time to time with the efforts of our own band. Presently the breeze ruffled the glassy surface of the stream, and with fluttering pennons and gay costume, the whole formed a picturesque view every way worthy a pencil.

Along the whole course of the Meinam on both sides, at short intervals, are built on posts the huts of fishermen, almost concealed in the luxuriant shrubbery. Near them were suspended in the branches, paper-cages and quaint figures, to keep off ghosts and evil spirits. Toy windmills were rattling away in the gentle breeze, placed on a tall bamboo before every door. We saw very few birds.

The course of the Meinam, literally the Mother of Waters, is very serpentine; it has an average depth of four or five fathoms, and is free from shoals. Its breadth is not half a mile. The tide, which rises and falls, perhaps seven feet, is not regular, ebbing and flooding but once in the twenty-four hours.

Towards midday our Albuquerque friends found their European finery too oppressive, and, as a sort of commentary on the title of "boat of ceremony," stripped to the skin before our eyes, and substituted for all their gaudy attire a simple sarong. Halfway up the river, we passed Paklat or "Cidade Nova," where there is a large fortress, on both sides of the river, which being brilliantly white contrasts finely with the green shrubbery. Here boats came off loaded with fruits as a present, for which our band paid in one of its best airs.

About nine o'clock P.M. we fancied we were at our journey's end. The day had been tedious and sultry, and we were glad to escape from our narrow accommodations. But we discovered to our great annoyance, that the anchor had been let go through the timidity and stupidity of our commander-in-chief. He urged that it was dark, the tide against us, many junks in the river, and we had better remain on board all night than run any risks; besides, if an accident should occur, His Magnificent Majesty would first apply the bamboo and then cut off his head. Finding ourselves only a mile from the anchorage, we scolded and threatened and delivered some pretty round Portuguese anathemata, which moved the worthy's compassion, who felt somewhat relieved of his responsibility by the arrival of Piadadè, and got the anchor up again. The distance was soon passed, and after sundry Siamese, Portuguese, and English objurgations, we were transported bag and baggage to the shore. We were received on a slip by another Albuquerque kind of cavalier, in an embroidered cocked-hat and coat (who afterwards proved to be a General), and his son, a child of ten years old, in red, trimmed with gold lace. Numerous torches were blazing along the street, which led to the quarters provided for us at the cost of the king, and where we were pleased to enter. The dwelling of the mission was a pretty-extensive storehouse of two shallow stories. The second one, which we occupied, was divided into four rooms, and opened upon a broad veranda, accessible from a narrow enclosure in front, by a rude ladder or wooden steps.

Piadadè had kindly anticipated our wants, and supper was ready to bring upon the table. Bedsteads and beds, furnished with half a dozen different sized and shaped pillows, were provided in ample numbers. They were all new, and sheltered by musquito curtains [sic], for which there was luckily no necessity, and some of them were ornamented by deep borders of satin, embroidered in flos silk. One of the bedrooms served as a dining hall, and the veranda as a drawing-room. Being shut in on all sides, it was almost insufferably hot, the thermometer ranging at about 92° F., and it was without ventilation. Yet it was the best that could be provided at the time. We were convinced of the good intentions of our host, though not precisely satisfied with their execution; the first were good, the last we attributed to ignorance.

Midnight closed our toils, and we sought to forget in repose all the petty grievances that had tended not a little to ruffle our equanimity. Our beds were comfortable, and our sleep undisturbed.

One circumstance would have been sufficient to destroy repose in people of delicate nerves. The walls were populous at night with varieties of lizards, and serpents were not infrequently seen "drawing their slow length behind," among the tiles and rafters, composing the roof of our abode. Snakes of hideous size and colour, were almost always to be seen, in the heat of the day, winking their lustrous eyes on the sunny side of the trees in the vicinity. Among them was a small species of asp, supposed to be the same as that used by Cleopatra for self-destruction.

# VOLUME II, CHAPTER I

CITY OF BANKOK—SAMPANS—AMPHIBIOUS CHILD—POPULATION—CHINESE RESIDENCE—COMMERCE—REVENUE OF SIAM—TAXES—GAMBLING—LOTTERY—COWRIES—DIVISION OF TIME—EXTENT OF THE SIAMESE EMPIRE—KING'S TITLES—GOVERNMENT, RELIGION, AND PRIESTS.

*April, 1836.*

The sun had set some time before we had attained even the outskirts of the capital, and the night was so dark that we could form no idea either of its appearance or extent. As we advanced along the last two miles of our voyage, nothing presented itself to our view, except the dark forms of vessels at anchor, and a few scattered lights along shore, and we had become so weary and selfish, that our whole attention was taken up with escaping from the boat of ceremony. It was certain, however, that the capital of the Magnificent King of Siam, did not impress us when seen at night with an idea of its grandeur.

The next day we awoke, strangers in a strange place; certainly the strangest I have ever visited, and sallied forth at an early hour to gratify our curiosity, in relation to a country of which we had heard much. We found the whole entirely new to us:—we saw nothing which is in common with Christian lands. Like Venice, the city seemed to have risen from the waters. Half the population is afloat. In Bankok every thing is peculiar, and though every moment was employed, I feel sure that we saw a very small part of the city, during the time we remained.

Bankok is built upon the river Meinam,[7] at a point where it is about half a mile wide, and perhaps twenty miles in a direct line from the sea. It extends about two miles and a half up and down the river, and from a mile to a mile and a half on each side of it. Bankok proper is on the right or western bank, while that on the left, from the palace

---

[7] The River Meinam is, of course, the Chao Phya, but was generally so called by foreigners at the time.

being situated there, is named Sia-Yut'hia,[8] but to the eye it appears all one town. It is irregular in its plan and is every where intersected by canals. The streets are dirty and narrow; the paved walk in the middle being scarcely wide enough for two persons to walk abreast. The reason for this, according to the Siamese, is that there are no two of the same rank in the kingdom, and etiquette does not permit individuals of different degrees to walk side by side! Many of the houses are extensive, but the greater portion of them are miserable bamboo huts, without any appearance of comfort. Trees are every where numerous, and the frequent 'Wâts' or Boudhist temples, with their gilt and glazed tile roofs and spires, sparkling in the sun, give to the city a picturesque appearance, and an air of wealth and magnificence.

Each side of the river is lined with houses, every one a shop, built on rafts of bamboo, moored or staked to the banks. The fronts are open like verandas, wherein various goods are exposed for sale. A row of Chinese junks, from two to six hundred tons each, extend for more than two miles, at anchor in the middle of the stream, where they often remain for months, retailing their cargoes; and though streets, canals, and river are crowded with people and boats, there is neither the bustle nor buzz of the multitude which would be found in an equally dense population in any Christian city. From daylight until dark the river presents an animated scene. The gondolas of this Eastern Venice, called sampans, are of every variety of size, from the mere nutshell, to that moved by half a dozen paddles; and there are some of large dimensions, permanently occupied by whole families, along the banks of the canals.

The better sort of sampan is a light canoe, moved by half a dozen or more short paddles, with a covered cabin in the centre, upon the floor of which the passenger reclines, and by drawing the curtains may be entirely concealed. Some are so small, that we are astonished they are capable of floating under the weight of a man, and others again are propelled like the Venetian gondola by a single oar, managed in a row-lock three feet high. The sampan of this description is usually sculled by a woman standing on the stern, without any other garment than a pair of drawers, with the occasional addition of a piece of black

---

[8] Ruschenberger repeats Roberts' statement that the new city of Bangkok was called Si Ayutthaya.

crape cast over the shoulders. The body is gently bent forward over the oar, and, to obtain a firm footing, one foot is placed in advance of the other, while the arms, in easy motion, impart speed to the vessel. The attitude and movement of these figures are eminently graceful, as they are seen threading their way through the mazes of junks and sampans of all sizes, which are all day gliding along from point to point, in every direction, and always occupying a very small space. The sampans are admirably adapted to the navigation of the canals and river, as we soon discovered, when one of our long-oared boats moved among them. They were often upset by us; but the Siamese always took the mishap in gentleness of spirit, and very quietly swam either to the shore, or to regain the sampan. Living so constantly on the water, they may be said to be a swimming people, though I am told they have a great dread of the sea. They are seen bathing at all times of the day, either swimming, or squatted on the veranda in front of the houses, dipping water out of the river with a basin and pouring it over themselves. Not long ago, Bankok presented the singular phenomenon of an amphibious infant, that forsook the mother's breast, and betook itself to the water on all occasions.

Luck-loi-nam, literally the child of the waters, swam when she was but one year old, and in 1832, when she had attained three years of age, was frequently seen swimming in the river. Her motions were not like those of other swimmers; she floated without any apparent exertion, turning round and round. When not in the water, she was cross and discontented, and when taken out cried and strove to return; if indulged, she tumbled and rolled about, seemingly with unalloyed pleasure. Luck-loi-nam, though well-formed, could neither walk nor speak, but uttered a gurgling, choking sound in the throat. Her vision was imperfect, and up to the time mentioned, she had never eaten any thing but her mother's milk. She usually applied to the breast, on being taken out of the river by her own consent. The mother of the child of the waters was a fine-looking woman, and had given birth to four children; two males and two females. The two brothers are dead, and the sister, eight or nine years of age, was always seen swimming in company, to protect the child of the waters against accidents, and give her direction that she might not get too near the boats, or the banks of the river. She has not been lately seen, and is supposed to be dead.

The population of Bankok, according to the Government Census of 1828, amounted to 401,300,[9] and is made up as follows:

| | |
|---|---:|
| Chinese, | 310,000 |
| Descendants of Chinese, | 50,000 |
| Cochin Chinese, | 1,000 |
| Cambodians, | 2,500 |
| Siamese, | 8,000 |
| Peguans, | 5,000 |
| Laos people, (old residents,) | 9,000 |
| Do. (new residents,) | 7,000 |
| Burmans or Bramas, | 2,000 |
| Tavoy people, | 3,000 |
| Malays, | 3,000 |
| Christians, | 800 |
| Total | 401,300 |

A tax of about three dollars is levied upon every China-man on entering the country, and is afterwards exacted triennially, which secures to him the privilege of following any trade or craft according to his pleasure, and also exempts him from the half-yearly servitude, required by the King from every other Oriental stranger resident in Siam. In 1836, the Chinese population had increased to four hundred thousand, so that we may safely state the city of Bankok contains half a million of inhabitants.

The Chinese residents are chiefly from Teo-Chew, a subdivision of the Canton province; but numbers from Hainan, Canton, and Seang-Hae [Shanghai], annually visit the place, and from the manner of conducting their commercial voyages, remain there from February until May or June. The number of junks in the river during that season is from thirty to seventy, each carrying from twenty to one hundred and thirty men.

Most of the mechanics, agriculturists, and tradesmen of Bankok are China-men. They are cheerful and industrious, but for want of other modes of diverting their leisure hours they are addicted to gambling and libertinism. The tax on Chinese and other gambling-houses in

---

[9] The exact population of Bangkok was (and remains) a vexed question. See B. Terweil, *Through Travellers' Eyes* (Bangkok, 1989) for a discussion of this subject. The Chinese population at 77 per cent seems extremely high, and was likely to be the Chinese population of the whole country. Ruschenberger's list is taken from Schuurman. The population of the city was probably about 400,000 though.

the capital brings a considerable revenue to the Government.

The commerce of Siam with other countries than China is very limited, though her internal resources for foreign trade appear to be every way ample. Within a few years it has increased with Singapore, which serves as an entrepôt between it and Europe, as well as the United States, to a considerable extent. In 1826, a treaty was concluded between the English[10] and His Magnificent Majesty, and the ratification of a treaty with the United States has just been exchanged. The advantages of this treaty, though not immediately apparent, may be in future very great. At one time no less than 2200 tons of American shipping were employed in the Siamese trade; but owing to the numerous and irregular exactions made in form of duties, presents, &c., to the delays incident to the slow mode of conducting business, being obliged almost always to make up the cargo by small purchases from different individuals, and to the rapid advance in the price of sugar when in demand, it dwindled away to nothing, and the commercial world in the United States almost lost sight of Siam. The Sachem, Captain Coffin, who introduced the Siamese Twins to the world, and the Maria Theresa, Captain O. Taylor, (now at Bankok,) are the only American vessels which have entered the Meinam, since 1828, a period of eight years; and probably the last-named vessel would not have ventured, had the commander been ignorant of the visit of the Peacock and its object. As will be seen in the sequel, the chief obstacles in the way of a profitable trade between the United States and Siam, namely, irregular and exorbitant charges, have been removed by the provisions of the treaty alluded to, and under its protection, the commerce may revive in a short time, and then the merchants of Bankok may perceive their interests in facilitating the business of sthose who come to buy or sell.

Siam is too distant for the Americans to send there, only, to purchase her products, most of which may be now obtained at Singapore for a small advance, and sugar, the staple article, can be obtained much nearer home; but she requires the American manufactures to supply her numerous though wretched population, and on the system of exchange only, can they hope to derive any solid advantage from commerce with so remote a country.

---

[10] The Burney treaty, which in practice meant as little as that secured by Roberts.

Nations as well as individuals are often deeply affected by the influence of example, though they may be too proud to acknowledge it, and are brought to the admission of principles and of the actions resulting from them, which without this influence they would have long resisted. It is true the prejudices of the Asiatics generally against all Christians, are so peculiar and so strong, that example may not have so extended an effect with them as among people of other nations; nevertheless, it cannot fail to exercise a powerful influence. The intercourse between Siam and Cochin China, has been until the present war very frequent;[11] it is also common between these two countries and China, and occasionally even with Japan. Should the Siamese derive a profitable trade under the provisions of the treaty, it will be perceived by their neighbours, and among commercial nations whose acquisitive faculties are large and active; to perceive a source of emolument is but a step short of desiring it for themselves.

The conclusion to be drawn, if these premises be correct, is, that this treaty will be the remote means of opening a wide field to American enterprise, and of new markets for her growing manufactures, and the increasing products of her extensive soil.

The chief merchants of Siam are the King, his ministers, the Chinese, and old women. They require from Europe and the United States arms and ammunition; perhaps a few military ornaments, coarse cutlery, glass ware, white cotton goods, which should not be less than two cubits in width; cotton twist, from No. 20 to 30; Siamese dresses, three yards long by forty inches broad, in star patterns, on red, green, and blue grounds, which colours should be bright; long ells, red and green; furniture chintz; ladies cloth, red, yellow, green, light purple, and light blue; steel, in small bars, the size of nail iron, which for this market should be put up in tubs instead of cases, one hundred of which are enough at a time. American cottons are now sought for, though afforded at a higher price, because they have been found to be much more durable. There is an opening for the introduction of American cottons, through Bankok, to the countries lying north of Siam.*

---

* For this commercial information I am indebted to Mr. R. Hunter, a commissionmer chant of several years' residence at Bankok, who kindly placed his manuscript diary in my hands, with permission to extract whatever I might think interesting. [Author's note]

[11] Siam and Vietnam were at odds over Cambodia from 1812 and Laos from 1828.

## Part II: The Ratification Mission of 1836

For the above articles they offer in exchange, sugars, tin, ivory, sappan wood, (*Cæsalpina sappan*,) rosewood, rattans, a variety of drugs, iron of a superior quality, &c. Sugar, the staple article, is at an average price of eight ticâls per picul of 133$^{1/3}$ lbs., and may be put on board for about five dollars per hundred: whether it will yield profit at this price, after paying freight, home duties, interest, insurance, &c., I am not merchant enough to decide.

Though the duties stipulated for in the treaty may appear high at first sight, 4275 dollars on a vessel measuring 25 feet beam, they will be found not to exceed ten or twelve per cent. on a valuable cargo.

An estimate of the Siamese revenue and resources of trade may be formed from the following Tables, made for one year:

Table exhibiting the Internal revenue, &c., of Siam, for one year, in Bats or Ticâls.

|  |  | Bats or Ticâls. |
|---|---|---:|
| *Tavern Licenses.* | Bankok, | 104,900 |
|  | Sia-Yut'hia, | 16,000 |
|  | Bang-xang,[12] | 8,000 |
|  | Suriburi, | 4,000 |
|  | Krungtap'han, | 4,000 |
| *Bazaars.* | Bankok, | 39,000 |
|  | Sia-Yut'hia, | 12,000 |
|  | Suri-buri, | 1,600 |
|  | Bang-xang, | 1,600 |
| Duty on floating houses, | | 36,000 |
| — on Chinese gambling-houses. | | 64,000 |
| — on Siamese ditto, | | 58,000 |
| Revenue from provinces under first minister, | | 32,000 |
| — — — — second minister, | | 24,000 |
| — — — — third minister, | | 12,000 |
| — — judiciary courts of Kromamuang, | | 4,800 |
| — — — — of tribunal, | | 8,000 |
| — — gold province of Bangtap'han, 180 ticâls' weight of gold equal to | | 1,880 |
| Revenue from gold province of Pipri, 60 ticâls' weight of gold, equal to | | 960 |
| — — tribute paid by Malays for working gold mines, 216 ticâls' weight of gold,* | | 3,456 |
| Total. | | 436,196 |

---

* Gold is estimated at sixteen times the value of silver. [Author's note]

[12] It is unclear whether these are subdistricts of the capital or separate townships.

TABLE OF COMMERCIAL REVENUE.

| Articles. | Quantities. | | Ticâls. |
|---|---|---|---|
| On Paddy, | 1,696,423 | koyans,[13] | 862,358 |
| Gardens, | | | 545,880 |
| Trees, | | | 17,800 |
| Teak wood, | 127,000 | trees, | 56,000 |
| Sappan wood, (3 qualities,) | 200,000 | piculs, | 84,000 |
| Cocoa-nut oil, | 600,000 | | 56,000 |
| Sugars, (5 qualities,) | 96,000 | | 40,000 |
| Jacra,[14] | 150,000 | jars, | 8,000 |
| Salt, | 8,000 | koyans, | 32,000 |
| Pepper, | 38,000 | piculs, | 23,000 |
| Cardammums, | 550 | " | 5,400 |
| Bastard do., | 4,000 | " | 16,000 |
| Stick lac, | 8,000 | " | 9,500 |
| Tin, | 1,200 | " | 18,200 |
| Iron, | 20,000 | " | 54,000 |
| Ivory, | 300 | " | 2,500 |
| Gamboge, (3 qualities,) | 200 | " | 1,200 |
| Rhinoceros' horns, | | | 1,600 |
| Deer's do. | 26,000 | pairs, | 3,600 |
| Cows' do. | 200 | piculs, | |
| Buffaloes' do. | 200 | " | |
| Deer's sinews, | 200 | " | 800 |
| Rhinoceros' hides, | 200 | " | |
| Tigers' bones, | 50 to 60 | | |
| Buffaloes' hides, in number | 500 | " | |
| Cows' hides, in number | 100,000 | | 1,600 |
| Gum Benjamin | 100 | piculs, | 400 |
| Birds' nests, (3 qualities,) | 10 to 12 | " | 32,000 |
| Dried fish, (3 kinds,) | 79,000 | " | |
| Dried shrimps, | 1,000 | " | 18,000 |
| Balachao,[15] | 1,400 | " | 4,600 |
| Azelu de Pao,[16] | 15,000 | " | 8,000 |
| Breu[17] | 10,000 | " | 6,000 |
| Rosewood, | 200,000 | " | 1,600 |

---

[13] By 'koyan' is meant a *kwien*, a cartload.

[14] 'Jacra' is jaggery, palm sugar.

[15] *Blachang* or fermented shrimp paste.

[16] 'Azelu de pao' is not identified. The quantities and volumes do not often correspond to Roberts' listing.

[17] La Loubère (1693) noted 'Brou is a green Bark or Skin which is on the Coco like as on our Nuts: but that of the Coco is three fingers thick, and its fibers may be twisted into a Cord.'

| | | | |
|---|---:|---|---:|
| Damar, | 200,000 | bundles, | 5,600 |
| Rattans, | 200,000 | " | 5,600 |
| Casca de pau,[18] | 200,000 | " | 1,600 |
| Wooden posts, (3 kinds,) | 203,500 | in number, | 8,000 |
| Bamboos, | 600,000,000 | " | 8,000 |
| Ollas, or Chak leaves,[19] | 95,000,000,000 | " | 8,000 |
| Firewood, | | | 14,000 |
| | | Total, | 1,960,838 |

These tables are derived from the Portuguese residents; and, though not complete nor perfectly accurate, proximative estimates may be formed from them.

The annual tax on cultivated paddy or rice fields is levied at the rate of three *fu-angs* per square *rai*, of 130 feet square. Being the custom of the country to plant the cane once every three years, sugar plantations pay one tical for the first, and for the two following years two *sa-lungs* per square *rai*. The reason assigned for the difference is, that the first year's growth is most valuable. A tax of one *sa-lung* per picul is also levied on the sugar before it is brought to market.

The taxes are separately farmed by the Government. The customs on wood, ollas or chak leaves, used for thatching, are one-fifth in quantity. Gardens are taxed per square *rai*, varying somewhat in proportion to their productions. Orchards pay according to their number of trees and the value of their fruits; on cocoanut and betel trees, &c., the tax is one *fu-ang* for twenty trees; on mango and other valuable trees, it is from one *fu-ang* to half a tical per tree.

The taxes on taverns, or more strictly speaking, tippling-shops, and on gambling establishments, are farmed to licensed individuals, without whose permission no one can sell spirituous liquors or open a gambling-house without incurring a heavy penalty. Individuals are not permitted to play in private, not even beneath their own rooftree, but in order to gratify this passion must repair to some one of the many licensed establishments, except at certain periods, when the law is suspended. A general permission to gamble is granted three times a year; three days at the commencement of the Chinese new year; three days at the commencement of the Siamese new year, and

---

[18] 'Casca de pao' are probably Roberts' 'barks, mangrove, etc.'
[19] 'Ollas or chak leaves': the mangrove palm used for thatch.

three days at another season. During these periods, all classes may be seen, assiduously waiting upon dame Fortune's smiles or frowns, read in the turning of cards or throwing of the dice. In these privileged times, wealth often changes hands; beggars become rich and the affluent are reduced to penury. In these periods too, a taste for play, under the influence of an almost universal example becomes irresistible, and when the law again becomes operative, those who have been unlucky resort to licensed tables to repair their shattered fortunes, and those who have been fortunate, in order to increase their gains. The honourable and productive avocations of society are forsaken or much neglected; wealth is squandered; intemperance and frequent quarrels ensue, and, often under the weight of overwhelming despair, the gambler, as in other countries, ends his not yet mature existence by suicide.

A species of lottery has been introduced by the Chinese, which has attracted much attention, and is much in accordance with the tastes of the people. An indefinite number of tickets are sold, upon which is written the name of some one of thirty-six titled cards, which the purchaser may designate. Once a week one card is turned up, and those whose ticket bears the title, win and receive thirty for one, the purchaser being at liberty to pay any sum he pleases for the ticket.

The circulating medium of Siam consists of silver and cowries exclusively; gold is occasionally coined, or rather stamped, but is held entirely as a curiosity, and cannot be considered as a part of the money system. The cowry shell (*Cyprea moneta*), circulates in many countries of Asia, but in former times to a much greater extent than at present. They were carried to various parts of the East in great quantities, from the Maldive islands, where they were fished twice, monthly; three days before and three after the new moon. Women alone were employed in the fishery. They waded into the sea, waist deep, and dug them from the sand; they were then made up into packages, each containing 12,000 shells, and thus shipped off to Ceylon, the Ganges, Siam, &c.; but in the Maldive islands they were not current money.

The silver pieces, in the form of short bars, doubled on themselves and impressed with a small stamp, closely resemble buck-shot and bullets. They are ticâls or bats, sa-lungs and fu-angs; all the rest of money divisions named in the following table, except the cowries, whose value is fluctuating, are imaginary. The ticâl or bat is the money-unit, and, according to the Calcutta assay, weighs 236 grains, and is valued at two shillings and sixpence sterling.

In April, 1836, dollars were at the rate of 150 ticâls for the hundred dollars.

SIAMESE MONEY TABLE.

| | | |
|---|---|---|
| 200 Cowries, | equal to | 1 P'hai-nung. |
| 2 P'hai-nungs, | - | 1 Song-p'hai. |
| 2 Song-p'hais, | - | 1 Fu-ang. |
| 2 Fu-angs, | - | 1 Sa-lung. |
| 4 Sa-lungs, | - | 1 Ticâl, or bat. |
| 4 Ticâls, | - | 1 Tumlung. |
| 20 Tumlungs, | - | 1 Catie. |
| 100 Caties, | - | 1 Picul, or $133^{1/3}$ lbs. |

The above are also used as measures of weight, whether apothecary, troy, or avoirdupois.

SIAMESE LONG MEASURE.

| | |
|---|---|
| 12 Fingers' breadth, | 1 Span. |
| 2 Spans, | 1 Cubit, = 19½ English inches. |
| 4 Cubits, | 1 Fathom, = 6½ English feet. |
| 20 Fathoms, | 1 Sen, = 130 feet. |
| 400 Sens, | 1 Yote, = 3 leagues, 271 yards, 81½ feet. |

The only land or square measure is the rai, of 130 English feet.

SIAMESE DRY MEASURE.

| | |
|---|---|
| 20 K:nàn, | 1 Tang, or bucket. |
| 50 Tangs, | 1 Ban. |
| 2 Bans, | 1 Kian, or Koyan. |

One k:nàn is equal to about 1½ English pints. Liquids are also measured by this table. Oil however is sometimes sold by weight.

The measure of time is not less singular than any other. The timekeeper, like that of the Hindoos, consists of a cup with an aperture in the bottom, floating in a vessel of water, which sinks at the termination of each watch.

SIAMESE TIME MEASURE.

| | |
|---|---|
| 10 Ak-san, | 1 Pran. |
| 6 Prans, | 1 Pùt. |
| 15 Pùts, | 1 Bat, or 1/10 of an hour. |
| 10 Bat, | 1 Tum, or hour of the night. |
| 3 Tum, | 1 Yam. |
| 4 Yam, | 1 K'hun, or night. |
| 12 Mong (hour of the day), | 1 Wan, or day. |
| 7 Wan, | 1 Kwap-a:tit, or week. |
| 29 and 30 Wan, | 1 Duan, or month. |
| 12 Duan, | 1 Pi, or year. |
| 12 Pi, | 1 Cycle. |

The day commences at sunrise. The forenoon is divided into six watches, and the afternoon until sunset into the same number. From sunset until midnight includes two watches, and from midnight till morning the same number. In Siamese, the day watches are called *Mong*, and those of the night, *Tum*.

The division of time into weeks of seven days was probably derived from the Portuguese. They are named, in Siamese, as follows:

| | |
|---|---|
| Wan-a thit, (literally day of the sun,) | Sunday. |
| Wan-chan, (moon-day,) | Monday. |
| Wang-ang-khan, | Tuesday. |
| Wan-put, | Wednesday. |
| Wan-prà-hat, | Thursday. |
| Wan-suk, | Friday. |
| Wan-sou, | Saturday. |

The Siamese reckon 29 and 30 days to the months, alternately, which, with the exception of the first two, are numbered. This gives their year 354 days; but they complete the measure by adding an intercalary month every third year, and omit reckoning three or four days, as the case may be, before the commencement of each new year. The month is divided into the bright and dark halves, corresponding to the increase and wane of the moon.

The Siamese year is divided into three seasons; the *hot season*, from the full moon in February to the full moon in June; the *rainy season*, from the full moon of June to the full moon of October, the remaining time being the *cool season*. The new year commences after the close of the fifth month, which, in 1836, falls on the 15th of April.

The great division of time is into two cycles, the greater of sixty,

PART II: THE RATIFICATION MISSION OF 1836      161

and the lesser of twelve years. The last is said to be employed for astrological purposes, in casting nativities, &c. The names of the years are nevertheless inserted in all important papers; they are named after different animals, as follows:—

| | | | | | |
|---|---|---|---|---|---|
| 1. Chuat, or year of the Rat. | | | 7. M: Mia, or year of the Horse. | | |
| 2. Ch-lú | — | Cow. | 8. M: Mé, | — | Goat. |
| 3. Khán | — | Tiger. | 9. Wak, (1836) | — | Monkey. |
| 4. Thô | — | Rabbit. | 10. R: ka, | — | Cock. |
| 5. M: Rong, | — | Dragon. | 11. Chá | — | Dog. |
| 6. M: Seng, | — | Serpent. | 12. Kun, | — | Hog. |

In dates of letters, &c., the Siamese mention, first, the day of the week, then the evening or morning of the day of the month, the increase or wane of the moon, and the name and number of the year. In all important documents, the year of the Siamese era is also inserted. The present year (1836), in their phraseology, is the 1197th from the commencement of the magnificent kingdom of Thai.*

The Siamese have two eras, a sacred and a popular one; the former, used by the Talapoins in all matters relating to religion, dates from the death of Guatama; the latter was introduced in commemoration of the introduction of the worship of Guatama into Siam, which happened in the 1181st year of the sacred epoch, corresponding with the A.D. 638, so that the God of Siam has been dead 2379 years.†

Of the precise extent of the Siamese empire we have no certain information; and from the frequent acquisition of territory by conquest, it is not easy to ascertain what are its precise boundaries. Crawfurd places its extreme western limit, including some desert islands in the bay of Bengal, in the meridian of 97° 50′ east of Greenwich, and the eastern limit in about the 105th. The northern boundary is under the twenty-third, and the southern under the fifth degree of north latitude, that is, on the west or Malay side of the gulf. Mr. Crawfurd commits a glaring error in placing the southern boundary on the Cambodian side, "in about the same parallel" as that on the side of the Malay peninsula. The island of Pulo Oby, at the southern extremity of

---

* For the above tables of weight and measure I am indebted to the kindness of Missionary Charles Robinson. [Author's note]

† Embassy to the Courts of Siam and Cochin China, by John Crawfurd, &c. [Author's note]

Cambodia, is situated in 8° 25´ north; so that, even if the Siamese possessions include that island, there is a difference of three and a half degrees of latitude—a space of open sea, claimed in vain for Siam. The area of the whole country is estimated at 190,000 geographical miles, including, besides Siam proper, Laos on the north, a part of Cambodia, and a large portion of the Malay peninsula.

Except in the vicinity of Bankok, the country is mountainous and well-watered. The soil is fertile, abounding in fruits, dye-woods, medicinal gums and timber. The teak, so useful in shipbuilding, grows in great abundance, and is of an excellent quality. The total population of the empire is represented to be 2,790,500.[20]

The Government is a despotism of the most absolute kind. The King is the god, the law of the land, and his name is known only to few, that it may not be taken in vain. He is mentioned by several epithets which are considered peculiarly soft and flattering; as, "The Sacred Lord of Heads," "The Sacred Lord of Lives," "The Owner of All," "Lord of the White Elephants," "Most Exalted Lord, Infallible and Infinitely Powerful." Even the members of his body are designated in adulatory terms; his feet, hands, nose, ears, and eyes, are never mentioned without the prefix of Lord, or sacred Lord. Every thing belonging to or attached to his Majesty's person is also styled golden. To visit him, is to come to his magnificent Majesty's golden feet, to speak in his golden ear, &c.

The country is divided into districts; each one is governed by a minister, appointed by the King, aided by a governor and other subordinate officers; and the more distant provinces are under viceroys or rajahs. There appears to be no written law; at least, there is none observed, the will or whim of the officer being often decisive.

All the people, with the exception of the Chinese, European and American residents, are virtually slaves, or in a state of slavery. The officers at the head of sub-divisions of districts require them to labour on public works one month out of every three or four, according to official pleasure, in building temples, junks, roads, or any thing else; which requisition is termed, "A call to public business." If a superior officer be engaged in any work, he calls upon one under him to furnish

---

[20] The population of Siam, like that of Bangkok, was always a subject of much discussion; it is not known how Rushenberger arrived at this figure.

a number of men, greater or less, according to circumstances, to labour for one month: when this term has expired, he calls on another for an equal quota, and so continues till the task be accomplished. The labourers support themselves and their families, and receive no compensation for their public services, except the glorious privilege of living in Siam or Thai, literally the "Free country." We may almost say, with Paudeen O'Rafferty,[21] "They work for nothing, and live upon less," content to be slaves, as long as they entertain the name of being free.

A number of people of various countries are held in perpetual bondage, including those who are taken in war, and those who are so unfortunate as to be in debt, because they have no hope of liberation unless some friend step forward and satisfy the claim against them. Debtors are allowed no compensation for their services, but on the contrary are charged for food, clothing, medical attendance, &c., so that the original debt is constantly increasing.

Except in case of debt, the Chinese are exempt from labouring on public works, by paying the triennial tax of four ticâls and a half, before mentioned. Some say this tax is collected yearly.

The religion of Siam is that of Boudha. The belief is, that after death the soul transmigrates through animals of the inferior classes, in gradation, according to the good or evil the individual has done in this world, until he arrives through meritorious deeds to the condition of supreme beatitude, which is the state of nonentity. Every animal is animated by some human soul, and hence the general respect for life. Though the Siamese will not kill an animal, they will generally eat of its flesh, because the sin lies only in driving the soul from its temporary abode.

The talapoins or priests, supposed to amount to at least one hundred thousand, are maintained by daily contributions of rice, &c., from the people, and annual presents from the King, consisting of money, and yellow cloth for their robes. At funerals they often receive valuable presents. They assemble daily in the wâts or temples, and repeat prayers which they do not understand, as they are in the Bali language, which they do not generally comprehend. This, however, is not an unfrequent occurrence in other countries. Not more than ten in the whole

---

[21] Paudeen (properly Paudien) O'Rafferty published in Dublin in 1825 *Together with the coronation*, *What's the use of fretting*, and *The sun that lights the roses*.

PRIESTS AT BREAKFAST

kingdom, it is said, are capable of understanding the sacred books which they read, and which are all in this language. They relieve the people from all devotional exercises and holy acts, except that of daily bestowing upon themselves boiled rice and other little offerings. For three months of his life, every Siamese is obliged to be a talapoin, and they generally assume the yellow robe at twenty years of age. They may doff this beggar's life when it suits them after the term has expired; but if they take up the robe a second time, it must be for life. The usual number in the capital is about twenty thousand, varying with the price of rice, and provisions; prosperous agriculture, abundant crops, making the fruits of the soil cheap, detract from the worship of the great Boudha, distinguished by being sixty-eight feet long, and having all his fingers and toes of the same length.

The talapoins are of different grades or classes, and are presided over by one, whom, from the nature of his office, we may in common parlance term the Pope. He has other priests below him, answering to the cardinals, archbishops, bishops and other dignitaries of the church of Rome. The whole system, including the monastic and beggarly lives of the churchmen, bears a strong resemblance to the Roman Catholic institution.

The wâts or temples are numerous, and costly, many of them indeed magnificent; and they occupy the best situations in the kingdom. They

PART II: THE RATIFICATION MISSION OF 1836            165

are the residences of the priests, and the places of education for all male Siamese.

The people seldom visit the wâts, nor do they ever perform any act of worship.[22] They as well as the priests are ever ready to acknowledge that Boudha died long, long since; but they believe there will be another incarnation of the Deity, and that all his fingers and toes will be of the same length. They are anxiously expecting such a person; and for this reason perhaps may feel more curiosity to see the foot than the face of the stranger. These being the marks by which his incarnation is to be known, it is said that Boudha before his death, caused some pattern statues of himself to be made, that he might be the more readily recognised on his second coming. For this reason all images of him in Siam are made after this fashion.

---

[22] This information, and much else in the latter part of this chapter, is suspect.

# VOLUME II, CHAPTER II

SUCCESSION OF THE THRONE—VISIT TO MOMFANOI—THE ROYAL ADELAIDE—MOMFANOI'S PETS—HIS PRIVATE MUSEUM—THE KHON PAA—A SIAMESE SWORD—MUSICAL INSTRUMENT—A TREAT OF ANTS' EGGS—PHRENOLOGICAL EXAMINATION—CHARACTER OF MOMFANOI—A WHITE APE—PHYSICAL CHARACTER OF THE SIAMESE—SIAMESE HEADS—SENSUALITY OF THE SIAMESE—THEIR ARROGANCE, ETC..

*April, 1836.*

THE morning after our arrival, we visited His Highness the Prince Momfanoi, literally, "Prince of Heaven, Junior." He is also called Chawfanoi, the ultimate syllable signifying the younger. he is half brother to the King, and in truth, rightful heir to the throne, which, on the late King's death, his present Magnificent Majesty usurped, and afterwards proposed to create Chawfaya[i] [Mongkut], the elder brother of the Prince and legitimate successor, second King. This proposal however was scorned by him; and, declaring that he would never bend to, nor do homage to the usurper, he assumed the yellow robe of the Talapoins for life. By this means he is enabled to keep his word, because they are excused from all the slavish ceremonies of Siamese etiquette, and in the presence of the higher grades, the King himself appears upon his elbows and knees. On the refusal of Chawfaya[i], an uncle of the reigning monarch was appointed second King; but since his death, which occurred about three years since, no successor has been named to this office, and it is asserted that His Majesty will not make another second King, because he is entitled, according to Siamese custom, to one-third of the revenue of the empire.

Chawfaya[i] leads a very holy life, measured by the Siamese criterion of sanctity, and enjoys a rank equal to that of a Bishop. His assumption of the yellow robe a second time, makes Momfanoi the legitimate heir; but his accession to the throne is not absolutely certain. The King has the power of naming his successor from among his lawful heirs. The reigning Monarch, though he possesses more than three hundred wives, has no children living, legitimate enough to wear the crown; and, since the death of his lawful son, Prince Momfanoi has "crept into favour," and rumour states that he is about being affianced to His Magnificent Majesty's favourite daughter, notwithstanding that he has already nine wives. If this report prove true, there is no doubt but he will succeed to the throne: *es mejor care en gracia que ser gracioso*.[23]

Being very popular and full of enterprise and military spirit, the Prince has been regarded with a jealous eye, or at least has been carefully watched. This state of things makes him very cautious and fearful of thwarting any of His Magnificent Majesty's views. He seldom goes abroad by day, therefore, but goes about, as he says good-humouredly, "like a thief at night." He makes frequent visits to the palace after sunset, the time selected by the King to receive his several ministers to hear their reports, after the cares of the day are done.

We found his Highness on board of his barque, where he gave us a hearty welcome. The size of this vessel is about two hundred tons, and is somewhat in the European style; but, having been at first intended to be a junk, and the plan after the work was well advanced being changed, she draws more forward than aft. He is now fitting her out with the aid of three English sailors in his employment, and so far, every thing is neat and well-finished.

Instead of the costume described when the Prince visited the Peacock, he wore upon the present occasion nothing but a heavy silk sarong or waist-cloth. He ushered us into his cabin, where he offered tea and cigars. His numerous attendants, all apparently on the familiar footing of companions, were resting on their elbows and knees around him, chewing arecanut, which His Highness does not use. He had two beautiful parrots from Borneo, of which he seemed to be very fond. We accompanied him over the vessel, and found every thing going forward actively: the workmen were generally seated on the deck, and therefore were not under the necessity of desisting from their labours, as would have been the case had they been standing. The Prince himself took the gouge from the hands of a mechanic, and squatting down began to apply it with skill, to a piece of wood which was turned by a man pulling a cord, passed about it like the string of a drill-bow, the ends of the wood revolving on points like those in the

---

[23] (Spanish): the *Diccionario de la Academia* says, rather flatly, that this is 'a saying which points out that a person's good luck may sometimes have more influence than his own merit.'

frame of a turning-lathe. While observing these things, we heard a shout or huzza from a hundred voices on the river, raised in a long canoe-like boat, pulling a hundred oars. The rowers were standing behind the oars, loudly marking time with the right foot, while one stood in the bows, striking together two pieces of bamboo, as a guide to their simultaneous efforts. The boat and crew belonged to the prince, who exercises them daily in this manner, which explained the salutation we had just heard. He has several thousand men whom he thus trains, or to the use of small arms daily. He delights in military affairs, but does not, on that account, omit any opportunity of acquiring general knowledge. On one occasion he borrowed our drummer to teach his own our rolls, calls, &c., and on another was very particular in having explained to him the object of lightning rods in ships. The day afterwards we found his armourer hard at work, making one for this vessel. He has called the barque the "Royal Adelaide:" and with his own hand has painted the name in English characters, on a rack for small arms, at the after-hatch. His taste for painting is displayed in several places; a large chest in the cabin is marked on the front with his own name, T. MOMFANOI, and he showed us several of his drawings.

The vessel was lying about ten yards from the shore, in front of his palace, which has the external appearance of a fort. The walls are snowy white, and surmounted by embrasures for guns.

We accompanied the Prince on shore, and as we walked to the palace gate, every native we met fell on his face till Momfanoi had passed. Within the walls we found, every where, evidence of the master's tastes. A number of people male and female were at work, some twisting or 'laying-up' rope, and others at various other occupations. Several of both sexes had chains on the arms and legs, and their naked backs bore recent marks of bamboo. It was the first time I had seen women in chains, and I felt a sudden recoil of mind at the sight, of mingled disgust and pity, and perhaps a desire that they should be at once free; but on reflection, I suppose it was correct, for they are not of the same comparative feebleness of body as in Christian lands.

Before entering his dwelling, Momfanoi led us to see his pets; a large baboon, half a dozen beautiful deer, a pair of large black bears from Borneo, with a white stripe over the fore part of each shoulder; these were tame and playful; a large cassowary from New Holland, so tame as to eat from one's hand, was running about at liberty. He now called our attention to a variety of parrots and krokotoas, in the corridor or veranda, surrounding the house; and then led us to his stables to see his fine stud of horses, and thence, to look at several storks, jungle fowls in cages, and half a dozen asses and monkeys. He had ordered three or four alligators to be brought from beneath the stable in the mean time, and their jaws to be secured, that we might examine them without risk.

In another part of the court or area were fieldpieces, and guns of various kinds and caliber, ships' spars, &c., neatly arranged beneath a shed. He had numerous questions to ask about every thing he exhibited, and was never satisfied till he felt sure that he clearly understood the answers which were given to him.

He now led us into the house, saying, "Gentlemen, you are welcome—I am glad to see you." The interior is lofty, though but of one story, and is divided into three apartments by two screens, which do not reach the ceiling. The centre apartment was furnished in the Anglo-Asiatic style, and as neatly as any house I have seen in India.

On a table near a sofa at one end of this drawing-room were violins, flutes, and a flagelet, upon which instruments His Highness performs. The adjoining apartment was filled as a study, furnished with a small collection of English books, a fine barometer, &c. A small room communicating with it is arranged as a private museum, in which there are many fine specimens of natural history; quadrupeds, birds, reptiles, &c., all preserved and set up by himself.

Among the strange animals belonging to Siam there is one described under the name of Khon Paa, which belongs to the known genus of natural history. This animal has been seen by the Prince and hundreds of others, yet we must confess that we are inclined to doubt the accuracy of description. The Khon Paa resembles man; it is five feet high, walks erect, has no knee-joints, and runs faster than a horse. Should he accidentally fall, he is forced to crawl to a tree or something else, by which he again raises himself on his feet. His skin is as transparent as a China horn lantern; his entrails are distinctly seen through it, and his abdomen shines like a looking glass—*credit qui vult, non ego.*[24] Under the superstitious notion that the presence of the animal in Bankok was unlucky, his owners were bambooed, and

---

[24] *credit qui vult, non ego* (Latin): let him who wishes to believe this do so, not I.

all their property confiscated by the King for bringing him there. This treatment caused so much terror, that no one has since ventured to bring a specimen of the beast from his native lurking-place.

When we returned from the museum to the drawing-room, the Prince ordered wine, Port and Madeira, which were excellent, and cigars of Siamese manufacture.

So gracefully did he do the honours of his house, in spite of his being nearly naked, that no one would hesitate to pronounce that Nature had stamped him a gentleman. He gave his attentions equally to all his guests, asked questions on almost every subject, and, when the answers were not perfectly clear, always repeated his inquiries, and on two or three disputed points, he referred to books in the library to support his opinions.

He showed us the sword used by the Siamese when they fight on elephants, which one might mistake for a spear. The handle was four feet long, of fine heavy wood, and perfectly straight, having a screw joint in the middle in order to make it more portable. The blade was one-edged, two feet long and gently curved; the guard was a disc set with gems, and the scabbard was enamelled. Such an instrument in a bold determined hand, might be used with the effect of a scythe.

A musical instrument, invented in Laos, the country to the north of Siam proper, was next exhibited. It consists of fourteen bamboos half an inch in diameter, and from eight to twelve feet long, placed in two parallel rows, containing seven each. The barrels or tubes are of graduated lengths, like those of an organ, and from the resemblance to that instrument, this might be termed the Laos organ. About two feet from the square end, the tubes pass through a short cylinder of wood at right angles, and about three inches above it, each tube is pierced by a small hole, to which a finger is applied when playing. The player holds the instrument between the palms, and blows into the open end of the cylinder.

We requested that some of his people would play for us. "Wow!" exclaimed the Prince in his usual manner of expressing surprise, "Wow—I will play for you myself," and, at once, calling an old man who was resting *à la Siamese*, he took the instrument between his palms. The old man crawled close up to the Prince's, feet, and sitting *à la Turque*, looked up into his face while his Highness played a showy interlude. The minstrel shut his eyes, and turning his withered countenance heavenward, began singing a melancholy air to his master's accompaniment. We were surprised at the power of the instrument, and much pleased with the performance.

He had no sooner ended his song, than the old man began to move back to his former station, but a word detained him at his master's feet. "Now," said the Prince, "I will give you another kind of tune," and at once struck up an air which might have been mistaken for Scotch, had we not been assured that it was Siamese. The minstrel gathered confidence from the music, and sang with much spirit and better effect than at first.

When we took leave, he detained some of us to dinner; and in the mean time entertained the company by showing them several Siamese curiosities, and conversing on all subjects. About three o'clock P.M., the table was spread in the Anglo-Asiatic style,—a mixture of English comfort and Eastern display; the dinner was remarkable for the variety and exquisite flavour of the curries. Among them was one consisting of ants' eggs, a costly and much esteemed luxury of Siam. They are not larger than grains of sand, and, to a palate unaccustomed to them, are not particularly savoury—they are almost tasteless. Besides being curried, they are brought to table rolled in green leaves, mingled with shreds or very fine slices of fat pork. Here was seen an ever-to-be-remembered luxury of the East. Two slaves stood waving fans behind the Prince's chair, and many other attendants were crouched upon elbows and knees around the room, to whom he occasionally translated such parts of the conversation as he thought would interest them. While he thus sat conversing cheerfully, circulating his choice wines, accurately cooled, and entertaining his guests, a slave was crouching beneath the table busily occupied in scratching His Highness' naked shins.

On another occasion we visited the Prince at night on board of the Royal Adelaide, which at present seems to be his hobby. We were no sooner on the deck than he exclaimed, "Wow—I am glad to see you; walk into the cabin." There we found him with several of his attendants. He showed us an American newspaper, which contained a list of the officers of the Peacock, and the announcement of the then projected Voyage to Siam. He had had the newspaper six months, but never had communicated the news to the King. He laughed heartily when he related the anecdote.

Among other subjects that of phrenology was mentioned, and I proposed to illustrate its principles by the examination of some of the heads of his attendants. This was agreed to, although there is a strong prejudice existing against putting the hand on the head of a Siamese. In relation to this point there is an anecdote told of the P'hra Klang. When the British Envoy[25] from the Government of India was here in 1822, he resided in the second story of a house; to avoid the ill luck and disgrace of having any body for a moment actually over his head, the worthy P'hra Klang (a man of some three or four hundred pounds substance) was in the habit of entering the Ambassador's apartments through a window, by a ladder placed against the outside of the building.

As the Siamese almost invariably burn their dead, it is almost impossible to procure a skull for phrenological comparison. I therefore determined to obtain the measure of some of them, and in order to do so, excited their curiosity, to lull the prejudices I have mentioned. I was lucky in guessing the predominant traits of those who submitted to examination. One of them was a brother to the second P'hra Klang, and, according to the Prince, a gentleman of pure blood. When the character given by me was interpreted to him, he seemed for a moment stupid with amazement; then seizing my hand, said, "You have told me much that I conceived impossible for you to know; there is one thing more which I entreat you to tell me. How long have I got to live?" At this the Prince and all of us laughed. He looked as grave as though he expected to hear me name the day of his death.

Momfanoi said he would submit his own head to examination at some other time in private; but no opportunity occurred.

The character of the Prince Momfanoi might be deduced from what has been already said. He is docile, active, determined, and considering he is of a race that has taken scarcely a step to emerge from ignorance and barbarism, he is liberal-minded and in a great degree free from the many prejudices, common to his countrymen. His manners are easy, but are rather of the kind which characterize naval officers than the carpet knights of royal courts. Possessing eminent qualities and quick perception, fitting him for a high and useful station, it must be a subject of regret to all philanthropists, if he be not nominated successor to the throne of "the free." The English language he acquired

---

[25] This is John Crawfurd.

from the American missionaries, and, delighting to diffuse the knowledge he acquires, he has already taught one of his slaves, a lad of sixteen or seventeen, to speak it intelligibly. Whenever he hears any thing novel, he immediately communicates it to his attendants, who always listen attentively to whatever he says. This disposition to communicate information is so great as to impart a puerile cast to his whole character, which is increased by the promptitude with which he appears ready to undertake or to execute any plan that squares with his fancy. On one occasion he was asked whether it were possible to procure a white monkey. "I don't know *that*—it is a rare animal; I have a white ape." At this moment he was interrupted, and the conversation took another turn. After a few minutes, though it was night and we were on board the Royal Adelaide, the white ape was brought in. By candle-light it appeared quite white and woolly like a sheep, but in daylight the colour is yellowish. The face, the palms and soles are black, and the eyes are of a very dark chestnut colour, or what might be termed without impropriety black. It is of the sort designated as the long-armed ape; the arm from the shoulder to the end of the middle finger of this specimen measured nineteen inches, and the whole height when erect was twenty-three inches.

The animal was for some time alive on board of the Peacock; it was grave and disposed to sleep a great deal; the stuffed specimen is now in the collection at the academy of Natural Sciences of Philadelphia.

In the event of Momfanoi ascending the throne, great changes will no doubt be effected in Siam. Improvements in every branch of useful industry may be anticipated; education will become more general, and liberal ideas will be diffused; the American missionaries will derive more beneficial results from their labours; Christianity will be established, and, last though not least to some of the community, the commercial treaty with the United States will be worth a great deal to America. In these things, the Prince will, in all probability, be the leader, and the people will follow —qualis rex talis grex[26]—

> "For princes are the glass, the school, the book
> Where subjects eyes do learn, do read, do look."[27]

---

[26] (Latin); as is the king, so are his subjects.

[27] 'For princes are the glass, the school, the book/ Where subjects' eyes do earn, do read, do look.' Shakespeare, *The Rape of Lucrece*, stanza 88.

We do not imagine that all these will be accomplished, but only believe that an impulse will be given by his example, which in the course of time, must lead to the result we predict.

The Siamese belong to that variety of the human species which writers on the subject denominate the Mongol. Their average height* is five feet two inches, which I suspect to be near the truth, from the few to whom I have applied the rule. The lower limbs are stout and well-formed; the body is long, and hence the figure is not graceful. The shoulders are broad, and the muscles of the chest are well developed; the neck is short and the head is in fair proportion. The hands are large, and the complexion of a dark olive, but not jetty. Among females of the higher classes, who pass their time generally within the harem of their lords, the skin is of a very much lighter hue; in some instances it might be described as a very dark brunette. The forehead is narrow at the superior part, the face between the cheek bones broad, and the chin is, again narrow, so that the whole contour is rather lozenge-shaped than oval. The eyes are remarkable for the upper lid being extended below the under, at the corner next to the nose, but it is not elongated like that organ in the Chinese or Tartar races. The eyes are dark or black, and the white is dirty or of a yellowish tint. The nostrils are broad, but the nose is not flattened, like that of the African. The mouth is not well formed, the lips projecting slightly; and it is always disfigured according to our notions of beauty, by the universal and disgusting habit of chewing areca-nut. The hair is jet black, stiff, and coarse, almost bristly, and is worn in a tuft on the top of the head, about four inches in diameter, the rest being shaved, or clipped very close. A few scattered hairs, which scarcely merit the name of beard, grow upon the chin and upper lip, which they customarily pluck out.

The occipital portion of the head is nearly vertical, and, compared with the anterior and sincipital divisions, very small; and I remarked, what I have not seen in any other than in some ancient Peruvian skulls from Pachacamac, that the lateral halves of the head are not symmetrical. In the region of firmness, the skull is very prominent; this is remarkably true of the Talapoins.

The following measurements, with callipers, of four purely Siamese

---

* According to the measure of Mr. Crawfurd. [Author's note]

heads, may convey a more definite idea than any description I call give.

|  |  |  | Inches. |  |
|---|---|---|---|---|
| Between openings of external ears, | 5½ | 5¼ | 5½ | 5½ |
| parietal protuberances, | 6 | 6 | 6 | 5¾ |
| root of nose and occiput, or antero posterior diam. | 7 | 7¼ | 7¼ | 6¾ |
| the temporal fossæ, | 5 | 4¾ | 4¾ | 5 |
| the external angles of the eyes, | 4¾ | 4¾ | 4½ | 4¾ |
| the cheek bones, | 5½ | 5½ | 5½ | 5½ |
| the angles of the jaws, | 5½ | 4¾ | 5 | 4¾ |
| From the incisors to root of nose, | 2¾ | 3 | 2¾ | 2¾ |
| the chin to root of nose, | 4½ | 5 | 4½ | 4¾ |
| root of nose to the crineal line, | 3¼ | 2¾ | 3 | 2 |
| the ear to the sagittal suture, | 5¾ | 5¾ | 5¾ | 5½ |
| Facial angle, | 59° | 67° | 67° | 59° |

Though active, the Siamese are not a warlike people. The only athletic exercises I have seen them practise, in my short sojourn, were rowing and playing shuttlecock with the feet.

Half a dozen were standing in a circle of about thirty feet in diameter, equidistant from each other. The shuttlecock, or bird, was a piece of leather, with numerous feathers stuck round it, which was kept flying from side to side, being struck only by the sole or knee. I have never seen a more graceful exercise, nor one requiring more activity and suppleness of limb.

The Siamese, like all Asiatics of low latitudes, are disposed to indolence, and to the indulgence of the animal propensities, where these do not contravene their religious notions, to which however they are not scrupulously wedded. They possess an inordinate self-esteem which places them above all nations, except the Chinese, whom they acknowledge to be superior and to whom they pay occasional tribute, and the Burmahs, whom they rank as their equals. All their superfluous wealth they devote to the building of temples, to obtain what they esteem the prospective benefit of their souls. They are mean, rapacious, and cruel; and never betray any of that high-toned generosity of feeling which wins our admiration or demands our respect. In proof of their cruelty, we have only to adduce their practice of enslaving those taken in war, without regard either to age or sex; and their wantonly barbarous treatment of the unfortunate King of Laos and his family, who were brought to Bankok in a cage, exhibited like criminals, and exposed to the rudeness of an ignorant and savage populace.* They are suspicious, vacillating, and procrastinating, and destitute of those principles of honour which give stability to society in the Christian world; the law which consigns the person of the debtor to slavery and stripes at the will of the creditor, has its origin in these traits of character. Cringing and servile to their superiors in the extreme, they are arrogant, haughty, and tyrannical in regard to those who are below them in rank. Though humble to the dust to their great men, in our presence, and with whom our intercourse was on terms of perfect equality, when no Siamese of distinction was present, they conducted themselves towards us with a hauteur bordering on insolence. They never manifested the slightest sign of respect, but crowded upon us at all times, when not kept off by reproof or by forcible means; and, had we not been looked on somewhat in the light of the King's guests, I question whether our treatment generally would have been tolerable, unless the hope of gaining something from us had purchased a more seemly entertainment. They were constantly begging for whatever they saw, with most shameless effrontery, not in the least abashed by the most contemptuous refusal.

Their virtues and their vices are venal; the services of the judge and the assassin are equally purchasable at a very moderate price, but will always be sold to the highest bidder of the contending parties, and they deem themselves fortunate, if by any chance they obtain fees from both sides.

The only commendable quality of the Siamese character, so far as I could learn, is their filial respect, which is kept up through life with all the punctilious exactness which characterizes it in infancy. The son never stands in the presence of either parent, nor assumes a seat on a level with his father. Even his Magnificent Majesty humiliates himself once a month, and appears before his mother on his knees and elbows. The Queen dowager and the chief of the Talapoins are the only two individuals in Siam who have no superiors.

Like all ignorant and uneducated people, they are superstitious. Without referring to a belief in ghosts, witchcraft, lucky and unlucky days, this trait is amusingly observed in their mode of detecting a thief. A gentleman, who has been long a resident at Bankok, related to me the following anecdote.

---

* Gutzaff's Voyages. Toumlin's Residence in Siam. Abeel's residence in China and the neighbouring countries. [Author's note, sic]

An individual lost from his apartment two bars of gold. Immediately on missing them, all those persons suspected of the theft were called together, and a conjurer summoned to declare who was the guilty individual. He came provided with several square bars of a metallic appearance, six or seven inches long, and thick as the little finger, which on examination proved to be of a species of clay. He charged each person with the theft, and asked individually whether any among them knew any thing of the gold, and was answered in the negative. He then lighted a small wax candle, and stuck upon each side of it a ticâl, obtained from the man who had lost the gold, and, muttering an invocation or spell, took a piece of clay and three times very ceremoniously raised it above his head. Then measuring it very carefully by the little finger, he broke it into pieces an inch and a half long, and gave to each suspected person three of them, which they were directed to chew as fast as possible, and prove their innocence by spitting, when the mastication was complete. All set to work chewing, and soon all were trying to spit; and as upon the success of the effort depends the innocence or guilt of the accused in the opinion of the Siamese, the scene may be readily imagined. In this case there were ten attempting to spit, and at last, after much labour, all succeeded, except a girl of fifteen, who was finally pronounced guilty; and the conjurer with the candle and ticâls walked off in triumph.

The test by clay is so much in favour, that, upon this ordeal alone, persons are often heavily ironed, and daily flogged, until they confess, or the stolen property be returned. In the present instance, the poor girl received only a promise of such treatment, and probably owes her escape altogether to the proverbial faithlessness of the Siamese to their words.

# [6]

# VOLUME II, CHAPTER III

PUBLIC VISITS—SIAMESE BADGES OF NOBILITY—VISIT OF THE PHYA-RATSA-PA-VADE—DWELLING OF THE SECOND MINISTER— A SIAMESE HAREM—DR. BRADLEY—SIAMESE LADIES—VISIT TO THE PHYA-SI-PI-PAT—DRAMATIC EXHIBITION.

*April, 1836.*

ON returning from our visit to Momfanoi, we found Mr. Roberts preparing to visit a distinguished officer of the Government, entitled, Phya-Ratsa-pa-vade.[28] Desirous of conforming as much as possible to the Customs of the East, on all occasions while in Siam, we were careful to appear with as much pomp and circumstance as our means would admit, and made all public visits in full dress, preceded by our band. We marched along the narrow streets to a military air, followed by a crowd, but observed none to crouch before us, as they are wont to do in the presence of the tea-kettled nobility of the magnificent kingdom of Thai.

A few minutes brought us to the dwelling of the "big officer," as the worthy captain of the port was pleased to call him. It is a large building of one story, enclosed in a spacious yard; and the centre of the front opens upon a broad veranda, exposing a hall of eighty by forty feet, the lofty ceiling of which is supported by numerous wooden columns. The floor is elevated about four feet above the ground, and was covered with mats. The hall was furnished with chairs, tables and Chinese mirrors, and many lamps hung from the ceiling. Close to the middle of the back wall reclined the great man on a däis, clothed in a silk sarong. Before him, on the däis, were his patents of nobility and badges of offices, consisting of a tea-kettle, chunam box, spittoons, and drinking-cup, all of pure gold. To his left lay crouched on the ground a fan-bearer and a sword-bearer, and on either hand were his numerous slaves and inferior officers.

Instead of looking at the dress of a Siamese to estimate his rank, it is necessary to cast the eye upon the slave following him, who bears

---

[28] Phya Ratchapawadi was apparently an official of the *phra khlang*.

upon a tray the badge which designates his master's rank. Tea-kettles of gold and silver, plain or ornamented, are patents of the highest grades of nobility, and are presented by the King as commissions of office.

A row of chairs stood beneath the veranda, facing the Phya-Ratsa-pa-vade, for our accommodation, to which we were showed by Piadadè who acted as interpreter. He bent down upon his elbows and knees, and crawled in the most abject manner to a spot halfway between us and our host, and there remained during the interview.

At the foot of each one of the pillars of the front row, were spittoons and quivers of cigars, placed on low stools. The doors leading to the inner apartments were concealed by silk screens. A crowd of naked rabble was in the yard, and another beyond the wall, gazing upon us to gratify their idle curiosity.

The scene was opened by the son of the General, who received us on our landing at Bankok. Dressed in his gaudy uniform and cocked hat, he crawled along at our feet, on his knees and one hand, as well as he might, offering cigars with the other to each of us as he passed: he then returned in the same manner with a lighted candle and paper matches.

A few commonplace questions were asked and answered through Piadadè, who made a salam at the beginning and end of every sentence. After a few minutes the Ratsa-pa-vade asked whether our quarters and situation were agreeable, and hoped we would waive all ceremony and make ourselves quite at ease. Tables loaded with fruits and sweetmeats of various kinds were now wheeled up before us, and during the interview tea without sugar or milk was served several times.

At the request of the Ratsa-pa-vade, our band played several airs, which, he was pleased to say, was the best music he had ever heard. At the end of half an hour we took leave by shaking hands, and returned in the order we came. Very soon after reaching the house, several slaves arrived laden with fruit presented by the officer we had just visited. It is an invariable custom in Siam to send presents immediately, by way of showing that the visit has been acceptable.

Early on the following morning, Ramòn, whom the reader may recollect as one of our interpreters at Paknam, requested me in the name of Phya-pi-pat-kosa,[29] familiarly known among foreigners as the

---

[29] Roberts specifies that it is the Portuguese who call Phya Pipat Kosa the second *phra khlang*. Crawfurd also mentions the office holder.

second minister, to visit him professionally. I appointed ten o'clock, and a little before that hour Ramòn appeared and announced that he was ready. Accompanied by a friend, I took my place in the Phya-pi-pat-kosa's sampan or gondola, rowed by seven men, and crossing the busy river, we entered a canal and pursued its course for nearly a mile, threading our way amidst boats of every description. Moored along the banks were many large sampans, with semi-cylindrical roofs, which were occupied as their permanent residence by large families. Some were salt-shops, and others were stored with earthenware. The people were nearly naked, and though wanting the dignity, they apparently possessed the ease desired by the poet. Some were whiling away time by industriously examining the bristly hair of each others' crowns. Many were swimming in the water. Fishermen with baskets slung upon their backs to hold whatever they might catch, were wading about waist deep, net in hand.

The scene was attractive from its novelty, and we wondered how so many people could exist in so small a space. They were wretchedly filthy in appearance, and so disgusting that we felt no regret at leaving the place.

The sampan stopped at the foot of a rude staircase, by which we mounted on the bank, and entered a large yard through an ornamented gateway. Within stood the dwelling of the second minister. This is extensive, but like most of the houses in Bankok, only one story high. The front presents an open hall with painted walls and carved joists, gaudy as the unsubstantial show of theatrical scenery. In this hall we were requested to remain; Ramòn disappeared behind a screen, and did not return before we had had time leisurely to examine the apartment. It had three sides, the front being open and supported by pillars of teak-wood, and protected from the weather by a great mat, swinging like a shutter from the eaves. The only furniture it contained was the dais or low table, upon which the great men of Siam recline when they receive their guests. Several slaves were lazily dusting and sweeping the mats upon the floor.

From the side of the screen Ramòn shortly afterwards beckoned us, and we passed through an inner court, upon which opened an apartment similar to that we had left, except that it was neither so neat nor so much ornamented. Here the Phya-pi-pat-kosa, a short stout man, with a round good-humoured face, clothed in a sarong of crimson silk, reclined upon a däis, in the midst of his family. Twenty of his wives were seated round *à la Turque*, with perhaps as many children. A female, resting on her knees, about two yards from the dais was fanning the minister. Thus we were introduced unexpectedly into a Siamese harem. The ladies were the fairest among their countrywomen that I had the good fortune to see; and I may add, they were graceful in their manners. They were all dressed alike, in silk drawers gathered full about the waist and ankles, and had a narrow scarf of black Canton crape thrown carelessly over their shoulders, which very partially and fitfully concealed the bosom. Their arms which were bare were folded across the chest, showing long taper[ing] fingers, which appeared longer on account of the long-trained nails. They sat silent with their eyes cast down.

The children were running about entirely naked, with the exception of one little girl of six or seven, years old, who wore a golden fig-leaf, supported by a heavy chain around her hips. This child was more grave than the rest, and stood, during the interview, with one finger in her little mouth, gazing at us strangers in wonder.

The Phya-pi-pat-kosa stood erect on the dais, and shaking us cordially by the hand, requested us to be seated on its edge along with him. Ramòn lay extended on his knees and elbows, salaming according to custom. The son of our host, a young man of twenty-two, was kneeling in the court, which was lower than the apartment, supporting his arms and chest against the floor of the hall.

Tea was immediately brought, and the minister stated, that he wished me to see his niece, whom he had caused to be brought in from the country for this purpose. She was spoken to, and my attention was called to a female of fair proportions, whose arm and hand a statuary might consider as a model, who, in a squat position, managed to move along the matted floor. Her features were regular, and countenance attractive, but a glance showed me that her situation scarcely admitted relief at my hands. She was totally blind, and had been so for nine years. I presumed her age to be twenty, but her uncle assured me it was twenty-seven. I asked him if she were married, whereupon he laughed heartily, saying, "Who would marry a woman without eyes?" which caused a general titter among all the ladies. I explained to the patient, that an operation might be successful in restoring sight, but it was doubtful; and at any rate that my short stay would prevent me from making any attempt. I therefore recommended her to take the advice of Dr. Bradley,[30] a resident American missionary at Bankok, who is daily employed in acts of benevolent usefulness in behalf of the Siamese. There was a sigh of disappointment, but not a word escaped the patient.

The minister next brought forward a child of two years old, labouring under a curvature of the spine, and inquired whether the deformity could be relieved. As in the first case, I referred him to Dr. Bradley. He appeared to be very fond of his children, to judge in the manner in which he caressed them.

Ramòn, having witnessed some of my phrenological examinations, related what he had seen to the Phya-pi-pat-kosa, whose curiosity was awakened, and he requested me to state the character of his son. In this instance, the father declared my remarks were correct and when I expressed an opinion that the young man was fond of female society, the ladies shouted in approbation.

The interview lasted nearly two hours, during which tea, fruit, sweatmeats and cigars were served. I remarked, that it was considered indecorous and impolite to smoke tobacco in the presence of ladies. "With us," replied the gay minister, "on the contrary, it is the sign of friendship, for your enemy will never allow you to smoke in his face." We now took leave of the "big officer," who shook us most socially by the hand, and invited us to repeat our visit.

Ladies of the better ranks are not actually excluded from sight, but strangers are very rarely permitted to see them. They are much more comely and of a lighter complexion than those commonly met with abroad.

We returned by the same route that we had come, Ramòn all the way lauding the minister for his goodness, wealth and wisdom.

In the afternoon we made a visit to the Phya-si-pi-pat,[31] who is acting for his brother, the Phra Klang, or minister of foreign affairs, now absent at Chantibun.

Just at sunset we landed from our several boats near the house of the first minister, where the band had been stationed to receive us. Along

---

[30] Dan Beach Bradley was the most famous of all American missionaries in Siam. Among other things, he introduced printing into the country, ran its first broadsheet, and initiated vaccination against smallpox.

[31] Ruschenberger correctly says 'the Phya Sipipat': this was a post, as Roberts confirms, held by the brother of the current *phra khlang*.

the narrow street as far as the house, there was a crowd of Siamese squatting and gazing upon us in wonder, as we marched on preceded by the music. We found the courtyard quite as crowded as the street. From it we were conducted into a lofty and extensive hall, two sides of which were a series of doors, opening upon surrounding verandas. On the right was a par-tition, or screen, covered with Chinese paintings, and Siamese arms; and to the left was a table, handsomely spread in the European style with fruits, sweetmeats, and wines. Along the wall in front of us, were three däis covered with Persian rugs, and there was a carpet on the floor. The pillars supporting the roof resembled polished marble, but were of wood covered with chunam. The Phya-si-pi-pat reclined on the first däis. He was a fat man, of about fifty, in a sarong of silk. A square pillow of crimson silk, embroidered in gold, supported his right side; and the right arm was extended straight over the edge of the däis, while the left hand grasped the sole of the right foot, which was turned upwards. The left leg was sufficiently bent to allow the sole to rest upon the rug. In front of him, on the däis were a large bowl of water with a cup floating in it, a spittoon, an arecanut and a chunam box, all of gold, and all surmounted by conical covers of crimson paper, figured with gold, together with a gold enamelled tea-kettle, china tea-pot, and gold quivers for cigars, the distinguished badges and patents of his nobility. A sword-bearer knelt upon his left, bearing a two-handed sword, cased in a crimson velvet scabbard, the hilt of which was set with brilliants; and beside him crouched a fan-bearer, exercising the functions of his office.

SIAMESE LADY.

On the next däis was the Phya-pi-pat-kosa, and next to him, another officer of less rank, both attired, and surrounded by the insignia of their respective ranks, agreeing, however, in character with those of the Phya-si-pi-pat.

The hall was illuminated by lamps suspended from the walls and ceiling, reflected by numberless small mirrors. Our band was still playing. A crowd of naked spectators stood outside, and about the floor crouched the numerous menials and inferior officers of the ministers. When we had entered a few steps, the Phya-si-pi-pat stood up on the däis, shook us individually by the hand, and motioned us to seats at the table. As we sat down, the music ceased, and the minister resumed his eastern position. A few observations, such as are common on such occasions, were made by Mr. Roberts and the Phya-si-pi-pat.

In a few minutes tea and coffee were served, and then wine. Mr. Roberts proposed, "The health of the King of Siam and his ministers," which was drunk standing, and followed by three cheers, no doubt much to the astonishment of the worthy natives present. Immediately afterwards he gave, "The President of the United States," which was drunk with two cheers; this was universally disapproved of by the officers, because it looked like yielding a degree of rank, and had the toast been distinctly heard, I doubt whether it would not have received a third cheer. After the wine, cocoa-nuts with the tops off, containing parched nuts, which add much to the flavour of the milk, and obviate the unpleasant effect which this beverage occasionally has upon the health, were served.

In a short time the company was scattered through the hall in groups, viewing whatever struck them as worthy of admiration, or conversing with the officers on their several däis. My friend, the Phya-pi-pat-kosa, recognised me by many smiles, and sent me a cup of tea from his own tea-kettle. He asked many questions relative to health, &c., and complained of pains in his knees, which were hard. The knees and elbows of the Siamese, from constantly kneeling, and crouching in the presence of superiors, are hardened like the soles of those persons who go habitually barefoot. This I found to be very common among people of all grades here. When we took leave, he shook my hand in both his; and then, in spite of my teeth, pushed his thumb and finger into my mouth, and there deposited a bolus of spices of most agreeable flavour.

The Phya-si-pi-pat was curious in examining the officers' swords, and by way of contrast exhibited his sword of state; but he appeared much disturbed when one of the officers drew the blade half out of the scabbard, it being contrary to Siamese etiquette to have naked weapons in the presence of nobles or great men.

When the Prince Momfanoi was on board, he was very particular in the examination of our great guns. In the course of the evening the Phya-si-pi-pat requested that one of them might be sent up to Bankok to look at, as they wished to mount some of their own after the same manner. The weight of a thirty-two pounder was, in their opinion, not the slightest objection to granting the request; and though a model was promised, which was afterwards sent, they did not seem to think us obliging.

As a mark of attention, and to testify their gratification upon the occasion of our visit, the minister proposed to entertain us with a dramatic exhibition, and requested to know whether we would like a long or a short play; one of an hour, or one of two, three, or four hours; and we pronounced in favour of the long one.

At the end of two hours we took leave; and, issuing out of the house, we found an open way from the door to the street, through a crowd of squatting Siamese, lighted by torches of sweet-smelling agila wood. Similar torches were held, a few feet apart, all the way to the boats, producing a novel scene, by their dappling light.

A large present of fruit followed us home.

# VOLUME II CHAPTER IV

AMERICAN MISSIONARIES—THEIR DISINTERESTEDNESS—BENEFICIAL RESULTS OF THEIR MINISTRY—DISPENSARY OF THE MISSIONARIES—MISSIONARIES IN BANKOK—APPEARANCE OF A WAT—MECHANICS AT WORK—THE BAZAAR BY DAY AND BY NIGHT—SIAMESE THEATRICALS.

*April, 1836.*

AMONG the most agreeable hours spent at Bankok, were those passed in the society of the American missionaries.

Whatever may be our opinions relative to the soundness of the policy under which they act, we cannot fail to accord to them admiration for their devotedness to the high cause which excites and cheers them in their philanthropic labours. We see them among a race of beings, whose degraded state of knowledge and morals, and whose wretchedness and poverty, call hourly for their sympathy and charitable exertions; while the strong passion which swells every breast remains controlled in their bosoms— I mean the affection which binds every individual to his own home and hearth-stone. Deprived of friends, of congenial society, of many comforts and all the luxuries or life—we behold them, still cheerfully toiling in a cause, the success of which appears to be almost hopeless, at least the most sanguine now living cannot expect to see it. While they contend against all these chilling circumstances, they are surveyed and watched by the eyes of individuals whose interests are opposed to the diffusion of knowledge, and the advancement of virtue and religion. These persons, often their own countrymen, are found in the ranks of the ignorant political rulers, encouraging them to persist in their ignorance, and even to curtail the few privileges which the missionaries may have already gained. I am not aware that this is the case in Siam, but in other parts of the world this is generally true. They misconstrue their motives, and most maliciously distort and misrepresent their acts and words. These persons certainly have not calmly investigated the subject, or they cannot be aware that they are standing in their own light. They will not believe that the march of the Christian religion will always be followed closely by intelligence and increase of commerce.

However my opinions may be swayed by philanthropic views, without discussing the question of its intrinsic necessity on the score of religion, I would encourage the Christian missions in all Asia, Polynesia, and indeed in all the world, because I think it is sound policy. By the introduction of the Christian religion, commerce must be benefited. Merchants, upon a candid investigation of the subject, will probably find their interest in doing all they can in behalf of those pious individuals, who sacrifice the honours of this world, in earning a glorious crown in the next, by attempting to put misbelievers in the path to sound morals, true religion and rational liberty.

To what extent the American trade in the East would be augmented by the conversion to Christianity of Siam, Cochin-China, China, and Japan, it is impossible to conjecture. When the half-naked millions of Asia shall attain Christianity, and with it, all the new wants which the necessary change in their social condition will produce, the soil of America, rich and vast as it is, will be scarcely adequate to supply them. A new and extensive mart must be opened for manufactures of the United States of all kinds, and even literary men will find an increased demand for their labours. Hundreds of ships will spread their sails to the eastward of the Cape of Good Hope, destined for the shores of Asia and the isles scattered in the Southern Ocean, and Commerce will pour her wealth, gathered in the Old World, into the lap of the New.

Dr. Bradley assisted by his wife dispenses medical advice and medicines daily, to at least one hundred afflicted Siamese. I spent several hours at their dispensary, and left them with feelings of admiration and respect for individuals, who appeared more in the light of ministering angels of beneficence, than in that of human beings. When I contrasted their present situation with what it must have been in the United States, and viewed their active and incessant labours in behalf of objects more calculated to excite disgust than call forth active pity, the risk of health and life they were daily incurring, I could not help suspecting them of acting under the influence of an enthusiastic zeal, tending rather to retard than advance their cause. Their efforts are too strong, and must defeat themselves: a more leisurely and cautious manner for the first few years at least, ought to be pursued. Of the truth of this opinion they are inclined to be convinced, but say, "How can we thrust away from us the afflicted who hourly petition our relieving charity?" They are aware that their own unaclimated constitutions are incapable of long enduring so much fatigue: they know from experience, that over zeal has been a rock upon which many bright prospects of the cause have been wrecked: they know that steady perseverance is likely to achieve more in this, as in every thing else, than interrupted efforts however strong; yet they pursue the impolitic course, unable to repress the ardent desire of doing good, notwithstanding that "doing good every day" is contrary to the laws of the land.

I accompanied Dr. and Mrs. Bradley from their humble dwelling, where they have all the little comforts which circumstances allow, to the dispensary, a small floating house on the river. The voyage was made in a sampan of the commonest kind, without shelter from a blazing sun.

We found nearly a hundred individuals crowded under the little veranda, and many, still in their boats, awaiting the doctor's arrival. Among the number was a considerable proportion of Talapoins in their yellow robes, and I thought all manifested pleasure at our coming.

The males on the veranda were separated, but a stranger would be unable to distinguish the sexes by their features, and, being aware of this, the doctor very kindly said, "These are the females, and those the males." The front of the dispensary is divided into two apartments. One of these is occupied by Mrs. Bradley, who dispenses prescriptions to the women, and, where the treatment of a case is continuous, manages the detail, thus leaving Dr. Bradley more time to bestow on new or more urgent cases. In every instance, the prescription is written on a slip of paper, upon the reverse of which is a text from Scripture in Siamese, and the patients have acquired the notion that this is an important part of the treatment. Whether this plan of disseminating the Scriptures be a feasible one I question; seeming very much like exhibiting chippings from the sculptor's chisel as a sample of a fine piece of statuary, or a brick as a specimen of architectural structure. Besides, it may lead to the impression that these texts are essential to the cure of disease.

I spent several hours here, and witnessed many specimens of disease, which I had never before seen; particularly a variety of the affections of the skin which are scarcely known in our country. The diseases of the eye are very numerous, which may possibly arise from constant exposure in the low sampans to the reflected glare of the sun from the surface of the river. Ulcers of various kinds abound.

I took leave of this scene, and left my best wishes for the philanthropic individuals who are instruments of almost incalculable charity.

On Sunday, the Rev. Charles Robinson delivers a sermon at the dispensary, in Siamese, which is attended by from one hundred to a hundred and twenty persons.

On one occasion, I passed nearly a day at the residence of the Rev. Messrs. C. Robinson and W. Dean, and feel indebted to them for their kindness and attention in showing me many things of interest, as well as for giving me much information. Mrs. Robinson will long be remembered by us with pleasure.

Mr. Dean devotes every afternoon to patients, prescribing for from forty to fifty Chinese, many of whom are sailors from the junks trading here, and on Sundays he preaches to a small congregation in Chinese. He has charge of the Chinese church, consisting of five members, three of whom he baptized. Besides the afternoon patients, he dispenses medicines to about a hundred individuals during the week. Professing but a limited knowledge of the healing art, his most difficult cases are referred to Dr. Bradley.

Some idea of the extensive field of his labours among the Chinese in Bankok may be derived from the following facts: The Chinese population of the city in 1836 was 400,000;[32] and from thirty to eighty junks, with crews numbering from twenty to one hundred and thirty each, annually visit the port, and remain from February till May or June, arriving in one monsoon and returning in the other. They are chiefly from the island of Hainan, Canton, and Leang-hâe; but their crews, as well as a majority of the Chinese residents of the city, speak the dialect Teo-chew, their native place, a subdivision of the Canton province.

Those who have laboured here, among the Chinese as missionaries are, Gutzlaff, Tomlin, Abeel, Johnson, and Dean; the latter arrived in July 1835, and is the only one now at Bankok.

Two or three schools have been begun here for Chinese children, and one is now in operation; but there is much difficulty in originating and sustaining them, for the reason that the children of the Chinaman here have Siamese, Burman, Laos, and other country women for mothers, whose prejudices are even stronger than those of the Chinese themselves.

The missionaries whose labours are exercised in behalf of the

---

[32] This increase has already been noted in the present chapter 4, though it is hard to credit.

Siamese are the Rev. T. R. Jones, the Rev. Charles Robinson, and Dr. D. B. Bradley. Mr. Jones has prepared some tracts in Siamese and has commenced the translation of the Sacred Scriptures. He is at present at Singapore, on account of the health of his family, but is expected to return soon.

The residence of the missionaries was moved, soon after their arrival, to its present place, by the Siamese authorities, because, as it was asserted, they were too near the residence of His Magnificent Majesty, who once a year passed that way. Besides, the missionaries were doing good every day, and thereby obtaining too much merit, which was contrary to law, His Magnificent Majesty himself not being allowed to "do good" for more than ten days successively.

The missionaries are not certain of permission to remain, for the Siamese are suspicious, and confine them strictly to the city. They applied for leave to visit the ancient capital of Yut'hia, a hundred miles up the river,[33] but were denied. Dr. Bradley visited Chantibun, and on his return made a chart or plan of the river; while copying it his teacher constantly expressed apprehension of being detected in the act, and thereby of incurring punishment. They have never had an audience with the King, and the request of Mr. Roberts in their behalf was denied.[34]

Among other matters of interest showed to us by the missionaries were several Siamese books. They consist of a long sheet folded alternately right and left, and some of them are ornamented with paintings, very much after the fashion of illuminated manuscripts, but far inferior in the style of execution. The reader sits on the ground it *à la Turque*, and unfolds the book before him.

Of the Roman Catholic missionaries I learned nothing.[35]

Soon after sunrise one morning we entered our sampan with Ramòn, and set off for the Bazaar. In our way along the river we met a number of Talapoins in small canoes, some of them containing two or three, collecting alms. It strongly reminded me of the beggars I have seen about the kitchen entrances of large hotels, receiving the broken meats of the previous day. The priests of the great Guatama are a filthy race;

---

[33] Ayutthaya is 76 km to the north of Bangkok. or just under 50 miles.

[34] Roberts makes no mention of this, and it may have been one of the items in his report which was suppressed.

[35] Ruschenberger clearly made no effort to find out. His prejudices in religion are as strong as those concerning race.

often the robes upon their backs were not yellow as they should be, and we may truly say, *ni perro, ni gato del mismo color*[36] could possibly be found.

At this hour the scene on the river is not so busy as later in the day. The Siamese find it more agreeable, on account of the heat of the climate, to pass the night, or a great part of it, in visiting and transacting business, The King usually holds his cabinet councils between sunset and midnight.

We turned into a canal, thronged with boats, among which our gondoliers threaded their way with a skill that at once surprised and pleased us. It is impossible to convey an idea of this singular scene. We landed in front of a wât, whose enamelled roof and gilded spire were glittering in the morning sun. The architecture is peculiar; particularly the roof, which in form may be compared to three saddles, placed one on the top of the other, diminishing in size from the lowest to the top. The effect is more pleasing than would be imagined, and, from the costliness of the structure, we might infer that religious feeling is very strong in the bosoms of the Siamese.

We passed over one of the high narrow bridges, resembling more what we might expect to find in the wilds of the western world, than a bridge in a metropolis numbering a population of half a million. It consisted of a rough plank, only wide enough for one person to walk upon, supported on lofty posts driven into each side of the stream. In our excursions along the canal we often passed under similar bridges, many of them fifteen or twenty feet above our heads.

After crossing the bridge we found ourselves before a row of huts, occupied by Chinese blacksmiths, who were seated beside their anvils, at work; not, however, wielding the huge sledge, with brawny arm, after the fashion of our own vulcans. Throughout the East, the mechanics are seen seated at their various labours. The carpenter, the tailor, the blacksmith, and the votary of St. Crispin[37] alike ply their tools, seated on the ground. The feet of the carpenter are as often employed as a vice, in holding the wood upon which be is working, as

---

[36] (Spanish): neither a dog nor a cat of the same colour.

[37] St Crispin and his brother St Crispinian died either in Rome or Soissons, France, about AD 286. They were born into a noble Roman family, travelled to Soissons, made converts to Christianity, and supported themselves by making shoes. The Emperor Maximian had them beheaded. Their feast day is 25 October and was much celebrated in the Middle Ages; in England it was also the day commemorating the battle of Agincourt in 1415.

his hands by the plane.

Just at this spot there was a crowd of fishing-boats, their bows wedging into the shore, and a noisy assemblage of men and women receiving into their baskets quantities of fine fish, all alive. The scene was enlivened by loud exclamation and vituperation, aided by the squalling of children and the barking of lank curs, that testified their displeasure by snarling and growling wherever we appeared. Why is it that fishermen and fishwomen, all over the world, are so given to vociferation?

The walk we were in, along a canal, terminated in a street about twenty feet wide, crossed at right angles, forming the bazaar, which is at least a mile in length. It is paved with large square bricks, which were now covered with slimy ooze. On either side were shops or stalls, five or six of one kind in a row, alternating with as many more of a different description. Here were five or six tailors' shops, and next as many stalls hung with fat pork; opposite were confectioners, and next them poulterers, the latter passing their time, seated on the ground, picking the pin feathers from dead fowls, with tweezers, making them look very clean, and much better than the plan of singeing followed by our cooks. Next were vegetables and fruits; and then, perhaps, shops filled with dried ducks, prepared for the use of Chinese seamen. The street was alive with people: fishermen with their kicking fish, and water-carriers with jars of water, slung from the ends of a bamboo over the shoulders: the purchasers, with their purchases and bags of cowries, all moving in heterogeneous streams, mingling and changing every moment, as they advanced in opposite directions. The hum of the multitude rose on the otherwise still air, and the curs barking at us, broke the monotony wherever we went. Then there was the disgust of naked bodies, shining in greasy perspiration, to detract from any thing like romance, with which the imagination might have clothed the scene.

At intervals of two or three hundred yards, the thoroughfare was partly interrupted by a sort of stage, eight or ten feet high, erected in the middle of it, for the exhibition of dramatic spectacles.

Having seen the Bazaar by day, we now paid it a visit at night. We found it much less crowded. Around the stages were knots of individuals, enjoying puppet-shows and a sort of diorama,[38] exhibited by

---

[38] A diorama was most commonly a small representation of a scene with three dimensional figures viewed through a window.

Chinese. The gambling-houses were open; and in front of them were spread tables, around which people were assembled, venturing their cowries, fu-angs, and ticâls, on the throw of the dice, or turning of the cards, by the light of numerous copper lamps, fed with cocoa-nut oil.

It is probable that similar scenes are witnessed in the towns of the Celestial Empire; for we may suppose from the great proportion of Chinese in the city, that they have imposed their own manners and customs upon the people, and something of their own style upon the character of the architecture of Bankok.

On Sunday morning the Phya-si-pi-pat informed us, by an officer, that, if it would be agreeable to us, we might that evening witness at his house a Siamese play. At once adopting the maxim *à Rome comme à Rome*,[39] the invitation was accepted.

About seven o'clock P.M. we proceeded, as on the former occasion, and, following our band, marched from the landing-place through a crowd of naked, squatting natives, lighted by great torches, and entered a court-yard, which was filled with people in similar primitive costume.

We were conducted to a large apartment, the floor of which was broken into three broad steps, and open upon a court, the front being supported by highly polished chunamed[40] pillars. On each of the several broad steps of the floor was a row of sofas and chairs, and, on our right, when facing the court, reclined upon his dais the Phya-si-pi-pat, surrounded by all the pomp and circumstance of his high office. The dais was placed near a small door, which opened into an apartment with tapestry of crimson silk. The silk curtain which closed the door, and those which shut a small window, with gilded trellis, by its side, were drawn back; and, though there was no lamp within, we perceived, by the reflection of numerous lights suspended in the hall, several females and children, dressed in silks and glittering with jewels, peeping upon the scene. One step below his father reclined the son of the Phya-si-pi-pat.

The court below was covered with fine white matting, and except a clear space in front, presented a mass of half-naked human beings on their hands and knees. On either side, at short distances apart, arose lambent flames, which at first sight seemed to proceed from entire

---

[39] When in Rome do as Rome does.
[40] 'Chunamed': covered in polished plaster or cement.

SIAMESE MUSIC.

barrels of oil; but on closer examination they proved to be metal pans, set upon cylinders of bamboo. On the left were about twenty musicians, who began their performance the moment we entered the court. Their instruments were gongs, hautboys, and pieces of wood about a foot long, which were struck together in time with the other instruments, producing altogether a great deal more sound than melody.

The Minister received us cordially, and, on taking our seats upon the upper step on a level with him, servants crawling on their hands and knees, placed gold quivers of cigars and lighted tapers at our feet. The representation of a pantomimic drama, entitled the 'Angels' now commenced. The plot seemed to be allegorical and illustrative of some portion of Boudhist religious history.[41] The actors were accompanied in their performance by the band, and a recitative in a squeaking female voice and an occasional chorus, altogether enough 'to split the ears

---

[41] It is far more likely that an episode of the Ramayana was enacted.

# Part II: The Ratification Mission of 1836

of the groundlings.'[42]

The first scene presented two individuals in close red jackets, which fitted the shape to the hips, where they were joined to short full skirts.

They wore masks, and conical caps terminating in a spire two feet high, ornamented with a profusion of tinsel and paint. Besides, they had long metallic-looking nails; in short, they were representing mongrel monkeys. Their first act on entering upon the stage, from a door to the right, was to prostrate themselves before the Phya-si-pi-pat and touch the ground with their heads. Then they enacted a series of antics in the slow time of the minuet, occasionally throwing side somersets[43] rapidly, and again knocking heads. At last they sat down, one on each side of the court, and were succeeded by twelve others, much more gaudily dressed, but in a similar fashion. One half represented ladies, and the other knights; and, if the drama has any influence upon taste in Siam, long fingernails are considered a mark of great elegance among the beauties of the capital; for those of the actresses were elongated and turned backwards, by metal appendages,

SIAMESE ACTOR AND ACTRESS

---

[42] The groundlings were spectators, usually low class.
[43] Somersaults, turning head over heels.

at least three inches in length.

These knights and ladies ranged themselves in two lines, confronting each other, as in a contra-dance, and, in time to the slow music, assumed various attitudes, some of which were very graceful. They now promenaded in circle and then changed places, the knights touching the ladies' hands, with due regard to their long nails, constantly manifesting by gesticulation their all-consuming love, which however the ladies were slow to accept. At the end of an hour they took seats *à la Turque* on opposite sides of the stage, to give place to a gallant knight, who, from the energy of his gesture, enacted the part of a challenger. After he had raved his time upon the stage, the ladies and knights again minueted for an hour, and again gave place. A lady now entered followed by a knight in a black mask, from whose pursuit she was flying. Whenever he approached she screamed and very gracefully eluded his grasp. They disappeared. The minuet of twelve was again performed, and, upon resuming their seats, a lighter female figure than any which had yet appeared, and more gaudily attired, entered bearing between her fingers a sparkling ball. She was the angel of light. The black mask soon pursued her, but the sparkling ball had talismanic powers, and he quailed before its flashing light, whenever he approached too near. After essaying in vain against the powers of the talisman, the black knight was encountered by the challenger. Both were armed with short swords. After strutting and motioning defiance at each other for half an hour, while the recitative became more squeaking, vociferating, and discordant than ever, and just as we thought their courage had oozed away, they crossed their blades. They made terrible passes at each other, but both were too cunning at fence to be soon overpowered. The challenger fell, and the black knight placed his foot upon the breast of his foe; but he struggled again to his feet, and overthrew the black mask, leaving the spectators to infer that virtue finally triumphs over vice.

The native musicians now brought their instruments in front of us and performed several airs, which were repaid by as many from our band. Their instruments are similar to those of the Javan gamelan which has been already described.[44]

---

[44] Ruschenberger and his party had earlier visited Java. In fact, Siamese musical instruments are markedly different from those in the gamelan.

Half and hour after the commencement of the play the Phya-si-pi-pat retired, offering us as an apology, the necessity of visiting His Magnificent Majesty. He had no sooner disappeared from amidst his golden badges of nobility and office, than his son filled the place.

The only refreshment offered besides cigars, during the entertainment, was water, served in basins of pure gold, and drunk from cups of the same metal.

We were heartily weary of the three hours' play, long before it was concluded, and at the proper time gladly took leave, and returned as we had come, lighted by torches.

On descending into the court, Piadadè inquired how I liked the actresses. I thought they acted well, and some of us were not a little surprised to be assured they were all males.

Most of the wealthy Siamese nobles entertain a company and a theatre in their own houses, for their private amusement, similar to that just described.

## VOLUME II, CHAPTER V

DELIVERY OF THE TREATY—SIA-YUT'HIA—HALL OF JUSTICE—PROCESSION OF ELEPHANTS—SPOTTED ELEPHANT—WAT P'HRA-SI-RATANAT—THE QUEEN'S WAT—LIBRARY—SIAMESE PRINCE AND PRINCESS—RETURN TO PAKNAM—THE GOVERNOR—DEPARTURE FROM PAKNAM—CHOLERA ON BOARD SHIP.

*April, 1836.*

THE following morning, the officers were formed into a procession headed by Mr. Roberts, two of them bearing a box, containing the American copy of the Treaty, and marched to the river, distant about a hundred yards, preceded by our band. At the place of embarkation, a canoe eighty feet long, rowed by thirty-four oars, both ends curving upwards, awaiting to receive it. A bright crimson silk canopy, embroidered in gold, overhung the centre of the canoe, with which all the ornaments of the vessel were in keeping. The rowers wore the red livery of the King.

On reaching the margin of the river Mr. Roberts took the Treaty in his hand, and, after holding it up above his head in token of respect, delivered it to a Siamese officer, the secretary of the P'hra Klang. He also held it above his head, and then, shaded by a royal chat, a large white silk umbrella, borne by a slave, passed it into the boat, where it was received upon an ornamental stand, and after covering it with a cone of gilt paper, it was placed beneath the canopy. At this moment our band ceased, and that of the Siamese began to play. The canoe shoved off, and we turned our steps homeward to the merry tune of "Yankee Doodle."

Immediately after the conclusion of this curious ceremony of delivering the Treaty, I set off, in company with several officers, for Sia-Yut'hia, the residence of the King, situated on an island about two miles from our mission house, and on the opposite side of the river. As we moved along, we saw several toys floating on the stream, which we were told, were offerings to the spirits of departed friends.

On landing outside of the wall, enclosing the palace and town, we were conducted to see a huge white elephant. He was dirty and wild, and, from being yet untamed, is called the mad elephant. Each of his legs was secured to a post driven into the ground, and he was attended by three or four slaves. The irises were white.

We now passed a gate, which was carefully closed after us, and we found ourselves in a broad street of mean houses in Sia-Yut'hia, the capital city of the magnificent kingdom of Thai. Following our conductor Ramòn, we passed a second wall enclosing a number of buildings, by no means neat in appearance. The principal one, situated in the centre of an open area, is called the Hall of Justice, and resembles an old storehouse. The hall of justice is a roof of tiles supported on stout columns of wood without walls. Horizontal shutters of coarse matting are so contrived that they may be made to exclude the rays of the sun, as they are cast either on one side or the other. The floor is raised about two feet above the ground, and was covered with mats, and along its edge were ranged several brass basins of water, with a drinking-cup of the same metal floating in each.

In the enclosure in which the hall stands, there are a number of mounted guns of heavy caliber, each protected by a kind of weather-house.

The day was oppressively hot, and we found the hall of justice an agreeable shelter from the sun. Here we met our friend Piadadè, and about a dozen Siamese. They examined us long and attentively; some of them were so curious that they laid their hands on the uniforms of some of the officers.

Soon after our arrival a considerable crowd of Siamese gathered around the hall, and presently His Highness, Prince Momfanoi, appeared seated *à la Turque*, on a palanquin, consisting simply of a platform between two poles, shaded by a silk awning supported by four staves. As he approached, the crowd fell upon their elbows and knees. He waved his hand and nodded familiarly to us as he passed, but received the salams of the prostrate hundreds without notice. He was followed by his faithful Sap, bearing the golden tea-kettle, and chunam-box, and a swordbearer. Although he continued on to another enclosure, all that part of the crowd within the range of the Prince's eye remained prostrate. I followed His Highness, and found him seated on a rude däis in company with one or two nobles, under a ruined roof of bamboo, and the widespreading branches of a large tree, which afforded them ample shade. He received us gaily, saying, "This is a better place to sit in than the King himself has got, because we have a fresh cool breeze." He was in fine spirits, and invited us to sit and take tea with him, and then a cigar.

A discordant screech of hautboys very soon announced the approaching procession, which was kindly got up for the gratification of those officers who were required to return on board ship before the presentation took place. The Prince laughed heartily, crying, "Go see, go see!", which we readily obeyed, prompted as we were by our curiosity.

A band of a dozen men in red and green uniforms, their cheeks swelled by their efforts, marched onward, closely followed by seven elephants. First came a huge black, fourteen feet high, then a large white, followed by another much smaller, and four spotted elephants of ordinary size. By the side of each walked a keeper, and several slaves bearing silver salvers, loaded with pealed sugar-cane and luscious bananas. The driver sat on the neck of each, in front of the houdah, or saddle-cloth, which was gold. Broad hoops of gold embraced each lusty leg, and jewelled rings glittered on the tusks of the white elephants; and from the ears of all of them were suspended tails of beautifully white hair.

The pageant wheeled round and halted on one side of the hall of justice. The slaves now set down their salvers before their respective elephants, and we were invited to admire and feed the animals, the possession of which, in the opinion of the Siamese, gives their King pre-eminence above every other monarch in the East.

The small elephant is the beauty of her race. She has a soft white skin, a beautiful chestnut-coloured eye, and a most complaisant manner of disposing of sugar-cane and bananas from the hand of the stranger. The other white elephant is a very much larger animal; but the skin is of a yellowish hue. Both are supposed to be animated by the transmigrated souls of Siamese monarchs.

The spotted elephants are all large. With the exception of the ears and shoulders, which are speckled rather than spotted, their colour is dark and uniform. The forehead of each animal is painted black, the outline of which is white, and traces the form of a headcloth.

The careful keeping and strict attention bestowed on these elephants, show how highly they are prized. The minute examination and admiration of our party gave visible satisfaction to the keepers, as well as to the crouching multitude around. When we turned away, the procession was again formed, and marched off in the direction in which it had come.

## Part II: The Ratification Mission of 1836

GATEWAY OF THE OLD PALACE

At the request of Piadadè, we now followed him about a hundred yards, and, passing through a gate, found ourselves in the Wât-P'hra-si-ratanat,[45] or great temple of the King. Here we were bewildered and dazzled by the splendour of gilt obelisks and temples sparkling in the sun. We stood under a broad corridor, surrounding the whole area, the sides of which are certainly not less than one hundred yards long. The pavement was chunamed, and shone like polished marble. The walls were painted with numerous quaint figures in bright colours representing events in the history of Guatama and the magnificent kingdom of Thai. How much did these walls express, had we been able to comprehend their language!

We were hurried to a great temple in the area. The walls were ingeniously inlaid with gems, and the roof and cornices were richly gilt and enamelled. We ascended a half dozen steps upon the floor of a magnificent portico. The door of ebony inlaid with ivory, stood open; but a splendid screen hid the interior of the sanctuary. We entered, and were not less dazzled with the view before us, than we had been by that of the outside walls. The ceiling was lofty and curiously carved. A large cut-glass chandelier hung from its centre, and many Chinese

---

[45] Wat Phra Si Ratana Satsadaram is the formal name of Wat Phra Keo, the Temple of the Emerald Buddha.

paintings and lamps were suspended around the walls. A subdued light disclosed the great altar of Boudha, not far from the middle of the temple. Its whole structure is of a pyramidal form, and is about thirty feet high. Two or three wax-tapers were burning at its base, and there was a rug spread before them on the floor. A large lotus-plant, at least five feet high, of virgin gold, stood upon the left. Numerous small figures of the god surrounded the richly-carved altar, which was surmounted by a figure of Boudha, two feet high, said to be cut out of a single emerald. This idol has two brilliants, flashing light through the temple, in place of eyes, which cost in Brazil 20,000 dollars. The value of the whole god is inestimable. I doubted its genuineness, but Momfanoi assured me he was positive that it was an emerald, and not a beryl, as I suggested.

We hastened from this temple to a second, smaller in size, designated I believe as the Queen's wât.[46] In our walk to it we passed many small figures, scattered through the paved area, among the beds of flowers and lotus-plants, representing elephants, horses, &c. The wât is white, and of a very chaste architecture. Within are three figures of Boudha, the past, present, and future, in white marble; one seated behind and higher than the other. They were surrounded by diamonds and gems of all kinds, suspended in festoons, in bunches, and a variety of forms.

Between the two wâts is the library[47] of sacred books, called, in the Bali language, Promodop. It is remarkable that in most religions, the priests have shut up the spirit and letter of their faith in some strange or forgotten tongue, thereby adding to its mysteries, which are always caught at by the vulgar. The exterior form of the libraries resembles the numerous 'prachadîs' or obelisks within the area of the temple. An ascent of two or three flights of stairs conducted us into a room about eighteen feet square. In the centre stood a prachadî of ebony, inlaid with ivory and mother-of-pearl, of the exact form of the exterior edifice containing it, and occupying about one-third of the area of the room, the rest of which was covered with a mat of fine silver, wrought of thin bars about a quarter of an inch wide. In this beautiful casket repose the learned dogmas of the false faith of millions.

---

[46] It is not clear which building Ruschenberger means. It may be the Phra Phuttha Ratana Sathan Monthiraram chapel.

[47] The *mondop*.

From this we strolled, almost bewildered, among beds of flowers and prachadìs, fifty in number, each ornamented by carving, figures of Boudha, and gilding. Aladdin's lamp never called up any thing comparable to the Wât-P'hra-si-ratanat in gorgeous ornament, or display of wealth in gold, in gems and in art. The greatest travellers among us declared that its beauties exceeded any thing they had before seen in any part of the world. The first glance was enough to enchant one of his senses. I wandered through the labyrinth, which is no doubt regular though cunningly planned, as one in a dream. The merry brain of a poetic beggar in a state of intoxication might possibly imagine something resembling it in character; but infinite credulity, aided by the most vivid imagination, would scarcely believe in the existence of such a place, were it described in detail; I had no definite idea of the place an hour after I left it.

There is no one thing in it grand or imposing. It bears no impress of a master genius; yet, there is nothing mean, or inelegant, or without taste. There are paintings by the best masters of the Chinese schools, there are beds of flowers; pools in the stone basins, upon which floats the sacred lotus; marble; gems of all kinds and of great price; gold in abundance; carving and inlaid work of ebony and ivory and tortoise-shell. The impression of a chaos of elegances rests upon my mind.

To have an idea of this temple it must be seen; but to comprehend its details, a month must be spent in it. It must be borne in mind that the Siamese are under the belief that their happiness in the next world will be in proportion to the honours they pay their god in this, and that this temple is the labour of successive monarchs, bigoted and zealous in their faith, who expended all their talents, and all the nation's gold in its construction.

In our last walk round the corridor we met a young prince of about fourteen. A rich sarong girded his loins, and the rest of his body was almost hidden under jewels; anklets and bracelets of gems surrounded his limbs, and chains of gold, curiously wrought, hung round his neck in profusion. A princess somewhat younger accompanied him. She wore a chased fig-leaf of gold, and stood, like mother Eve, all naked, but not alone. The complexions of these two individuals were much lighter than those of the numerous male and female servants in their train. They were the fairies of the scene. They stopped to gratify their curiosity by gazing at us, and we imitated them, and returned the compliment. We here received a message from His Magnificent Majesty, expressing his good will to us and all Americans, and a wish that we would examine and look at every thing freely, and without constraint.

We took leave of the temple, fully convinced that it is well worth visiting, but not worth a voyage from Europe or the United States to see; and, after a few minutes' conversation with the Prince, who had been all the time sitting in the shade with his noble friends, returned to our place of sojourn. Our descriptions were cautiously received by those who did not accompany us, but they afterwards declared them to be far short of the truth. For the sake of our veracity, I hope the reader will bear this in mind.

Commodore Kennedy was now taken seriously indisposed, and we learned with regret that that dreadful disease, the Asiatic cholera, had appeared on board our ship, and that a seaman, Daniel K. Thomas had fallen the first victim. Under these circumstances, I bade farewell to Bankok, and, in the morning of the 12th of April, set off with the Commodore in his gig under a glaring sun, and without a breeze.

At four o'clock P.M. we landed at Paknam, after a sultry pull of seven hours. The governor was sulky, and seemed to think that he had already seen enough of us. I charged him with insolence, and delivered him a letter from the acting P'hra Klang, enjoining him at the peril of his shoulders and head, to treat us with all the attention and hospitality in his power. He at once apologized for the reception he had given us on the plea of indisposition, and ordered supper, which was mean in the extreme, consisting of rice, fried fish, and boiled duck-eggs, all cold.

The Commodore retired to his mat, overcome by the fatigues of his journey and indisposition, and I, after insisting that a better supper should be furnished, sought repose on a bamboo settee, while His Excellency sat doggedly smoking his long pipe. He is subject to frequent corporeal castigation for his petty delinquencies, and receives the paltry salary of eighty ticals per annum; so that he literally gets "as many kicks as halfpence," though deserving many more of the former.

Before sunset a party of officers, who had left the city before us, arrived. The servants now bustled about, and spread a table, under the superintendence of an interpreter, who professed to be well skilled "in custom of Europe gentleman." He was an active, officious, half-caste Portuguese, in a dirty sarong, and a beggar withal. After the table was spread, he reviewed it very carefully, and, to give the whole a proper polish, as well its to enhance his own qualifications in our eyes, commenced wiping out the tumblers with his naked fingers, which had been last applied to scratching his own skin. He was reprimanded for this proceeding, showed much contrition for his error, and to retrieve himself, gathered pieces of waste paper, which had enveloped tobacco or cigars from the floor, and began anew to clean the soiled glasses. In spite of our disgust, we could not but laugh at his notion of "custom of Europe gentleman."

We had fallen very much in the estimation of the people of Paknam, and even the servants were disposed to be disrespectful. A young slave on being directed to bring fire to light a cigar, flung the match across the floor at my feet. With these people a positive and almost imperative manner is the most successful. If intercourse be attempted on an equal footing, they become arrogant and consequently insolent.

At daylight next day we left Paknam, and reached the ship at ten o'clock A.M., and on the same day another party of officers set out for the city.

Though a second individual had died of cholera (William Waggoner, marine), it was very satisfactory to find that the epidemic had abated. As soon as it had made its appearance on board, the ship was got underway, and kept close hauled upon a wind, and, her sides being alternately offered to the breeze, she was thus kept thoroughly ventilated. Though all the cases on the list wore the type of cholera, cold shrivelled surface with blue nails, no new case occurred, nor did any one terminate fatally after the ship was under way. The disease prevailed at Chantibun, epidemically, about a hundred miles from the anchorage, and sporadically at Bankok. No cases occurred on board of the Enterprise.

# [9]

# VOLUME II, CHAPTER VI

THE KING OF LAGOR—ENTERTAINMENT ON BOARD—SIAMESE CURIOSITY AND ETIQUETTE—MEASUREMENT OF THE BRIG—AUDIENCE WITH THE KING OF SIAM—THE PROCESSION—SIAMESE SOLDIERS—THE AUDIENCE HALL—HIS MAJESTY AND COURT—CEREMONIOUS ENTRANCE—FORM OF AUDIENCE.

*April, 1836.*

ON the 12th of April Mr. Roberts had an interview with the Rajah or King of Lagor,[48] who had been appointed by His Magnificent Majesty to settle the important matter of affixing the regal seals to the Siamese copy of the Treaty exchanging, as well as to the certificate of ratification.

The Rajah is the monarch or rather Viceroy of Lagor, a tributary state to Siam, situated on the Malay Peninsula. The object of his present visit to Bankok was to assist at a funeral ceremony, which took place eight days before our arrival. Six months ago the only legitimate son of the King died; and, according to the Siamese custom (and "old custom," with them is as binding as law) the body was embalmed, and recently committed to the funeral pile. So important was this ceremony, that all the tributary princes and governors of the empire were summoned on this occasion by His Magnificent Majesty.

On landing, Mr. Roberts was met by the King of Lagor, seated on a palanquin, consisting of a cushioned seat, borne on two poles, with his bare legs hanging down on each side. He was followed by many attendants, one of them bearing a large silk umbrella over his head. So soon as the interpreter came up, the King offered an apology for not inviting Mr. Roberts to his house, at the same time requesting his company on board of his junk. His house was merely a bamboo shed; preferring to spend his time in his own country, he will not build himself a palace as he has been urged to do, because, so long as he has none, he has always a ready excuse for making brief visits. He is short and fleshy, and possesses an agreeable countenance and polite manners. He is

---

[48] Chao Phya Sithammarat, the hereditary ruler of Ligor, now Nakhon Sithammarat, was already encountered in Roberts' text.

sixty-one years of age, an able minister and the oldest courtier in Siam.

The sword of Mr. Taylor attracted his attention, and he requested permission to examine it, and for the purpose put on his spectacles. He regretted that no business could be transacted that day, and hoped that Mr. Roberts would not be angry for causing him so much unnecessary trouble.

While on board of the junk, tea was served in earthen pots, and drunk from porcelain cups without saucers. A tea-pot and cup were placed before each person present, on a salver of pure gold, set with precious stones. Water-basins and cups, chunam-box and spittoons of fine gold, were borne on salvers of the same metal. Fruit and confectionary were presented on salvers six feet in circumference, with pedestals two feet high, of richly embossed silver. Silver spoons and forks were on the several dishes from which the company were expected to help themselves, without using a separate plate. The King was very polite, and often helped his guests with his own hands.

At eight o'clock the following morning, Mr. Roberts, accompanied by Mr. Taylor, again waited on the Rajah on board his junk. They were received by the Rajah's eldest son, a young man of twenty-two, who entertained them with tea, eggs, &c., in the same style as on the preceding day. The Rajah soon made his appearance, and stated that the royal seal of Siam could be affixed only to the certificate of ratification. Mr. Roberts replied to the preamble, that the King had promised to affix his seal to the articles of the Treaty, and he would therefore unquestionably do so; and that it was indispensably necessary to the certificate; for the Treaty could not be considered as ratified without it. After some discussion the Rajah unwillingly yielded the point, and declared that it should be completed in accordance with Mr. Roberts's wishes.

One of the secretaries requested a list of the officers who had visited the Wât-P'hra-si-ratanat a day or two previously, that it might be entered on the archives of the Government.

The curiosity excited by the officers among the Siamese was scarcely to be restrained. We were frequently felt from head to foot, and to-day the Rajah had his hands in Mr. Taylor's pockets, while at the same time his son had rolled up his pantaloons to feel his boot-leg. The Rajah, his son and two grand-children, wore round their waists, besides the sarong, cream-coloured crape shawls of beautiful texture. The Siamese, like the Chinese, wear the finger-nails very long and the ladies have them sometimes tipped with silver.

About eleven o'clock, Momfanoi accompanied by another prince and a medical practitioner,[49] on their way to visit his priestly brother, who was unwell, appeared on board. The Rajah left his seat, and knelt upon the deck during the visit, and Momfanoi assumed the vacated place. The prince was pleased to say on this occasion, that the swords, the genuineness of which had been doubted at first, as he remarked, only by "small officers," had been tested by the King's assayer, and were pronounced to be good gold. This doubt had arisen from an appearance of verdigris at a point in the brazing, and from their light colour. The Siamese use no alloy in their manufactured gold, which is very fine, and of a very deep colour, almost orange. The prince who accompanied Momfanoi, though on terms of intimacy and in the boat sitting on the same seat with him, so soon as he got on board the junk, made his obeisance in form, and took a seat a little above the Rajah. The costume of both was simple, but costly. The under garment was of purple silk with a highly embroidered edge, over which was an exquisite scarf. When they took leave, the Rajah resumed his seat.

At one o'clock P.M. a dinner consisting of soups, curries, cutlets, ducks, chickens, and pork, with fruit and sweetmeats, was served up in gold and silver. There were twenty-six dishes for three persons, and no fewer than fifty-four gold vessels were used in the entertainment. There was no ostentation or seeming attempt at display; all appeared to be a matter of everyday occurrence. The hospitable old Rajah forced upon the plates of his guests, litchis, from China and 'Romania,'[50] a fruit resembling a date. He sat quietly the while chewing his betel, but occasionally got upon the table, that he might the more readily assist and point out to his guests those articles which he himself liked most. While arranging the dishes, the servants did not hesitate to mount the table and walk about upon the cloth. Before dinner was over, Momfanoi again visited the junk, when the same ceremonies as on his first visit were enacted; and after his departure the Rajah again took his seat.

At the end of nine hours the certificate of ratification, in Siamese,

---

[49] One of these might have been Prince Wongsathirat, Chudamani's half-brother, who had studied Western medicine and gained a correspondence diploma from a medical school in Philadelphia.

[50] The fruit called 'Romania' resembling a date may be the *mayom*.

Chinese, Portuguese, and English, was ready to be appended to the Treaty. The same labour would have been performed in the United States, or Europe, in one-third of the time.

On the same evening Mr. Roberts waited on the acting P'hra Klang, to discuss a difficulty which had arisen, under the third article of the Treaty, relative to the measurement of the brig Maria Theresa. Mr. Roberts stated that the officers of the Government had measured from outside to outside of the vessel, instead of the deck. The P'hra Klang insisted that such was the manner of measuring both Siamese and Chinese junks, the decks of which extend between the timbers. Mr. Roberts remarked that the Treaty had reference only to American built vessels. The P'hra Klang replied, that it was "an old custom, and therefore could not be altered." Mr. Roberts observed, then he should recommend the captain to protest at home against the violation of the Treaty, which would be referred to the Government at Washington, and result in an unpleasant controversy between the two countries. But as nothing could be decided without reference to the King, Mr. Roberts took leave and visited him on another occasion.

The Minister appeared to be inflexible. Mr. Roberts then stated, that unless American vessels were measured in conformity to the third article of the Treaty, it would become his duty to make it known forthwith to the Government of the United States, adding, that the Captain of the Maria Theresa would certainly protest against such departure from the Treaty. During the day the brig had been measured, but Mr. Roberts had not been informed of it until after this discussion.

The captain and supercargo were now sent for, and stated that the vessel had been measured, by taking half her length, and at that point, to ascertain her breadth of beam. The deck was there measured across from one waterway seam to the other, entirely omitting the waterways, and taking in only a part of the gunwale, which mode was so favourable as to lessen the duties to the amount of 170 ticâls. The P'hra Klang asked whether they were satisfied with the mode of measurement. They replied, "Entirely so." "Then," said the P'hra Klang, "I am glad that all difficulties have been surmounted; this shall be the precedent for measuring all American vessels in future."

The sixteenth of April had been appointed, four or five days previously, for admitting the American Embassy to an audience with the King. The day was oppressively hot, the thermometer in an airy apartment standing at 98° F. It was calm, and not a breath ruffled the tranquil bosom of the river, which was like a stream of molten gold, stirred only by numerous gondolas, skimming with feathery lightness over its bright surface. Many persons had come forth to view the passing procession, and many crowded the verandas of the floating-houses, though no "Morning Herald," or "Evening Post," circulates the news through this vast population; they seemed to be aware of the event from instinct.

At nine o'clock, accompanied by twenty-two officers from the squadron in full dress, and the master and supercargo of the Maria Theresa, Mr. Roberts embarked in three gondolas, each rowed by thirty oars. Though permission had been granted for the gentlemen of the Maria Theresa, the request of Mr. Roberts in behalf of the American missionaries was refused on the ground that it was not according to the Siamese custom.

The boats proceeded at a rapid rate, our band making the still air resound with "Hail, Columbia!" and we were much surprised at the crowds of spectators who awaited our landing. Orderlies armed with rattans and bamboos, the application of which was not spared on the naked backs of the Siamese, were constantly active in making way for the procession.

On entering the first gate, they found a number of fleet ponies, caparisoned in the Eastern style, each attended by two grooms. The scene was as novel to the animals as to the American officers; and they testified their impatience by kicking their nettlesome heels merrily among the crowd. Here the procession was joined by several Arabs, Persians and Jews, in the rich costumes of their respective countries. After some little delay, arising from time occupied in selecting horses, the company mounted, the short stirrups bringing the knees almost to the chin, and made their way through the multitude to the second gate, where the officers left their swords, it being contrary to etiquette to appear armed in the presence of Siamese royalty.

They were received in the Hall of Justice by the Phya-pi-pat-kosa, who was as usual full of life and conversation. Water, betel, and cigars were offered. While waiting for the King to signify his readiness to receive them, they found time to discover a large green snake coiling itself among the tiles of the Hall, over their heads. Lizards and ge-kôs were numerous. The Siamese expressed their astonishment that such trifles should attract attention; habit makes men indifferent to the most loathsome objects.

At the second gate, files of soldiers encumbered with uniforms of red and green, and arms which they could scarcely manage, amounting to several thousands, lined the various avenues. The bayonets were fixed with the scabbards upon them. The artillery were armed with sheathed broadswords, and stood with the hand upon the hilt, ready to draw. Pikemen and clubmen also appeared in the military array. Whoever has seen at any large theatre, a grand army badly drilled, may imagine the Siamese troops, and conceive what genuine "food for powder," they would make before a handful of disciplined troops.

At this gate the band was compelled to await the return of the embassy.

At the Hall of Justice, the elephants were paraded as on a former occasion. The crowd was great, but whenever they encroached beyond bounds, they were at once severely repulsed by the rattan. At the end of half an hour, the procession again moved forward through two other gates. The number of troops were here much augmented, and near the palace was a body armed with shields and swords. On each side of the path along which the procession advanced three hundred musicians in double files were ranged, screeching out on hautboys and beating on tomtoms, producing a most percusive monotony. The walks now became broader. The eye here and there caught a glimpse of a rich building, or spire glittering in the sun, through the foliage of the trees and shubbery planted in the enclosures.

The exterior of the audience-hall is not very remarkable. It has three entrances on each side, the doorways are ornamented with carving and Boudhist divinities, and within stood screens, painted in quaint devices, which conceal the interior.

The extent of the audience-chamber is thirty-five by seventy feet. The middle of the floor, about one-half of the whole width, is raised eighteen inches above the rest, leaving a sort of lobby on each side, equal to one-fourth of the breadth of the whole room, and extending its entire length. A row or six pillars, three feet square, stood on each edge of the middle floor; and the wall, ceiling, and pillars, were hung with red gilt paper, and the floors were carpeted. Chandeliers and lamps of various patterns were suspended from the ceiling, and numerous Chinese paintings and mirrors adorned the walls. From a central point, the floor gently rises in an inclined plane up to the throne, at the farthest end of the apartment. The throne itself is about six feet high, and large enough for one man to sit upon cross-legged; it is of gold, or richly gilt, and ornamented with diamonds and other precious stones. Behind it is a piece of ornamental architecture resembling an altar. A royal chat, an umbrella having five tops, one above the other, and diminishing in size, shades the monarch's seat; and on each side, extending to the pillars, were six other chats or chattahs, arranged so as to form an arc, which separates the King and court.

Mr. Roberts and his companions entered the middle door of the front of the hall, and, passing round the screen, found themselves in the presence of His Magnificent Majesty, and the royal court of the magnificent kingdom of Thai. His Majesty, a fat man of about fifty,[51] sat like the god Boudah, cross-legged upon his throne, enveloped in a rich mantle of gold tissue, chewing betel, and squirting saliva into a golden urn. Numerous attendants prepared his betel, and with large fans circulated the air about his Majestic Obesity, as he sat in the pomp and circumstance of state.

Except a long space, eight feet wide, in front of the throne, the whole floor was covered by nobles, courtiers and magnates of the land, in silk and gold costume, the fashion of which was a long tight jacket with short skirts, somewhat resembling the cut of an ancient coat of mail. There were several Arabs and Persians present, in rich Cashmere shawl turbans, contrasting their splendid statures with the squat forms of the Siamese; and their expressive countenances, strongly marked by the jetty whisker and antimony-shaded eye, outshone them in intelligence. Perhaps three hundred individuals composed this goodly company; every one crouching upon his knees and elbows, with the head bent upon the ground. The hall only admitted a subdued light. Jewels appeared to advantage, and the diamonds and carbuncles on the King's person glittered and flashed all around like miniature lightning.

It was particularly remarked by several officers, that, notwithstanding the stipulation that our party should not appear in the presence armed, being contrary to court etiquette, many of the Siamese wore swords.

Such was the spectacle hall and court presented when the American Embassy passed the screen. There they removed their hats, and, as they advanced to the open alley above mentioned, made three bows according to previous agreement. At the lowest end of this al-

---

[51] Phra Nangklao was born in 1788 and so was 48 in 1836; he did not die until 1851.

ley, at a great distance from the throne, they sat down upon the carpet, carefully turning their feet behind, that His Magnificent Majesty might not be shocked by the sight of those lowly, booted members; for they did not consent, like the Anglo-Bengal mission under Mr. Burney, to leave their shoes outside and appear barefoot, at the risk of finding as he did, that they had been stolen.[52]

Previously to his audience with the King in 1833, when negotiating the Treaty which was now being concluded, Mr. Roberts positively refused to take off his shoes on entering the presence, except on the condition that he should keep on his hat. After a great deal of discussion, it was no longer insisted on that he should appear barefooted, and he was the first foreigner who, with his shoes on, saw His Majesty of Siam.

After being seated in this novel, and therefore somewhat uncomfortable position, they made three Siamese salams, and the whole court knocked their heads three times on the ground. His Magnificent Majesty expressed his satisfaction by squirting saliva into the golden spittoon, and renewing his quid of betel and areca-nut.

In front of the mission were displayed a part of the presents brought by Mr. Roberts, the whole being too bulky for such a pageant. Immediately after the salams were performed, a low, murmuring sound arose from behind the throne, which the interpreter stated proceeded from the King's secretary, reading the list of presents from the government of the United States to His Magnificent Majesty.

This over, the King addressed to Mr. Roberts several questions, which were filtered through three interpreters or secretaries. One crouched near the throne, and repeated in a low tone His Majesty's words to another, more than halfway down the hall, who repeated them in a still lower tone to Piadadè, the interpreter, who, being crouched near Mr. Roberts, whispered the sentence in his ear. The replies were made through the same medium in the same manner.

When the King finishes his question, the secretary makes three salams and mentions the King's titles before he repeats to the second, and he goes through the same ceremony to the third. The answer begins with three salams from the interpreter, who repeats a string of titles, "P'hra, Putie, Chucka, Ka, Rap, Si, Klau, Si, Kla, Mom, Kà P'rah

---

[52] It was Crawfurd's mission of 1822 that lost its shoes; Burney's in 1826 kept theirs, saying they would either keep their shoes or their hats; the Siamese preferred that they removed their hats. This was already mentioned in Roberts' account (Ch. 2 / XVII).

Putie Chow," Mr. Roberts, "Ka P'hra Râchâ, Tan, Krap, Thun, Hie, Sap, Thi, Fa, La, Ong, Thule, P'hra, Bat;"[53] then follows the answer and three salams. As this form is invariable, it may be readily conceived how slow and fatiguing the intercourse with His Majesty must be. Nor is one certain that his expressions or words are faithfully conveyed to the "golden ear." Mr. Robert Hunter told me, that some years ago he had an audience with the King, who inquired whether he was not then making a great deal of money in his business. Mr. Hunter replied, that at first he had done very well, but for the past year he had lost a great deal. The interpreter conveyed the answer thus: "Mr. Hunter made money very fast the first years, but the last, he has not made so much." When Mr. Hunter explained the difference he had made in the answer, the interpreter replied, that he dared not tell His Magnificent Majesty any thing so unpleasant as to say, "Mr. Hunter had actually lost Money!"

A similar incident occurred in the present audience. The King stated that the Americans were on a footing with the English, which Mr. Roberts denied; saying, that such was not the spirit of the Treaty. The secretary nearest the King translated the reply; that Mr. Roberts *admitted it, and was very much obliged to His Majesty*. Mr. Hunter, who was present, informed Mr. Roberts of the misinterpretation. He repeated what he had at first said, which was then correctly rendered.

During the interview, the King inquired after the health of the President, after that, of "all the great men of the United States," that of the crews of the Peacock and Enterprise; when they left America; where they had been; what had been Mr. Roberts's state of health in the three years he had been absent from Siam, &c.

At the expiration of three quarters of an hour, a sharp metallic sound was heard, and the audience was closed by drawing a curtain of silk and gold across the hall, in front of the throne, hiding His Majesty from view. The embassy then made three salams, and the whole court bent their heads three times to the floor.

During the audience water and betel were served. As the chamber was open, swallows flew in and out, and occasionally alighted on the chandeliers.

The gentlemen were now conducted to see His Majesty's stud, several elephants, and, last the Wât, which has been already described.

---

[53] This rather garbled version is still the form used to address the king.

# [10]

# VOLUME II, CHAPTER VII

DELIVERY OF THE SIAMESE TREATY—VISIT TO THE PHYA-SI-PI-PAT—
DEPARTURE OF THE EMBASSY FROM BANKOK—COPY OF THE TREATY.

*April, 1836.*

THE 18th of April had been appointed for the delivery of the copy of the Treaty, ratified on the part of Siam. The barge of ceremony in which we had come from the ship was ready to return. Owing to a superstitious notion of the Siamese that it would bring misfortune upon any house into which it should enter after being delivered into our hands, the Treaty was to be received on board the vessel, and not landed again on any account, as such an act would be the cause of distress in many minds.

About one o'clock P.M. Mr. Roberts was informed that the golden barges of the King were in sight. Accompanied by the officers in full dress and the band, he repaired to the vessel of ceremony, where he found the Phya-pi-pat-kosa had already arrived. There were three long barges, richly gilt, decorated with pennons, and each rowed by one hundred oars. The curtains were of cloth of gold with scarlet ground. That which bore the Treaty led the van. The Treaty was in a box, covered with coarse yellow silk interwoven with gold. This was placed on a silver dish, which rested on a salver with a high foot of the same metal. Over it hung a scarlet canopy, itself shaded by a royal chat. The scarlet uniforms of the men, and the measured stroke of their hundred oars; the flaunting banners, the music of their pipes and drums, and the glitter of gold and silver in the sun, formed a pretty pageant, and indicated with what scrupulons ceremony every thing is conducted at the Magnificent Court of Siam.

As the casket was raised, the Siamese band played plaintively and soft. The Phya-pi-pat-kosa conveyed it to Mr. Roberts, at the same time making a salam, to the royal seal, attached to the Treaty. Mr. Roberts received it, and, in respect to the King, raised it as high as his head, at the same time our band struck up "Hail, Columbia!" He then placed it upon a stand which had been provided, and deposited it in the cabin of the junk of ceremony.

Speedy preparations were now made for leaving Bankok. Mr. Roberts, in his private capacity, signed a memorial to the Chao Phya P'hra Klang from the missionaries, praying that sufficient ground might be allotted to them whereon to erect a church and suitable dwellings, with permission to appropriate a part as a place of sepulture, the same having been granted to the Portuguese Roman Catholics, Mussulmans, Chinese, and others.

Before leaving the house wherein the Embassy was lodged, the Phya-Ratsa-pa-vade paid a farewell visit, attended by a numerous retinue. He expressed a strong feeling in behalf of Americans, and requested Mr. Roberts to furnish American ship-masters coming to Siam with letters to him, that he might to the best of his abilities facilitate their business. He assured Mr. Roberts that he was entirely disinterested, and would receive no compensation for any service he might render. To manifest his regard for Mr. Roberts, he presented him with several toys for his children, but Mr. Roberts would receive no present *for himself* from any individual of the court.

In the evening Mr. Roberts paid a final visit to the Phya-si-pi-pat, and met there the Phya-pi-pat-kosa. He was entertained by a band of amateur musicians, playing singly and in concert, on instruments resembling guitars, hautboys, &c. It was stated that the Siamese use more than a hundred different musical instruments.

At midnight, the Embassy being concluded, the junk of ceremony weighed anchor, and was towed by three galleys, assisted by the ebb tide. At noon the next day they anchored at Paknam; and at midnight again got under way, and reached the ship about noon on the 20th of April.*

Of the history of Siam, we have been able to collect very little information. It appears to have early attracted the attention of commercial adventurers from Europe, and as early as 1610 an English factory was established at Bankok by Captain Middleton, which subsisted for some years; but it appears to have been withdrawn subsequently to 1623, when the King of Siam, and the English of Jacatra were in correspondence. In 1662, the King expressed a desire that the English should settle a factory in his dominions, though the

---

* For an account of the events which transpired at Bankok after my departure from that city on the 12th of April, I am indebted to Mr. Roberts and to Mr. Wm. Rogers Taylor of the Navy, who kindly placed their journals in my hands. [Author's note]

Dutch had at that time a large commercial intercourse with Siam, lading their forty ships yearly. In 1664, they quarrelled with the King and the next year threw obstructions in the way of the English trade in those seas, which was the chief object that provoked their jealousy and resentment. The settling of a factory was, under these circumstances, deferred, although it is stated, about this time the nation was in high favour with the King of Siam, who gave them a recommendation to the Emperor of Japan, whose sister he had married.[54] The subject was resumed in 1671, and the directors of the English company approved the proposal of establishing a factory at Bankok, if practicable. In 1674, the King renewed his overtures for an English factory in his dominions, which was accordingly established in 1676, with the view of eventually opening a trade with Japan. At the commencement of this intercourse great expectations were formed of the tin trade of Siam, which was then almost exclusively in the hands of the Dutch; and it was thought that the Siam trade generally would prove more beneficial than even that of Japan. That country was also considered capable of affording a market for a great quantity of broad-cloth; and the English agent at Bantam, wrote to the King of Siam, recommending to him the encouragement of a broad-cloth trade, as necessary to the maintenance of an English factory in his dominions. In 1679, it was discovered that Siam itself consumed but little broad-cloth; the sale of that commodity depending on China and Japan; it was therefore decided the next year, to recall the factory from Bankok. But in 1683 and 1684, it was resolved to re-establish it, the station being favourable to the prosecution of a Japan trade, in which great hopes were indulged. Accordingly Sir John Child, in 1685, addressed a letter to the Prime Minister of Siam,[55] explaining the difference between the Company's servants and private traders, concerning which some misunderstandings had arisen. Another letter was afterwards addressed to the King. It was observed, that this prince was favourably disposed towards foreigners, and that Siam was a place of considerable commerce; and therefore the Company's former losses were to be attributed to mismanagement, and the malignity of the Prime Minister, Constantine Faulcon.

---

[54] There is no evidence for this.
[55] Presumably a letter to Phaulkon.

In 1687, an insurrection of the Macassars took place at Bankok, by which the country was thrown into confusion, and the Prime Minister narrowly escaped. The Macassarese were all destroyed. The Company's losses arising out of the troubles, as appears from a letter from the President of Fort St. George to the King of Siam, dated in 1687, amounted to 65,000*l*.,[56] which satisfaction was demanded, or war would be declared. The next year there was a massacre at Bankok.[57] The Company were also advised that six French men-of-war, with 1400 soldiers, had arrived to assist the King, and that Constantine Faulcon had been made a Count of France.

In 1705, the Governor of Fort St. George addressed a letter to the King of Siam, desiring a renewal of former friendship, which had been interrupted by the ambitious minister. In 1712, the P'hra Klang invited them to make a settlement, offering the same facilities as had been granted to the Dutch. At this time, however, Siam appears to have been in a state of internal disorder, and to have continued so for many years afterwards.*[58]

In 1822, the Anglo-Bengal Government despatched a mission to Bankok, under Mr. Crawfurd, accounts of which were published by him, and by Mr. Finlayson, both of which have already been referred to. Mr. Crawfurd concluded a Treaty of amity and commerce, which is probably advantageous to English trade. In 1833, the Government of the United States sent an agent to the capital of Siam, who succeeded in negotiating a Treaty, which was ratified by both governments and exchanged in April, 1836.

As early as 1672, the Siamese evinced a very friendly disposition towards the French, and particularly towards Louis XIV, which is attributed to the labours of some French missionaries who visited Bankok about that time.[59]

---

* Asiatic Journal for 1822. [Author's note]

[56] The EIC's losses arose, not out of the Makassar uprising in 1686, but the effects of the Mergui massacre of the English in 1687, of Samuel White's actions in the Bay of Bengal, and the unpaid supply of jewels through Phaulkon to the King of Siam.

[57] There was no massacre in Bangkok; the French troops arrived in 1687 with the embassy of La Loubère and Céberet, and after the May 1688 coup d'état in Lopburi were largely confined to their fort in Bangkok, from which they withdrew in November.

[58] The death of King Thai Sa in 1733 was followed by a hotly disputed succession, the victor being the *upparat* and full brother of Thai Sa, Song Tham (Boromakot).

[59] French missionaries first came to Ayutthaya in 1662, not Bangkok in 1672.

At this period, a Greek, or, some say, an Italian adventurer of restless and ambitious spirit, named Constantine Faulcon,[60] had so crept into the sovereign's favour as to be appointed P'hra Klang. Forgetting himself in his prosperity, the minister aspired to wear the crown, and circumstances seemed to countenance a hope of his success. Opportunity brings out the scoundrel: many a villain has probably died with a reputation for virtue, simply because he has never been lured to vice by circumstances offering an easy accomplishment of his wishes for wealth and aggrandizement. The Prince was weak, valetudinary, and without posterity, and his minister ruled him, as well as his people, despotically. He formed a project for succeeding to the crown, and it appears he afterwards contemplated the idea of dethroning his benefactor. For the execution of his plan, he fancied he could make use of the French, and, in 1684,[61] sent ambassadors to France, offering to the monarch the alliance of his master, and to the French merchants the ports of Siam.

The haughty genius of Louis XIV drew advantages from this Embassy. His flatterers persuaded him that his glory was so universal, that it attracted to him the homage of the East. He despatched a squadron, with Jesuits and merchants, and a Treaty was concluded between the two Kings, the French ambassadors acting under the instruction of Father Tachard.[62] The Company anticipated great advantages from their establishment; and their hopes were not without foundation.

In the sixteenth century, numbers of ships visited the roads of Siam, from eastern Asia, when agriculture, mining, and manufacturing flourished. Soon afterwards, despotism grew to its full height, and consequently the affairs of the kingdom fell into confusion and languor. In this condition of decay, the French found the country on their arrival; it was very poor, without arts, and subject to a despot. The little costly merchandise used in the court, and in the houses of the opulent, was from Japan; the Siamese had taken the manufactures of

---

[60] Phaulkon, born in Cephalonia (then Venetian), did not come to Siam until about 1679, and did not assume full powers, without any formal title of post other than Ok-phra Wichayen, until 1683.

[61] The mission of 1684, as noted under Roberts, was to find out what had happened to the lost embassy of 1680. The Siamese embassy which reached France in 1686 with the returning French embassy of 1685 was purely formal. Fr Tachard, though, was party to Phaulkon's plans for installing Frenchmen in key positions in Siam.

[62] It is largely true that La Loubère and Céberet were, unwillingly, in the hands of Tachard.

that country into exclusive favour, and maintained a high respect for the Japanese.

It was difficult to change their opinions in this respect, however necessary it was to do so to effect the sale of French goods. If any thing were likely to bring about such a change, it was preaching the Christian doctrines, which the missionaries had done with some success; but the Jesuits were too much attached to Faulcon, and abused their favour at court; they became odious, and the odium fell upon the religion itself. The people, and particularly the Talapoins, were shocked that they should erect churches before they were converts enough to require them.

The fort at the mouth of the Meinam was conceded to the French, and they possessed many advantages, which, had they been properly managed, might have led to many others. It was an opening to the trade of Ava, Pegu, and Laos, but the Company's factors and officers, their troops and the Jesuits did not perceive it. Finally, they became so closely connected with Faulcon, that, lending him their aid, when that minister fell, just as he was on the point of perpetrating his designs, they were also involved in his ruin, and the fortresses of Bankok which had been garrisoned by the French, were wrested from them by this indolent and cowardly people.*[63]

---

* Establecimientos Ultramarinos. Madrid, 1786. [Author's note]

[63] The French Jesuits (as opposed to Portuguese Jesuits, who had come to Siam in the sixteenth century though in small numbers) had barely established themselves in Siam before the death of King Narai and their withdrawal with French troops in November 1688. The French Missionaries, who had been working in Siam since 1662, suffered persecution but remained.

# TREATY OF AMITY AND COMMERCE

BETWEEN HIS MAJESTY THE MAGNIFICENT KING
OF SIAM, AND THE UNITED STATES OF AMERICA.

His Majesty, the Sovereign and Magnificent King in the city of Sia-Yut'hia, has appointed the Chao Phya P'hra Klang, one of the first ministers of the state, to treat with Edmund Roberts, Minister of the United States of America, who has been sent by the Government thereof, on its behalf, to form a Treaty of sincere friendship and entire good faith between the two nations. For this purpose the Siamese and the citizens of the United States of America shall, with sincerity, hold commercial intercourse in the ports of their respective nations as long as Heaven and Earth shall endure.

This Treaty is concluded on Wednesday, the last of the fourth month of the year 1194, called Pi-marong chatava-sok (or the year of the dragon), corresponding to the 20th day of March, in the year of our Lord, 1833. One original is written in Siamese, the other in English; but as the Siamese are ignorant of English, and the Americans of Siamese, a Portuguese and a Chinese translation are annexed, to serve as testimony to the contents of the Treaty. The writing is of the same tenor and date in all the languages aforesaid it is signed, on the one part, with the name of the Chao Phya P'hra Klang, and sealed with the seal of the lotus flower of glass; on the other part it is signed with the name of Edmund Roberts, and sealed with a seal containing an eagle and stars.

One copy will be kept in Siam, and another will be taken, by Edmund Roberts, to the United States. If the Government of the United States shall ratify the said Treaty, and attach the seal of the Government, then Siam will also ratify it on its part, and attach the seal of its Government.

ARTICLE I. There shall be a perpetual peace between the United States of America and the Magnificent King of Siam.

ART. II. The citizens of the United States shall have free liberty to enter all the ports of the kingdom of Siam, with their cargoes, of whatever kind the said cargoes may consist; and they shall have liberty to sell the same to any of the subjects of the King, or others, who may wish to purchase the same, or barter the same for any produce or manufactures of the Kingdom, or other articles that may be found there. No prices shall be fixed by the officers of the King on the articles to be sold by the merchants of the United States, or the merchandise they may wish to buy: but the trade shall be free on both sides to sell, buy or exchange, on the terms and for the prices the owners may think fit. Whenever the said citizens of the United States, shall be ready to depart, they shall be at liberty so to do, and the proper officers shall furnish them with passports, provided always there be no legal impediment to the contrary. Nothing contained in this article shall be understood as granting permission to import and sell munitions of war to any person excepting the King, who, if he does not require, will not be bound to purchase them; neither is permission granted to import opium, which is contraband; *or to export rice, which cannot be embarked as an article of commerce.* These only are prohibited.

ART. III. Vessels of the United States entering any port within His Majesty's dominions, and selling or purchasing cargoes of merchandise, shall pay, in lieu of import and export duties, tonnage, licence, or trade, or any other charge whatever, a measurement duty, as follows:— The measurement shall be made from side to side, in the middle of the vessel's length, and if a single-decked vessel on such single deck; if otherwise, on the lower deck. On every vessel selling merchandise, the sum of one thousand seven hundred ticâls or bats shall be paid for every Siamese fathom in breadth so measured; the said fathom being computed to contain seventy-eight English or American inches, corresponding to ninety-six Siamese inches: but if the said vessel should come without merchandise, and purchase a cargo with specie only, she shall then pay the sum of fifteen hundred ticâls or bats, for each and every fathom before described. Furthermore, neither the aforesaid measurement duty nor any other charge whatever shall be paid by any vessel of the United States that enters a Siamese port for the purpose of refitting, or for refreshments, or to inquire the state of the markets.

ART. IV. If hereafter the duties payable by foreign vessels be diminished in favour of any other nation, the same diminution shall be made in favour of the vessels of the United States.

ART. V. If any vessel of the United States shall suffer shipwreck on any part of the Magnificent King's dominions, the persons escaping from the wreck shall be taken care of, and hospitably entertained, at the expense of the King, until they shall find an opportunity to be returned to their country, and the property saved from such wreck

# PART II: THE RATIFICATION MISSION OF 1836    223

shall be carefully preserved, and restored to its owners :—and the United States will repay all expenses incurred by His Majesty on account of such wreck.

ART. VI. If any citizen of the United States coming to Siam for the purpose of trade shall contract debts to any individual of Siam, or if any individual of Siam shall contract debts to any citizen of the United States, the debtor shall be obliged to bring forward and sell all his goods to pay his debts therewith. When the product of such *bonâ fide* sale shall not suffice, he shall be no longer liable for the remainder; nor shall the creditor be able to retain him as a slave, imprison, flog or otherwise punish him, to compel the payment of any balance; but shall leave him at perfect liberty.

ART. VII. Merchants of the United States coming to trade in the kingdom of Siam, and wishing to rent houses therein, shall rent the King's factories and pay the customary rent of the country. If the said merchants bring their goods on shore, the King's officers shall take account thereof, but shall not levy any duty thereupon.

ART. VIII. If any citizens of the United States, or their vessels or other property shall be taken by pirates and brought within the dominions of the Magnificent King, the persons shall be set at liberty and the property restored to its owners.

ART. IX. Merchants of the United States trading in the kingdom of Siam, shall respect and follow the laws and customs of the country in all points.

ART. X. If hereafter any foreign nation, other than the Portuguese, shall request and obtain His Majesty's consent to the appointment of consuls to reside in Siam, the United States shall be at liberty to appoint consuls to reside in Siam, equally with such other foreign nation.

### CERTIFICATE OF RATIFICATION.

"This is to certify, that Edmund Roberts, a Special Envoy of the United States of America, delivered and exchanged a ratified treaty on the day and date hereafter mentioned, and which was signed and sealed in the royal city of Sia-Yut'hia, being the capital of the kingdom of Siam, on the twentieth day of March, one thousand eight hundred and thirty-three, corresponding to the fourth month of the year of the Dragon.

"In witness whereof, We, the Magnificent King of Siam, do ratify and confirm the said Treaty, by affixing thereunto our Royal Seal, as well as the seals of all the great ministers of State, at the city of Sia-Yut'hia on the fourteenth day of the fifth month of the year, called the Monkey, being the Sakarat or year Eleven hundred and ninety-eight, and which corresponds to the fourteenth day of the month of April, being the year of Christ, one thousand eight hundred and thirty-six."

Here follow the seven seals of the Empire. They are blurred impressions, in red ink, about two inches and a half in diameter, bearing curious devices.

1st. The royal seal of Siam, or P'hrah, I, Era Pot, presents an elephant with three heads, having on each side two royal chats, and bearing on his back something resembling a castle; perhaps it is the gateway of a wat.

2nd. The device, which is almost illegible, is an animal compounded of a dragon, lion, &c. This seal is called P'rah Ra-chasè, and is used by the Chao Phya Bodin Desha, or Khroma-ha-thai, formerly called Phya Chakri. He has the general superintendence of the northern provinces, adjoining Pegu, and of the principalities of Laos and Cambodia.

3rd. The device, a griffin. This is the seal of Chao-Phya-Mahasena or Khroma Kalahom. He is of equal rank with the last, and holds the office of Commander-in-chief of all the land and sea forces, with the general superintendence of the south-western provinces, even to that of the last tributary Malay Rajah.

4th. Is called, Trah Boa Kean. Its device is a Boudha in the usual position, holding in one hand a blown lotus flower, and in the other its leaf. This is the seal of the Chao Phya P'hra Klang, or Khroma-tha, the minister of commerce and foreign affairs. He superintends the southeastern provinces adjoining Cochin-China.

5th. Is named Trah Prah None Tak An, and the device is an angel astride on the shoulders of a man or demon. It is the seal of the Chao Phya Therema Terat, or Khroma Wang governor of the royal palace.

6th. Called Trah P'hra Peroon, the device of which is an angel riding on a serpent, holding a flaming sword. This is the seal of the Chao Phya Phollatape, or Khroma-na, who is minister of agriculture and produce.

7th. Is the Trah (seal), P'rah Yame Kesing, bearing for device an angel riding a lion and bearing a lance. It is the seal of the Chao Phya Somarat, or Yomarat; or Khroma Merang, the minister of criminal justice.

The presents made by the Government of the United States, consisted of lamps, nankins, carpeting, male and female costumes of the United States. Two very large and elegant mirrors, an American flag, shawls, a set of United States' coins, and two splendid swords in gold scabbards.

The Envoy distributed presents among several of the Siamese officers, consisting of pistols, fowling-pieces, money, &c.

The exception of rice as an article of export, made in the second article of the above Treaty, robs it of a great part of its value, because rice is an important article in the trade with China. Vessels loaded with it are exempted from paying, what is known as "cumshaw duties," amounting, in many cases, to three thousand dollars; and for this reason, they often put into the rice ports of Java, or into Manilla, on their outward voyage from the United States to Canton, to load with this article. Therefore, it is desirable to add to the places beyond the Cape of Good Hope whereat rice may be obtained, for the advantage of the Chinese commerce of America.

# [11]

# VOLUME II, CHAPTER VIII

DEPARTURE FROM SIAM...

May, 1836.

On the 20th of April, Mr. Roberts and the officers, all of them unwell and some of them seriously ill, returned on board. The Prince Momfanoi attempted to visit us, but was so much affected by sea-sickness after clearing the mouth of the Meinam, that he put back. In testimony of his regard, he sent to several of the officers little curiosities, as books of the talipot leaf, &c., which they reciprocated in such books as they thought might be useful and entertaining to him. Among them were, Hinton's Views of the United States, Herschell's Astronomy, Duponceau's Constitution of the United States, Cobbett's Advice,[64] and several works on gunnery and military tactics, &c., far exceeding in value the presents of Momfanoi.

At sunset we were under way, and I believe no one in the squadron felt the least regret upon taking a final leave of Siam. In all probability not one of us will ever visit it again, and we hope it may be long before any of our ships of war will be found in the waters of the Gulf. The officers and crews now felt severely the effects of Eastern tropical climates; all, with few exceptions, had been seriously ill once, some of them twice; the last two months had been spent in contending against wind and currents; the ship was almost an hospital; four men had died since leaving Batavia, the provisions were of inferior quality, and were fast lessening in quantity; a general languor possessed our bodies, and even the stoutest hearts were at times dejected. We looked for relief in clearing the Gulf, and hoped to find fresh and favourable breezes in the China Sea, which would soon waft us to some invigorating climate.

The passage down the Gulf of Siam was retarded by calms and very light winds. The air was moist and sultry, and the "sun appeared as if

---

[64] John Howard the elder, *The History and Topography of the United States*, edited by J.H. Hinton, London 1830-1832; Sir John Herschel, *A Treatise on Astronomy*, London 1833; Pierre-Etienne Duponceau, *A brief view of the Constitution of the United States*, Philadelphia 1834; William Cobbett, *Advice* ('Having, in America, witnessed the fatal effects of Revoluton...'), London 1800, with many subsequent editions.

shining through a wet blanket." The number of sick was augmented, and in almost all the cases, as in cholera, the skin was cold and clammy (the Genius of the disease still hovering over us), evincing a strong predisposition to internal congestions. Nor did this state of things change immediately after reaching the China Sea.

For several days, while in the Gulf, we were visited by many pretty flycatchers, which hopped about with perfect confidence, picking up flies on deck; they often received food from the hand, and sometimes, when we were sitting quiet, would alight upon our persons. They flew in and out of the cabin during the day, and took shelter there at night.

In the Gulf we saw several white dolphins. Siam presents us with a great number of animals, which differ in a remarkable manner from the same species in other parts of the world. The white elephant, the white squirrel, the white ape, the white monkey, white as snow, white lizards, white dolphin, &c. Mr. Finlayson is of opinion that they are white for the same reason, which is not known, that produces the variety in the human species, known as albino. But after a pretty careful examination of several of the above animals, I am disposed to differ from that gentleman. The iris of the white elephant is not white in all specimens; nor was it white in any specimen of the white squirrel which fell under my observation.

On the 2nd of May, we were near the island of Pulo Oby, situated in latitude 8° 25´ north, not far from the coast of Cambodia, which is low and beautifully green. The island is high and clothed in a luxuriant vegetation from its summit to the water's edge; but from want of level land, adapted to cultivation, is incapable of supporting any considerable population, and has only two or three inhabitants. It is often visited by vessels for water, which is of good quality and easily procured.

This day we had the melancholy duty of committing to the deep the remains of Henry Mount (marine), who died from the effects of repeated attacks of dysentery and diarrhoea.

The next morning the Peacock anchored on the northern side of the island, and procured about a thousand gallons of water. The watering party brought off a pigeon of a yellowish white colour, the wings tipped with black, several squirrels and crows.

On the 4th we got under way, and pursued our voyage along shore, the sea being smooth and the wind fair, but the currents were found to be strong and rapid. The temperature became more tolerable, but there was no diminution of the sick list...

# CHRONOLOGY

| | | |
|---|---|---|
| 1809 7 Sep. | | Rama II ascends to the throne of Siam. |
| 1822 | | Dr John Crawfurd's mission, representing the Governor-General of India, in Siam. |
| 1824 21 July | | Rama III, Phra Nangklao, succeeds to his father's throne. |
| 1826 Feb. | | Treaty of Yandabo between Britain and Burma. |
| June | | Treaty signed between Capt. Henry Burney on behalf of the East India Company and Siam. |
| 1832 26 Jan. | | Edmund Roberts nominated by Levi Woodbury, United States Secretary of State for the Navy, to negotiate trade treaties with Siam, Muscat, and Cochin-China. |
| 1833 18 Feb. | | Roberts' mission arrives in Siam on the *Peacock*; treaty dated 20 March. |
| 6 April | | Roberts' mission leaves Siam. |
| 1834 April | | Roberts returns to Portsmouth, New Hampshire. |
| 1835 March | | Roberts instructed to exchange ratifications of the treaties with Muscat and Siam: left, with William Ruschenberger as ship's surgeon for Rio, Muscat, Java and Siam. |
| 1836 25 Mar. | | Roberts and Ruschenberger arrive in Siam on the *Peacock*; treaty ratified 14 April. |
| 20 April | | Roberts' mission leaves Siam where cholera breaks out. |
| 2 June | | Roberts dies in Macao. |
| 1837 | | The *Peacock* returns to Norfolk, Virginia. J.H. Moor, as editor, published in Singapore *Notices of the Indian Archipelago and Adjacent Countries*, with unflattering remarks about Roberts' mission. |
| | | Posthumous publication of Edmund Roberts' *Embassy to...Siam...*, New York. |
| 1838 | | Publication in Philadelphia and London of William Ruschenberger's *Narrative... of an Embassy to... Siam*. |
| 1840-41 | | F.A.Neale in Siam; published in London in 1852 his account mentioning the mission of Roberts ('Mr Eliot'). |
| 1851 3 April | | Rama III died. Prince Mongkut declared king, with his younger brother Prince Chudamani as *upparat* or second king. |
| 1852 | | The Second Anglo-Burmese War. |
| 1855 24 Mar.-25 April | | Sir John Bowring and party in Bangkok; treaty signed 18 April. |
| 1856 29 May | | Siamese-United States treaty of trade and amity signed in Bangkok by the American negotiator Townsend Harris. |
| 1857 | | Sir John Bowring published in London *The Kingdom and People of Siam*. |

# INDEX

Abeel, Mr D. 69, 189
Africa 20, 22
Agincourt 191
Alaungphaya, 'Alompia' 101
Albuquerque, Afonso de 80, 144, 145, 147, 148
America, see United States
Anderson, J. 109
Anglo-Burmese War, First 10
Anglo-Burmese War, Second 15
Anu, see Chau Anu
Arabia 128
Arakan 10
Arkansas 27
Asia 20
Assam 10
Assumption Church, Bangkok 79
Ava 70, 220
Australia, 'New Holland' 168
Avignon 79
Ayutthaya, 'Jutaya', 'Yuthia' 31, 40, 80, 100, 190

Bahia, Brazil 13
Balestier, Joseph 10
Bangkok, Bang-kok, Bankok, Sia-Yut'hia 10, 11, 13, 26, 31, 32, 40, 62, 83, 109, 112, 113, 114, 132, 135, 137, 142, 149, 150, 151, 152, 153, 162, 169, 176, 182, 185, 186, 189, 198, 204, 205, 216, 217, 218
Bangkok Yai canal 62
Bang Plasoi ('Bang-pa-soe'), see Chonburi
Banka, Strait of 142
Bantam 217
Batavia 11, 72, 226
Battambang, 'Batalang' 102, 111
Bencoolen, Sumatra 23
Beneditto or Benedito de Arvellegarai, Sur, see Ribeiro
Bengal 111, 112, 114, 161
Behar 97
Bombay 11
Borneo, Kalimantan 168
Bowring, Sir John 15
Bowring Treaty 14, 16
*Boxer* 12, 20
Bradley, Dr Dan Beach 182, 187-8, 189, 190
Bradley, Mrs 187-8

Brazil, 127
Brent, Lt 27
Britain 10
British East India Company 12
Brooke, Sir James 10
Buddha, Gautama 23, 31, 57, 60, 63, 64, 65, 68, 71, 79, 82, 96, 97, 106, 111, 161, 163, 165, 190, 203
Buenos Aires 11, 127
Bunker, see Chang and Eng
Burma, Burmah 17, 27, 47, 57, 63, 68, 71, 100, 109, 111
Burgess, Captain 68
Burney, Major Henry 10, 12, 14, 16, 47, 53, 70, 88, 103

Calcutta 114, 159
California 13
Cambodia, Camboja 80, 83, 85, 96, 102, 109, 111, 112, 114, 129, 161, 162, 227
Campbell, Lt 13
Campbell, Captain 12, 128
Canada 140
Canton 13, 75, 89, 127, 152, 189, 225
Cape of Good Hope 22, 80, 112, 126, 187, 225
Cape Horn 13, 20
Cape Liant 25
Carrol, Midshipman 27
Catalani, Mrs 38
Céberet, Claude 218, 219
Cephalonia 219
Ceylon 13, 158
Cham 95
Chang and Eng Bunker 140, 153
Chantibun, Chantaburi, 'Chautabun' 112, 182, 190, 205
Chao Fa Noi, see Chudamani, Prince
Chao Phya Bodindesa 83, 84
Chao Phya River (the Menam, Meinam) 25, 27, 28, 36, 50, 51, 62, 65, 67, 69, 76, 80, 86, 89, 111, 113, 117, 118, 129, 135, 142, 147, 149, 153, 220, 221, 226
Chao Anu, Chao Vientiane, 'Chow-vin-chan' 84, 86, 175
Chaumont, Chevalier de 100
Chetsadabodin, Prince, see Rama III
Child, Sir John 217

China, Chinese  40, 57, 60, 71, 75, 76, 78, 83, 89, 109, 112, 113, 114, 115, 187, 225
China Sea  22, 27, 85, 226, 227
Cholburi, Chonburi, Bang Plasoi  25
Chongs  109
Chromachiat, 'Chromas Chit', Prince, see Rama III
Chudamani, Prince, Chao Fa Noi  17, 44, 49, 102, 133-4, 166-74, 178, 185, 199-200, 208, 226
Cleopatra  148
Cobbett, William  226
Cochin-China  11, 12, 13, 20, 21, 24, 26, 30, 34, 57, 78, 84, 85, 100, 114, 154, 187
Coffin, Captain  153
Cokai, Thonburi  68, 70
Confucius  23
Crawford, Midshipman  27
Crawfurd, Dr John (sometimes here 'Crawford')  10, 44, 47, 52, 71, 88, 161, 172
Crispin, Saint  191
Crispinian, Saint  191
Cuba  140

Dean, Rev. W.  189
Demerara, British Guiana  11
Domingo  33
Downes, Commander  21
Duponceau P-E.  226

Eliot, Mr see Roberts  13
*Enterprise*  12, 128, 132, 138, 205, 214
Europe  147, 153

Finlayson, G.  227
Forsyth, Secretary of State  12
Fort St Geroge, see Madras
Fowler, Lt  27, 90
France  100
*Friendship*  20

Ganges, River  158
Garcia, Mrs  38
Gautama, see Buddha
Geisinger, Captain David  23, 27, 35, 36, 43, 103, 127
Goa  100
Governor-General of India  10
Greenwich  161
Gutzlaff, Charles  48, 69, 189

Hainan  152, 189
Harris, Townsend  17
Haw peninsula  100
Hawaii  13
Henry, Captain  49
Herschel, Sir John  226
*Highland Chief*  49
Hinton, J.H.  226
Hong Kong  14
Hué  79
Hunter, Mr Robert  68, 69, 70, 90, 138, 139, 214
Hsinbyushin, 'Shembuan'  101

India  24, 34, 70, 75, 76, 109, 129, 144, 169, 172
Indian Ocean  20

Jackson, President  11, 15
Jakata, Jacatra  216
Japan  12, 22, 187, 217
Java  10, 13, 22, 127, 225
Johnson, S.  189
Jones, Rev. John Taylor or T.R.  62, 68, 69, 70, 189, 190
Juliet  141
Junk Ceylon, 'Junti Ceylon', see Phuket
Jutaya, Jutia, see Ayutthaya

Kariangs  109
Kas  109
Kedah, Sultan of  10, 47, 70, 88, 111
Kelanten, 'Calantin'  114
Kennedy, Commodore  12, 13, 128, 146, 204
Ko Kam, Koh-kam  26
Ko Kong  111
Ko Sichang  25, 26, 129
Krek  99

La Loubère, Simon de  218, 219
Lanchang  111
Langdon, Catherine, Mrs Roberts  11
Laos  37, 57, 83, 84, 90, 96, 109, 111, 113, 162, 170, 220
La Plata, River  27
Lawas  109
Louis XIV  100, 218, 219
Ligor, 'Lagor', Nakhon Sithammarat; 'Chau Phya Ligor', Chan Phya Ligor  88, 101, 105, 206-7
Lopburi  100, 218

Louisiana 30
Low, Captain James 106
Luang Nai-Sit 46, 59
Luang Prabang 111
Luk-loinam, 'Luck-loi-nam' 151

Macao 12, 27, 79
Madras 49, 218
Magadha 96
Makassar 218
Maine 68
Malacca 47, 111, 114
Malay 11, 27, 57, 109
Malay Peninsula 23, 68, 86, 88, 102, 109, 111, 114, 161, 162
Maldive Islands 158
Manila 34, 127, 225
Manipur 10
*Maria Theresa* 153, 209, 210
*Mary Ann* 11
Maximian, Emperor 191
Mekong River 111
Menam or Meinam River, see Chao Phya
Mergui, 'Magni' 100
Mexico 13
Middleton, Captain 216
Minh Mang, Emperor 12, 84
Mississippi, River 27
Mom Fa Noi, see Chudamani, Prince
Mongkut, Prince, Chow Fa Yai 10, 14, 17, 47, 102, 166
Moor, J.H. 15, 16
Moors, or Chuliahs 49, 54, 57
Morrison, J.R., Mr 26, 27, 35, 36, 90
Mount, Henry, marine 227
Mulmein, 'Maulmein' 68
Muscat 11, 12, 13, 20, 21, 23, 127, 127, 143

Nakhon Sithammarat, see Ligor
Neale, F.A. 13, 14, 17
New Hampshire 11, 20
New Holland, see Australia
Norfolk, Virginia 13
North Carolina 140

Obi, Oby, Pulo 161, 227
O'Rafferty, Paudeen 163

Pachacamac 174
Pacific Ocean 22
Pahang, 'Pakhang' 111

Paklat, Pack-lac 30, 147
Paknam, Packnam 26, 27, 28, 30, 132, 135, 137, 145, 179, 204, 205, 216
Pasig River 34
Pasqual, Colonel 54, 105
Pattani 86
*Peacock* 12, 13, 14, 20, 21, 36, 103, 126, 127, 128, 129, 167, 173, 214, 227,
Pegu, 'Peque' 54, 57, 83, 109, 220
Peking 110
Penang, Pulo, Prince of Wales Island 10, 47, 88
Perak 10, 111
Peru 13
Phaulkon, Constantine 100, 217, 218, 219, 220
Philadelphia, Academy of Natural Sciences 173
Philippine Islands 22
Phitsanulok, 'Piseluk' 101
Phra-klang, 'Prah Khlang', 'P'hra Klang' 26, 33, 35, 45, 52, 57, 59, 69, 70, 85, 90, 128, 132, 138, 172, 182, 198, 204, 209, 216, 218, 219
Phya Pipat-kosa 179, 180, 181, 182, 183, 184, 210, 215, 216
Phya Ratsapavade 178, 179, 216
Phya Sipipat 182, 183, 184, 185, 193, 197, 216
Phya Viset 32, 105
Phuket, Junk Ceylon 102, 111
Piedade, Joseph, 'Piadadè' 26, 33, 36, 46, 105, 137, 140, 142, 148, 179, 197, 201
Pigneau, Bishop 100
Polynesia 187
Portsmouth, New Hampshire 11, 12, 126
Portugal, Portuguese 11, 26, 29, 33, 39, 43, 80, 99, 109, 115, 144
*Potomac* 20
Prasat Thong, King 100
Prince of Wales Island, see Penang
Province Wellesley 10
Purveyance, Lt. 27

Qualah Battu 20, 21
Quedah, see Kedah

Raffles, Sir Stamford 10
Rama 88

Rama I, 'chakri' 101
Rama II, 'Prince Chow Fa' 101
Rama III, Phra Nangklao, formerly Prince 'Chroma-Chiat' 10, 14, 17, 47, 56-57, 62, 70, 102, 128, 138, 212-4, 221, 223
Ramathipodi II, King
Ramon 137, 179, 180, 181, 182, 190, 199
Rangoon 68
Raymondo 90
Red Sea 127
*Reliance* 68
Ribeiro de Alvergarias, Pascal, 'Sur Beneditto' 32, 46, 105
Rio de Janiero 13
Roberts, Edmund 11, 12, 13, 15, 16, 18, 90, 126, 127, 128, 129, 131, 132, 137, 138, 145, 146, 178, 184, 190, 198, 206, 207, 209, 210, 212, 213, 214, 215, 216, 221, 223, 226
Roberts, Captain Joshua 11
Robinson, Mr 90
Robinson, Rev. Charles 189, 190
Robinson, Mrs 189
Romeo 141
*Royal Adelaide* 198, 171, 173
Rumford, Midshipman 90
Ruschenberger, William 12, 13, 18

*Sachem* 153
Saigon, 'Longuar' 83
Saint Crispin, see Crispin
Saint Joseph's Church, Ayutthaya 80
Sakdiphonlasep 104
Salem, Mass. 20
Santa Cruz, Bangkok 39, 80
Sap, Nai 134, 199
Sattahip 25
Selangor 10
Semang 23, 109
Shanghai, 'Seang-Hae' 152
Silveiro, Mr, Portuguese consul 43, 68, 69, 70, 79, 85
Singapore 10, 47, 68, 75, 114, 127, 153
Siracha 25
Sogkhla, Singora 86
Soissons 19
Sommoma Kodom 96
Song-khiam 105
Sontag, Mrs 38
South America 20

Sozopolis, Bishop of 79
Stribling, Captain 12, 128
Sudhodana, Sukodana 96
Sumatra 20, 22
Suriburi 155
Suriyamarin, King 101
Surat, 'Surak' 75, 112

Tachard, Fr Guy 219
Taiwan 13
Taksin, King, 'Pla-tah', Phya Tak 101
Tartary 96
Taylor, Captain O. 153, 207
Tenasserim 10
Terweil 152
Texas 30
Ticknor, Dr 13, 27, 62, 79, 90
Thai Sa, King
Thomas, Daniel K., Midshipman 27, 204
Toby Filpot 74
Tomlin, J. 189
Tompkin, Rev. Mr 69
Tonkin, Tung-king 85
Trengganu, 'Tungano' 111
Tumbah Tuah 23
Turane Bay 34, 100

United States 10, 11, 23, 28, 70, 115, 126, 128, 173, 187, 221-3

Vasco da Gama 80
Venice 149, 150
Vietnam 34
Vunglam 34

Waggoner, William, marine 205
Wat Chan-Tong 62
Wat Phra Si Ratana Satsadaram, Wat Phra Keo 58, 201
Weed, Midshipman 90
Wells, Midshipman 27, 90
White, Samuel 218
Wongsathirat, Prince 208
Woodbury, Levi 11, 13, 20, 127

Yandabo, Treaty of 10
Yunnan 113
Yuthia, see Ayutthaya

Zanzibar 11, 13